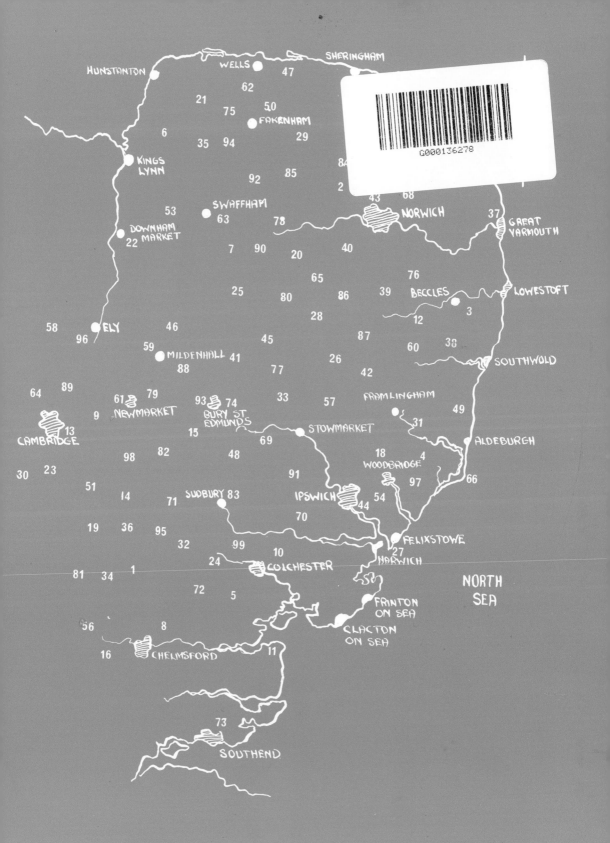

AVIATION

AVIATION

Flight Over the Eastern Counties Since 1937

by

GORDON KINSEY

TERENCE DALTON LIMITED
LAVENHAM   .   SUFFOLK
1977

Published by
TERENCE DALTON LIMITED
ISBN 086138 032 0

Revised edition 1984

Text photoset in 11/12pt. Baskerville

Printed in Great Britain at
THE LAVENHAM PRESS LIMITED
LAVENHAM   SUFFOLK

Contents

Index of Illustrations

In memory of Travers Leefe Dodman, a friend and companion in many adventures.

Acknowledgements

IN compiling this book many people and organisations have drawn on their memories and delved into the background and furnished me with valuable and interesting information. Whilst I would like to write notes and personal thanks here to everyone space will not permit. Main sources, first individual and then organisational, have, I hope been recorded alphabetically. My sincere thanks to everyone.

Warrant Officer Peter Barker; Mr David Barton; Mr Bert Beecroft; Mr W. Begbie; Mr Keith Bowman; Mr Michael Bowyer; Mr C. Chandler; Mr David Cook; Sergeant Michael Cooling; Mr W. L. Cope, Canada; Mrs J. Dale; Mr Christopher Elliott; Mr Michael Elmer; Mr Stewart Evans; Mr Alan Farrow; Mr R. J. Finch; Mr Roger Freeman; Mr A. R. J. Frost, A.I.I.O., A.R.P.S., M.I.R.T.; Flying Officer John Fuller; Mr and Mrs Hall of Hengrave; Mr and Mrs C. E. (Holly) Hall; Mr Harry Hayward; Squadron Leader Holmes; Mr A. J. Jackson; Mr R. C. Johnson; Captain and Mrs R. J. King; Mr John Langford; Mr and Mrs K. Leighton; Canon W. M. Lummis, M.C.; Mr Robert Malster; Sir Arthur Marshall; Mrs Mollie Martin; Mr Ian McLaughlin; Squadron Leader Clive Mitchell; Mr Hugh Moffatt; Mr Russell Nunn; Mr Parkes; Mr L. A. Patient; Harold Penrose, O.B.E., C.Eng., F.R.Ae.S., A.M.R.I.N.A.; Mrs E. Pettitt; Mr John Rayner; Mr Charles Riches; Flight Lieutenant D. P. Riordan, D.F.C.; Inspector Claude Rush; Mr Donald Smith; Mrs Lena Smith; Group Captain R. P. Stanford-Tuck; Mr W. Strong; Mr E. E. Swain; Mr E. Symonds; Group Captain Peter Townsend; Major John Venmore-Rowland; Wing Commander K. H. Wallis, E.Eng., A.F.R.Ae.S.; Mr and Mrs Stanley Ward; Mr Ron Webb; Mr Peter Whatling and Mrs Gladys Wilton.

Air Anglia of Norwich; The Air Historical Branch; Anglia Cameras, Mr Jim Empson; The British Aircraft Corporation, Warton and Mr Les Harris, Filton; Colmans Foods, Norwich, Miss Honor Godfrey; The Department of the Air Force, Captain L. W. Barry, Bentwaters and Captain W. D. Palmer, Mildenhall; Essex County Standard, Mr Reginald Clarke; Felixstowe Dock and Railway Company, Messrs Butcher, Minns and Palmer; The Friends of the Eighth Air Force; Great Yarmouth Library, Mr A. W. Bridges, F.L.A.; Hawker Siddeley Aircraft, Mr J. I. Treddell, Kingston, Mr K. J. Stalker, Hatfield and Mr G. Allen, Middleton; Ipswich and District Historical Transport Society; Ipswich Library, Miss King and Miss Wood; 1361st Photographic Squadron, Arlington, Virginia, U.S.A.; Rolls Royce (1971) Limited, Mr Jack Tetley; Royal Air Force Careers Centre, Ipswich, Warrant Officer Hunter; Shorts Limited, Belfast, Mr Jim White; United States Air Force Headquarters, Washington, U.S.A.; The United States Embassy, London, Lieutenant R. M. Grace, U.S.N.; Vickers Limited and Westland Helicopters, Mr Elfan ap Rees.

Sincere thanks to Air Commodore, The Honourable Peter Vanneck, C.B., O.B.E., A.F.C., A.E., D.L., who honoured me by writing the foreword at very short notice.

Finally my gratitude and thanks to my wife, Margaret, for tolerance and assistance in every sphere and my daughter, Sallie, who assisted with the preparation of copy. My thanks also to my publishers and their staff for full co-operation, quiet guidance and excellent workmanship.

Gordon Kinsey
Roundwood Road
Ipswich
August, 1976.

Square fields and dark woods quilt the scene as this Wellington flies over the area portraying the very flat nature of the region's northern areas. *Mrs M. Martin*

Foreword

by

Air Commodore the Hon. Peter Vanneck, C.B., O.B.E., A.F.C., A.E., D.L.

IT gives me great pleasure to write this short foreword to *Aviation — Flight Over the Eastern Counties Since 1937* by Gordon Kinsey, whose efforts in research and presentation deserve all praise.

If I may hark back even earlier than the period covered it is to put it in perspective with the evolution of aviation in general. Readers will appreciate that it was natural for the first efforts to be made with balloons and man-carrying kites for artillery spotting by the Royal Engineers to take place near Farnborough, with the concentration of the Army in the Aldershot area.

The second phase when aeroplanes were first used for mobile reconnaissance and troop spotting in support of the cavalry moved those concerned out, for instance, to Salisbury Plain and, from the naval point of view, to Gosport so handy to Portsmouth and the Isle of Sheppey equally handy to Chatham.

However East Anglia was not long to come into its own. The safety of operations in our area is so obviously enhanced by the flat nature of the countryside and the excellent weather factor, evidenced by our low rainfall compared to areas further west.

Those of us who hail from Suffolk note three particular events over the years, first the destruction of the Zeppelin in World War I, that fell near Theberton where some of the crew were buried: I believe the successful fighter was built by Ransomes Sims and Jefferies, who certainly were making aircraft in what, when I was apprenticed, was their Lawn Mower Factory. It must have been a great occasion for the people of Ipswich to see it fall in flames.

The second was the arrival of intensive test flying by the Royal Air Force at Martlesham Heath and Felixstowe and of course whenever there was a dispute about an aircraft's performance it was always the "Martlesham figures" that were quoted as finality.

Thirdly there was the hush-hush establishment of Sir Robert Watson-Watt's radar development at Bawdsey Manor which helped the ultimate victory of the Battle of Britain, and comes into this book.

This may seem a little parochial, for now Mr Kinsey's book takes us ranging over four counties, and up to 1975. We must be grateful for his enthusiasm which provides us with this extremely interesting book.

King George VI, Queen Elizabeth, Princess Elizabeth and Princess Margaret visit R.A.F. Bircham
Newton, Norfolk, during 1940.   *Mr E. Swain*

CHAPTER ONE

Days of Peace

THE term Eastern Counties for the purpose of this book embraces the Counties of Norfolk, Suffolk, Essex and Cambridgeshire.

Always susceptible to invasion, the coast and hinterland throughout the centuries has been ever ready to repulse intruders and when this was not possible they believed in the theory, and proved in practice, if you can't beat them join them.

It is hoped that this book will rekindle in the memory of the older men the machines and wide open spaces where they lived and bring knowledge to the younger ones of the not far distant days of aviation in the Eastern Counties. The days when men and women, many not of these counties or even of this country, joined with the inhabitants in staving off yet another potential invader and acquitted themselves well.

Three decades ago it was almost impossible to journey more than a few miles without encountering an airfield, many of which remain, either active or derelict. Many more are marked only in the memory of those who knew them, their existence merely plotted by heaps of broken rubble and tumbledown rusted huts.

The Eastern Counties never could boast large participation in the aircraft manufacturing industry, but what they lacked in the making of the machines they overwhelmingly gained in the flying. The terrain allied itself to the requirements of flattish country for airfields, but during the late thirties its military position was even more important and was the nearest part of the British Isles to what was assumed would be the next enemy, Germany.

Several long-established Royal Air Force stations existed in the region such as Martlesham Heath, Bircham Newton, Duxford and Felixstowe, and these had over the years become part of the local scene, their silver aircraft colourful with bold red, white and blue cockades a daily sight in the local skies. Martlesham Heath, the home of the Aeroplane and Armament Experimental Establishment, and its counterpart, the Marine Aircraft Experimental Establishment at Felixstowe, were the great centres of interest, housing as they did the fastest and greatest products of the British aircraft industry.

Squadron aircraft with colourful markings graced the pre-war scene at stations such as Duxford and Bircham Newton, flown by many a junior officer who over the next few years was to rise rapidly to fame in the service of his country. On the mercantile side only the minor airlines plied their routes, some on a seasonal basis, but the light aeroplane clubs were in the ascendent, with a sizeable membership at Ipswich, Norwich and Cambridge.

A Wellington bomber flies over its pre-war home aerodrome at Marham, Norfolk, during the last days of peace. The layout of the station is interesting and the flatness of the countryside is clearly evident. *Mrs M. Martin*

With schemes to build up the strength of the Royal Air Force rapidly, these counties were the main centre of growth and airfields for both fighter and bomber units appeared in the countryside. Many of them appeared similar in construction, their layouts being very much alike, but in one aspect they were all identical, they were the new and up-to-date image of the air arm. Wattisham, Stradishall and Honington were commissioned in Suffolk, Watton, Marham, Feltwell and Coltishall in Norfolk, and Debden in Essex. The new airfields housed new aircraft, now no longer glinting silver but in drab shades of green and brown, with black undersides. The long serving biplane gave way to the sleeker monoplane, and the increased performance of the new machines called for longer runways which in turn consumed more of the countryside, within the airfield perimeters. The local inhabitants were fortunate in that they were among the first to see the new aircraft of the R.A.F., as when the prototypes had left Martlesham Heath the production models came in their numbers to the new aerodromes, the Spitfires, Hurricanes, Wellingtons, Blenheims and Wellesleys. Sometimes the airfields were ready before the aircraft and in the case of Stradishall, the last biplane bomber of the past era, the Handley-Page Heyford, finished its days in a new home before being replaced by the monoplane Wellington bomber. Feltwell and Marham housed one of the less numerous of the Expansion types, the Handley-Page Harrow, a high-wing twin-engined monoplane bomber already obsolete by the time hostilities broke out.

The local newspapers of 10th July, 1935, reported that there was a very fine programme at Sir Alan Cobham's air display at Trimley, near Ipswich. The aerodrome was a large field off Drabb's Lane, and to this spot a large number of people made their way. The proceedings opened with a cleverly carried out formation flight, passengers being taken up in the various machines. Some of the passengers were lucky in obtaining tickets for free flights, these being supplied through competitions arranged by the *East Anglian Daily Times* and the *Felixstowe Times,* and it is interesting to note that in practically every instance the free flight passengers were making a first trip in the air.

At the same time about a dozen members of the Eastern Counties Aeroplane Club Limited formed a Flying Flea Club, and a fortnight later they assembled a Flying Flea aircraft at Ipswich Airport, at a cost of £75. Mr A. J. Adams, of Bixley Road, Ipswich, was the Club's honorary secretary.

"Pou de Ciel", the infamous Flying Flea and this example G-AEEI was powered by an Austin Seven water-cooled car engine. It is pictured at the Flying Flea Rally at Ashingdon, Essex, 6th April, 1936.

Mr A. J. Jackson

The Cievra C-30A autogiro, a pre-war attempt to obtain short take-off and landing performance. The absence of any mainplanes amazed the public when it first appeared. A three-bladed rotor was driven by the airflow and provided total lift for the aircraft. *Myron Burak*

The R.A.F. Station at Marham, which had been in a reserve condition, reopened on 1st April 1937, under the command of Group Captain A. P. V. Daly, A.F.C., within No. 3 Group. No. 38 Squadron took up residence on 5th May, equipped with the twin-engined Fairey Hendon night bomber with a crew of five. No. 115 Squadron was reformed a month later with the Handley-Page Harrow, another twin-engined bomber, a monoplane but still fabric covered and with a fixed undercarriage. These remained for two years, and then No. 115 Squadron re-equipped with the Vickers Wellington I.

Holiday makers and keen observers alike were enthralled with the flying boats and seaplanes from the M.A.E.E. at Felixstowe as they roared or cruised along the seafront and to a small extent contributed to the holiday amenities.

From air to sea to land, a Supermarine Walrus runs up the slipway at Felixstowe. Amphibians of this type carried out numerous rescues around the East Anglian coastline and also far out into the North Sea. *Vickers*

The Short Singapore IIIs of No. 209 Squadron presented a majestic sight and Empire Air Day drew its usual large crowds, who eagerly inspected the large flying boats and the small faster seaplanes of the Royal Air Force, together with the new large Short Empire commercial aircraft. Of particular interest was the new shape gull-winged Short Knuckleduster flying boat K.3574 but without a doubt the event of the year was the arrival of the Short Mayo Composite aircraft designed by a former Martlesham Heath test pilot Major Mayo. This was a means of getting a heavily loaded seaplane airborne on the back of a large "mother-plane" which when it had safely released its "baby" returned to base, the upper unit winging its way to a distant destination.

The 9th May was the great day, when a full load separation was made off Felixstowe, the composite aircraft being flown by two Short Brothers pilots but later by two M.A.E.E. pilots, Squadron Leaders Martin and Pickles. The two units were the lower four-engined flying boat "Maia" G-ADHK and the upper four-engined

The Short-Mayo Composite aircraft which carried out full load separation trials from Felixstowe. The upper component "Mercury" G-ADHJ later served as a trainer at Felixstowe, whilst the lower component "Maia" G-ADHK was lost by enemy action. *Shorts*

seaplane "Mercury" G-ADHJ. This was almost a repeat of the experiment carried out from Felixstowe during May 1916 when a Porte flying boat carried a Bristol Scout aloft on its upper wing and safely released it.

The first of the grand ladies of the air, the prototype Short Sunderland K.4774, arrived at Felixstowe on 8th April 1938 for evaluation and trials, the first of the many that were to perform such valuable duties in later years.

The same year one of the first of the new high speed rescue launches was based at Felixstowe. It was developed by the Marine Craft Experimental Unit also based at Felixstowe.

The first Suffolk Air Day was held at Ipswich Airport on 9th July, 1938 and attracted an interested crowd estimated at 30,000. New airport buildings designed by Messrs. Hening and Chitty gleamed in the bright sunlight, the first phase of a really ambitious scheme which included tennis and squash courts, a swimming pool and a whole host of other recreational amenities. The then Under Secretary of State for Air, Captain Harold Balfour, M.C., M.P., arrived in the Air Council's De Havilland DH.86B to open the new buildings and was greeted by Councillor E. C. Ransome, Chairman of the Airport Committee and Mr Whitney Straight, Managing Director of the Straight Corporation who leased the site.

The proximity of Martlesham Heath and Felixstowe and their goodwill enabled several new types to participate and a Handley-Page Harrow, Bristol Blenheim, Vickers Wellesley, Westland Lysander, Blackburn Skua and the graceful De Havilland Albatross flew over from Martlesham and landed. Unable to join in the ground activities, but coming down close to it were a Short Sunderland, Saro London and Supermarine Scapa from the M.A.E.E. Felixstowe.

Vickers Wellesley bombers of No. 148 Squadron run up prior to taking off on a pre-war exercise. These single-engined aircraft did not see operational service in the United Kingdom, but were used on operations in East Africa. *Vickers Ltd*

The Percival Mew Gull G-AEKL owned by Giles Guthrie, later Sir Giles and Chairman of B.O.A.C., and flown by him from his private airstrip at Brettenham Park, Suffolk was impressive and noisy during its high speed passes. Three Gloster Gladiators performed aerobatics in formation whilst the new Wellingtons of No. 9 Squadron from Stradishall flew over in formation.

The crowds went home happy, air-minded and confident that Ipswich Airport was well established, 272 of the visitors taking to the air for the first time in the joy-riding aircraft.

A Volunteer Reserve flying training school was also planned as well as the Civil Flying Club. The flying club at Norwich had been established for some time, known as the Norwich and Norfolk Aero Club, and at Cambridge Marshall's were well organized and passing out a steady stream of qualified pilots. The small airport at Clacton, Essex, was also controlled by the Whitney Straight Corporation, and the Straight Flying schools were governed by a notable airman, Captain Cumming, who had just left Imperial Airways as a senior flying boat captain.

A daily Straight operated air service between Ipswich and Clacton commenced on 20th June, 1938, the aircraft leaving Ipswich at 10.30 a.m. and returning at 20.30 p.m. the flight taking 15 minutes. The return fare was 9/6d. and the single fare 6/6d. The aircraft used was the Short Scion five seater feeder airliner.

Six Taylorcraft Model A two-seat high wing monoplanes were imported by C. N. Prentice of Ipswich who held the British licence for this type of aircraft, which cost, at that time, £450. One of the first, G-AFDN, was based at Ipswich with its partner G-AFKN at Bury St Edmunds with the West Suffolk Aero Club. Another, G-AFHF, was operated by Cambridgeshire Flying Services Limited. To illustrate the ruggedness of these machines, a Taylorcraft Plus C2, G-AFTZ used by the Suffolk Aero Club during 1939, was impressed as R.A.F. Serial No. HH.987 and then served for a further twelve years as a communication aircraft for a large aircraft manufacturer. Another of the originals of 1938, G-AFJP, crashed at Woodbridge during 1953.

The flying club used a unique two-seat light monoplane, the Czech designed Hillson Praga and the weekend air buzzed with the hum of their Praga 36 h.p. 2-cylinder motors, although these gave trouble and were replaced with the 40 H.P. Aeronca J.A.P. J.99 motor. The Ipswich machines were registered G-AEUP, G-AEUT, G-AEYL and G-AFYM.

September 1938, saw the first Supermarine Spitfire squadron in being, No. 19 at Duxford, Cambridgeshire. Only a month after their re-equipment came the Munich Crisis and the squadron was put on a two-hour notice. However, better times came on 8th October when the squadron gave a display at the official opening of Cambridge Airport. The first Spitfire for No. 19 Squadron, K.9789 arrived at Duxford on 4th August, 1938, and caused quite a stir when compared with the Gloster Gauntlet biplane which had been the unit's previous equipment. Commanded by Squadron Leader Henry Cozens, the unit "worked up" and eliminated

Hillson Praga G-ADXL two-seat light trainer as used at Ipswich Airport during 1938 by the Straight Corporation.   *Flight 12273*

many of the problems such as motor starting troubles, oil leaks in the Merlin engines, and an adjustment of the cockpit end of the hydraulic system. Another Spitfire squadron joined No. 19 at Duxford, No. 66, whose aircraft were the first to be fitted with the new V.H.F.* radio sets, whilst a little later No. 19 were the first to receive cannon-firing Spitfires. Unfortunately shell feed problems cropped up and the cannon-equipped Spitfires had to be taken out of service temporarily.

On 24th March 1939, all Royal Air Force Stations in East Anglia were put on alert as a precautionary measure due to the growing tension in Europe, and the aircraft changed their image, unit markings giving way to squadron identification letters. All leave was stopped and those away from their units were urgently recalled. No person was allowed off the stations, except in exceptional cases, and then his movement was restricted to a mere five miles, whilst all officers and senior N.C.O.s had to report to their respective station headquarters every six hours. The storm passed and on 28th March the alert was called off and normal life resumed.

Once a year, on Empire Air Day, numerous R.A.F. stations were opened to the public, usually from 12.00 hours until 18.00 hours. In 1939 this, the sixth such occasion, occurred on 20th May, with Martlesham Heath and Stradishall open in Suffolk, seventy-eight aerodromes in all being opened throughout the British Isles. Empire Air Day, which was organised by the Royal Air Force in conjunction with the Air League of the British Empire, was the only occasion when the Air Force was at home to the public. In a special message to the public, the then Secretary of State for Air, Sir Kingsley Wood, appealed to the British nation to become air-minded as during 1939 no fewer than 75,000 men and boys were required by the Royal Air Force, the Reserve and the Auxiliary services.

R.A.F. Stradishall, unlike Martlesham Heath with its large variety of aircraft, was an operational bomber aerodrome but still managed to put on an interesting display. Among the aircraft taking part were Bristol Blenheim, Avro Anson, Vickers Wellington, Miles Magister, Blackburn Skua of Naval Air Branch,

*Very High Frequency.

Gloster Gladiator, Fairey Battle and Supermarine Stranraer and Short Sunderland flying boats. They demonstrated navigation, radio telephone, parachute droping and air and ground attack. They raced, dive-bombed burst balloons and carried out aerobatics. Air Raid Precautions (A.R.P.) also staged a demonstration.

Throughout the summer the number of Service aircraft greatly increased on the new aerodromes, whilst the experimental stations at Martlesham Heath and Felixstowe now held their largest ever complement of new aircraft for trials. No longer did they have the solitary prototypes of a new type, but several all being tested for different things over the same period, thereby saving valuable time in their development. Reference to the aircraft lists in the author's book *Martlesham Heath** will give the reader an insight into the tremendous amount of work carried out at this time.

During September 1938, the Civil Air Guard was launched to bring within the reach of the average man and woman the opportunity to learn to fly. It was estimated that for £10 a member of the Civil Air Guard could pay for full uniform and a full year's flying training, with no other incidental expenses. Training expenses during subsequent years did not exceed £5 a year. Many civil pilots obtained their licences through this scheme and served shortly afterwards in the Services, but the organisation did not have a chance to prove itself before the outbreak of hostilities. The fees for the Civil Air Guard seem ridiculous by present-day standards but it must be remembered that at this period the Ford Prefect car cost £145. Also for comparison, flying instruction fees at civil clubs at this time averaged about 35 shillings per hour, which included petrol and oil, instruction and insurance.

During the last days of peace, the often colourful private and club aircraft droned their way through the East Anglian skies, the sound of the Gipsy motors audible for long after their passing. With the growing number of clubs cross-country flights were the order of the day, and on rally days quite a number of aircraft gathered for the occasion.

It was thus that the peace-time students, club fliers, and the Auxiliary Air Force, backed up by the Royal Air Force, were ready for the day when the peaceful joys of flight became matters of necessity and deadly business.

The new Wellingtons were beginning to show their paces, as on 19th July 1939 when nine aircraft flew to Marseilles and on the 25th another nine flew to Bordeaux.

Britain's maritime aircraft fleet grew with the advent of the large Short flying boats and during March, 1939, the Short Empire S.30 flying boat "Cabot", G-AFGU, was being tested at Felixstowe for fuel jettison systems, the tests being conducted by the M.A.E.E.'s Chief Technical Officer, Mr Harry Garner.

A great deal of Army co-operation flying was carried out from Ipswich, regular evening sorties being flown in connection with the Observer Corps. The area of

*(Published by Terence Dalton Limited 1975).

action was situated near Norwich and at Weybourne in Norfolk, and as many as nine aircraft were used simultaneously on any one night. Flares were used for take-off and landing at Ipswich, and emergency landing arrangements were available at Mousehold Aerodrome, Norwich and in a field near Weybourne which could have been quickly illuminated by Army searchlights.

The contracts involved flying at specified heights and courses over a roughly oval route covering some 200 square miles. Navigation lights were switched off and the searchlights did their best to seek out the "raiders". A pilot relating this experience remembers how on taking off from Ipswich during the late evening he used to set course to the north and climb into the last light. Navigation was by map, as only the twinkling lights of the towns and villages could be seen below, but if you cheated it was possible to follow the railway line to Norwich. Having made that city, patrols were flown at various heights for set periods between 4,000 feet and 8,000 feet, with intermediate levels for good measure. The searchlights would switch on and grope about the sky for the aircraft, and if you were fortunate it was possible to escape the terrific glare of the beams. If one picked you up, then the others would converge and the aircraft became engulfed in a brilliant halo of light, with all bright parts reflecting the glare. A break with a run outside the scheduled zone and then back again for some more action, lucky or otherwise, and then after three hours or so flying, home to Ipswich where refreshment awaited the cramped and often very cold pilot.

With the uneasy peace of summer 1939 almost exhausted, the units throughout the district were in a state of full preparation, and when the day did arrive, only a few tasks remained to be done to put them on a war footing. The Aeroplane and Armament Experimental Establishment moved from Martlesham Heath to Boscombe Down, Hampshire, and the Marine Aircraft Experimental Establishment from Felixstowe to Helensburgh on the River Clyde, whilst civil flying ceased, the majority of the light aircraft being impressed for R.A.F. communications duties.

All civilian employees on R.A.F. stations were closely screened and issued with new identity cards, roads through the camps closed, and in many cases armed guards patrolled the newly erected barbed-wire fences around the perimeters of the aerodromes. So the Eastern Counties went to war. Many of its native population went to the uttermost ends of the earth, whilst as if to keep the scales balanced members of the Commonwealth Forces and later those of the overrun countries, in exile, made their temporary home in the region.

CHAPTER TWO

Single Handed

ALTHOUGH the Eastern Counties were, in the main, "bomber country", there were several fighter stations prior to the Second World War, mainly in Essex. It was thought that any attack would come from the Channel shores, whilst the bombers, if based in the Eastern Counties, would shorten their flights to bomb Continental targets.

The Annual Air Exercises were held during August, 1939, the two opposing "sides" being named, for the purpose of the operation, "Westland" and "Eastland", the former being the "friendly" force. The new R.A.F. fighter force of Hurricanes and Spitfires rose to attack the invading Blenheims, Wellingtons, Whitleys and Hampdens.

22nd August, 1939, saw all R.A.F. personnel recalled from leave and all stations placed on full alert. Readiness "C" order was put into operation on 24th August, this brought all operational aircraft onto twelve hours standby. Personnel on special leave were told to be prepared to be back at their stations within six hours of recall.

Readiness "D" came into force on 26th August, putting the R.A.F. on an even more practical war footing with all personnel recalled from leave and all aircraft dispersed around the airfield perimeters. Flying was limited to air tests, and this only when of a necessary nature, although as yet no armament was at "war-readiness".

War with Germany came on 3rd September, 1939. The Auxiliary Air Force, which had several squadrons of fighter aircraft, flown mainly by "weekend pilots", was renamed the Royal Air Force Volunteer Reserve for the duration of the war.

An early casualty was Pilot Officer H. Fiddes, who was killed when his Spitfire 1, P.9985, crashed near Wattisham, Suffolk, due to engine failure and in attempting a forced landing.

The first R.A.F. fighter aircraft to pass over Nazi territory were six Blenheim 1Fs from No.601 (County of London) Auxiliary Squadron, together with six similar aircraft from No.25 Squadron. Taking off from Bircham Newton aerodrome in Norfolk on 27th November, 1939, they attacked the German seaplane station at Borkum, inflicting considerable damage to the installations. All twelve aircraft returned safely and landed at Debden in Essex.

No.604 (County of Middlesex) Auxiliary Squadron were resident at Martlesham Heath during January, 1940, equipped with Blenheim IV's fitted with early Air Interception or A.I. sets for bomber detection and interception. A feature

Bristol Blenheim Mk. I K.7045 in pre-war finish with large serial numbers beneath the mainplanes. Several regional squadrons were equipped with this type until they were superseded by the Mark IV.

B.A.C.

of this unit was that when the Blenheims were dispersed around the airfield perimeter they were positioned so that their turret guns could be brought to bear on any attacking enemy aircraft.

The Meteorological Flight still operated from Duxford, Cambridgeshire, and Bircham Newton, Norfolk, during the early months of the war, and twice daily, in all kinds of weather, pilots wearing normal Sidcot flying gear and oxygen equipment would take to the air. Flying specially instrumented single-seater Gloster Gladiator biplane fighters, they climbed to an altitude of 25,000 feet to take readings and make observations. This information was of the greatest value to the R.A.F. Commands, because during wartime the former source of weather information from ships at sea was cut off. It was of the greatest importance to prevent Atlantic weather information getting into the enemy's hands.

The first Boulton-Paul Defiant squadron, No.264, received its aircraft at Martlesham Heath and worked up to operational efficiency during the early months of 1940. Coded with the squadron letters PS, the new aircraft were plagued by many technical troubles during December, and a grounding order was issued during the following month delaying flying until February. On 12th May, 1940, No.264, flying from Duxford with its "A" Flight at Horsham St Faiths near Norwich, sent six aircraft on patrol off the French coast, but they were surprised by Messerschmitt 109s and five of the patrol were shot down, only Defiant L.6974 returning home. Fortunes changed on the following day when No. 264 shot down fourteen enemy aircraft without loss, but it was the Germans' turn again two days later when seven Defiants were lost.

Boulton-Paul Defiant 4-gun turret fighter, the first squadron of which, No. 264, commanded by Squadron Leader Philip Hunter, was worked-up at Martlesham Heath. The turret housed four .303 Browning machine guns but there was no forward armament. *Rolls-Royce*

East Anglian-based fighter squadrons helped the Dunkirk evacuation, code-named "Operation Dynamo", with over 200 Spitfires and Hurricanes taking part, but many casualties resulted. Flying Officer Ayne of No.609 Squadron, badly wounded, managed to make Harwich and attempted a forced landing in his Spitfire I, but lost his life when the damaged fighter spun into the grounds of the Royal Naval Mine Depot at Wrabness. Flying Office Howell from the same unit managed to make the airfield at Rochford*, whilst Flying Officers Dawson and Dundas successfully carried out forced landings in the vicinity of Frinton-on-Sea, Essex. Flight Lieutenant Stoddart of No. 611 Squadron forced-landed at Martlesham Heath, his Spitfire so riddled with enemy machine-gun fire that the holes almost equalled the area of untouched metal. The Commanding Officer of No.505 Squadron, Squadron Leader Watson, was killed when attempting a forced landing at night in his Hurricane near Bungay, Suffolk.

This operation, which at the time was described as a miracle, brought back to the shores of these islands 225,000 British and 111,000 Allied soldiers who reformed and became the nucleus of the new Allied land strike force.

After Dunkirk Fighter Command moved its squadrons around in order to face the expected onslaught on the bases by the Luftwaffe. One example of these moves was No.92 Squadron, which in the space of a few days moved from Duxford to Martlesham Heath, then to Feltwell and back again to Duxford. Mr W. L. Cope of Niagara Falls, Canada recalls those hectic days:

"I was with No. 17 Squadron from April 1940 and at the time we were operating from Martlesham Heath and Debden, on a two-week basis. We flew to

*Now Southend Airport.

Martlesham and back to Debden in a decrepit Bristol Bombay transport and it was from Martlesham that one of our pilots made his first kill. Moving from Martlesham to Hawkinge and then Kenley, on the 6th June, 1940 we moved to France in Handley-Page HP.42 airliners. Things turned bad and after only a short stay on the Continent we made our way to St Malo. Burning all the documents and technical books on the town green, the last act was to drive the transport into the dock and board a cattle boat to the Channel Isles. After three days, Southampton was the next port of call and then back to Debden. August saw the squadron back at Martlesham Heath again where a section was placed on Air-Sea Rescue duties and this eventually became a flight of No.277 Squadron. My recollections, after all these years are still clear and I well remember playing the piano at the Kesgrave Bell which was kept at the time by Mr and Mrs Abbott."

Early one morning No.92 Squadron landed at Martlesham Heath in a steadily thickening mist, which the "locals" assured the visitors would soon clear with the morning sun. Grounded by natural causes, it was frustrating for the eager pilots to hear the enemy passing overhead in clear air. Among the pilots were Flight Lieutenant Stanford Tuck of No.92 and Flight Lieutenant Douglas Bader of No.222 who later were able to get airborne for an operation off the French coast.

On 2nd June, operating again from Martlesham, No.92 Squadron together with two other units made a big formation sweep off the Dutch coast, the first such operation of the war, from which all the aircraft returned safely to Martlesham, although several were damaged by enemy gunfire.

During June, No.264 Squadron were back at Duxford and Martlesham Heath with the Defiants, but now engaged on coastal convoy patrols which continued until the end of July.

A new success came on the night of 18th/19th June, 1940, when Flight Lieutenant "Sailor" Malan, D.F.C., of No. 74 squadron took off from Rochford at 23.00 hours in his Spitfire I, K.9953. Locating enemy aircraft in the Southend area, he stalked a Heinkel 111 for some time and then managed to get several hits on the enemy bomber, which crashed in flames near Chelmsford. He then spotted another Heinkel 111 and after a long chase shot it down off the Essex coast. This was a considerable feat as the aircraft was basically a day fighter and was not equipped with any special radio aids.

On Monday, 26th August, a damaged Hurricane endeavouring to make Martlesham Heath crashed into a field near Brightwell Church. Fortunately the pilot was only slightly injured.

No.54 Squadron was at Rochford with its Spitfires and on 8th July three aircraft took off led by Flight Lieutenant MacMullen to intercept a formation of Me.110s. In this action two of the Spitfires were shot down, and the survivor returned home badly damaged. Two days later No.66 Squadron at Coltishall took off with their Spitfires early in the morning and climbing, sought out the enemy. Sergeant Robertson in N.3035 picked out his target and getting into position, fired, the Dornier shuddered, rolled into its back and dived into the sea 20 miles off the Norfolk coast, the first German victim of the Battle of Britain.

The feel of the coming battle was in the air, and the thunderstorms which rumbled across East Anglia during the middle of July seemed to indicate the noise in the sky which was to come. The gas masks which had been issued were tried on in earnest, more sand bags were filled, yet life still carried on with "Gone with the Wind" in the local cinemas, although the B.B.C. had broadcast a message that if the British Isles were invaded the population would be given instructions in good time.

Sea fog was a hazard during the summer months, and on 10th July it enabled several enemy aircraft to avoid visual detection. A Coltishall-based Spitfire intercepted a bomber near Great Yarmouth just after sunrise and a little later two Hurricanes drove off some enemy bombers which were shadowing a coastal convoy off Lowestoft. Another convoy proceeding through the same area, however, lost a ship when attacked at mid-day by another group of enemy bombers.

With the growing need for more light alloy metals for aircraft production, Lord Beaverbrook appealed to the housewives to give him their frying pans, saucepans and kettles and he would make Hurricanes, Spitfires, Blenheims and Wellingtons with them. On 24th July, when No.54 squadron was in action again from Rochford, a pilot who was to be a great name in aerial warfare was a section leader, Flight Lieutenant Alan Deere. Also involved in the mêlée that day was another pilot who was to be the top German ace, Adolf Galland.

Just prior to the Battle of Britain, more fighter units had been drafted into East Anglia and on 8th August, 1940, No.56 Squadron was at Rochford with Hurricanes, Nos. 85 and 25 at Martlesham Heath with Hurricanes and Blenheims 1Fs, Nos. 66 and 242 at Coltishall with Spitfires and Hurricanes and No.19 at Duxford.

Hawker Hurricane of No. 56 Squadron with air and ground crews at R.A.F. Martlesham Heath, Suffolk, just before the outbreak of war. The state of preparedness is evidenced by the men carrying gasmasks.

On 11th August, No.85 Squadron scrambled its Yellow Section led by Flight Lieutenant Peter Townsend from Martlesham Heath to go to the aid of Convoy "Booty", proceeding off the coast between Walton-on-the-Naze and Clacton and being attacked by a Dornier 17 bomber. After a cloud chase, Flight Lieutenant Townsend set the bomber's starboard engine on fire, but just then twenty Me.109's which had been lurking above dropped down and a massive battle ensued. Group Captain Peter Townsend recalls those days with clarity:

"In May 1940 I had taken command of No. 85 Fighter Squadron (Billy Bishop's and Mick Mannock's in World War 1). We were based at Debden, Essex, but soon one flight, and then the other, were moved forward to Martlesham Heath.

Major maintenance jobs on our Hurricanes were done in the hangars where I had seen the Beardmore Inflexible and the Hawker Hoopoe prewar, but our serviceable aircraft were dispersed around the airfield and we lived there in tents. During the hot, sinister summer when we fought in the sky for our country's survival, death was an everyday event among our little band. But the scented air of Martlesham Heath full of pine and heather, of birds' cries and the drone of bees, was a blissful reminder that life was stronger than death despite the carnage and sadness.

Often other fighter squadrons would fly into Martlesham at dawn, among them those led by Douglas Bader, Bob Tuck and the gentle-spoken Philip Hunter who, at the head of No.264 Squadron, died on a suicide mission.

Our Hurricanes, with their strident Merlin engines and their thrilling oily reek rent the peaceful atmosphere of the Heath. They churned the sandy soil into clouds of brown dust and when it rained cascaded through the small shallow lakes which undated the airfield. Coming in late one evening off a convoy patrol I was warned that the airfield was unserviceable. I found a way among the lakes then, stationing my Hurricane at the leeward end, switched on my landing lights and called my two wing men to land alongside. Young as they were, they made a fine job of landing in these tricky conditions.

One morning as I flew out from Martlesham Heath to relieve a convoy patrol, I spotted far away a reconnaissance Dornier 17. After five minutes of hide and seek among the clouds I got in a fleeting burst at the German who dived and disappeared. As I continued searching seaward, strains of the old song 'September in the Rain' came drifting over the radio, louder and louder. The clouds suddenly cleared and there below me were thirty Messerschmitt 110's circling. It was their leader who was providing the vocal refrain, interspersed with orders to his Staffel in German.

At 06.00 hours on the 11th July I was ordered off to investigate a 'bogey', an unidentified enemy aircraft. The Hurricane slid through the ground fog and climbed towards the rain-clouds above. The controller steered me out to sea, searching. Suddenly I spotted a Dornier 17 above me heading south for home. I spun my Hurricane round, nearly screwing my head off my shoulders to keep the

Dornier in sight. My only hope of avoiding detection was to climb stealthily directly beneath the Dornier, but when I levelled out 200 yards behind him, he spotted me. In the machine-gun battle which ensued our red tracers criss-crossed for some seconds then — bang! — a yellow explosion filled my cockpit. My engine was hit and I began to lose height. The last I saw of the Dornier was as it, too, slid downwards into the clouds.

Nearly thirty years later, researching for my book *Duel of Eagles*, I found the Dornier's rear-gunner. His name was Werner Borner. 'It was good to shoot you down', he told me, 'but it's better to see you alive today'.

Borner and his companions, all wounded, had crash-landed at their base, their Dornier holed by over 200 bullets. I baled out, watching sadly as my Hurricane 'K for King' plummetted into the North Sea. Fished out myself by the Hull trawler *Cap Finisterre*, I got back to Martlesham Heath that evening in time for the dusk patrol — this time in Hurricane 'Q for Queen'."

Two ships were seriously damaged off the Norfolk coast on 11th August by bombers which had managed to elude the protecting fighter screen, whilst the following day convoys were attacked off the Essex coast. The 12th August was a day of action with aircraft from all the regional airfields engaged against the Luftwaffe, with No. 56 at Rochford and the units at Debden protecting the south of the region and Martlesham Heath, Duxford and Coltishall looking after the other end.

It was the turn of Martlesham Heath on the afternoon of Sunday, 15th August when the Luftwaffe's crack Erprobungsgruppe 210, which had been developing fighter-bomber techniques, made an attack on the airfield. The formation consisted of twenty Me. 110s carrying 250 kilo bombs and a Staffel of Me. 109s. No. 1 Squadron attempted to intercept the formation at 15,000 feet near Harwich and Flight Lieutenant Brown's Hurricane was badly damaged by a group of Me. 109s. He was forced to bale out over the sea, eventually to be picked up by a trawler and landed at Harwich. Whilst on the final approach to Martlesham Heath, two more Hurricanes of No. 1 Squadron were shot down and Pilot Officer Brown and Sergeant Pilot Shannahan were both killed. Pilot Officer Mann engaged the 110s and caused damage to one, but was eventually forced to land on the now heavily bombed airfield at Martlesham, through lack of fuel. Pilot Officer Elkington chased the departing raiders and managed to destroy a Me. 109 over the North Sea. No. 31 Squadron from Biggin Hill attempted to intercept the raiders near Harwich, but Pilot Officer Grice, D.F.C. was shot down off Harwich, being picked up by a naval vessel. So fierce was the opposition that one Polish pilot, Pilot Officer Wlasnowalski found himself attacking nine Me. 109s at one time. After getting one, he was himself shot down in Essex.

During the late afternoon of 18th August, 1940, No. 85 Squadron patrolling between Chelmsford and Colchester ran into a massive formation of enemy aircraft, Junkers 87s, Heinkel 111s, Me. 109s and Me. 110s. Once again Flight Lieutenant Townsend was in the thick of the fray, leading Red Section, whilst Flight

Lieutenant Hemmingway led the unit's Blue Section. The latter's Hurricane was hit off the Essex coast and he was forced to bale out, being picked up about 18 miles off Clacton. The Squadron log book for the day records; "Six Messerschmitt 110s, three Messerschmitt 109s and one Heinkel 111 destroyed, six enemy aircraft damaged and four probably damaged. Two Hurricanes lost and one destroyed."

Fighter airfields in the Eastern Counties were the Luftwaffe's prime targets on the 18th August and heavy raids were directed against Rochford in order to cripple the fighter squadrons resident there. No. 1 Squadron again rose to the challenge and ran into a mess of enemy aircraft at 15,000 feet, mainly Me. 109s and Dornier 17s. One Dornier crashed into the sea near the Tongue lightship whilst another crashed on the airfield at Rochford.

The tension of the times was reflected in an incident which occurred on 20th August, 1940, when a fighter squadron climbed to meet the enemy over Essex and the leader spotted another squadron of Hurricanes apparently attacking a force of bombers. Rushing in to assist in the attack, at the last moment the leader realized that the bombers in question were Bristol Blenheims and that the Hurricanes were on a bomber affiliation practise. What could have been a tragic error was narrowly averted.

Aircraft of Lufteflotte 2 attacked the fighter aerodrome at Debden on 26th August, causing considerable damage, and although the enemy were chased by two squadrons from No. 11 Group and one from No. 12 Group, they escaped without great loss. Two days later, just after mid-day a large group of enemy bombers and fighters attacked Rochford aerodrome, but were engaged by several squadrons.

Heinkel HE 111 H-3 of the type which operated from France against the British Isles during 1940. This was the heavy bomber of the Luftwaffe and was adapted to carry out a number of duties such as torpedo bombing, high and low level bombing, and later air launching V.I. flying bombs.

The Defiants of No. 264 Squadron, on the ground for refuelling, were forced to take off hurriedly. At the end of the day, the Luftwaffe had lost two fighters and one bomber, whilst the home team had lost three fighters but no pilots. On 31st August, the Luftwaffe mounted a heavy attack on Duxford but the force was engaged by Hurricanes of No. 111 Squadron and little damage was done to the airfield, although Debden was not so lucky and suffered considerable damage.

Another ace of later days came into the region during late August when "Johnny" Johnson, then a Flight Lieutenant, was posted to No. 19 Squadron at Duxford, whilst, at Coltishall, Wing Commander Douglas Bader led No. 242 Squadron.

No. 54 Squadron, still at Rochford, had a new squadron commander when ex-Olympic hurdler Squadron Leader Don Finlay arrived to take over. Being in the front line, this unit had been under constant pressure; not only had the Luftwaffe fighters depleted its ranks, but bombers constantly raided its home airfield. Soon after arriving at Rochford, Don Finlay was shot down on 28th August, spending many weeks in hospital, and not returning to the squadron.

On the 31st August, the Luftwaffe's fighter forces tore into Duxford and Debden in order to ground the fighters as they were refuelled, but some managed to get off and do battle with the following bomber force. That day the squadrons lost 39 fighters and 14 pilots, whilst the Luftwaffe had to settle for 41 aircraft lost.

Relentless as ever, the Luftwaffe still attempted to smash the fighter squadrons on the ground, and massive attacks were aimed against Rochford and Debden on the 2nd and 3rd of September.

What was estimated to be the largest air battle in history took place over the Thames Estuary and Essex on 7th September, 1940, when over 1,200 aircraft took part. Squadrons from all over the region were drafted into the battle with the complete wing of No. 12 Group, including the Hurricanes of No. 242 Squadron led by Wing Commander Bader, taking off from Duxford.

No. 242 was in action in a big way on 15th September over the East End of London and Essex. During the battles of that afternoon the Northolt sector commander, Group Captain Vincent who lived at Bury St Edmunds, took on an enemy formation single-handed and so impressed the opposition that they fled. This was the result of great experience, as Group Captain Vincent had flown as an operational fighter pilot in both World Wars. Three days later, Wing Commander Bader, leading a formation of thirty-six Hurricanes from the Duxford Wing, escorted a large evening bomber formation. Bader shot down two enemy aircraft, a Dornier and a Junkers, out of the total of nineteen destroyed that day.

During the "Battle" No. 257 Squadron commanded by Squadron Leader Stanford-Tuck returned to Martlesham Heath and made daily interceptions against the masses of the Luftwaffe, mainly over the Thames Estuary. Discipline was strict and the master of the rules was the Commanding Officer who on one occasion arrived back after being "left" in the battle by two non-commissioned officer pilots who had "funked". Drawing a revolver, he walked over to the two culprits, pointed the firearm at them and commenced to give them his views on the subject. As a result of the later Court-Martial one of the pilots was reduced to the rank of Aircraftsman Second Class, whilst the younger pilot was given another chance and later proved his mettle.

When No. 302 (Polish) Squadron was based at Duxford during the "Battle" one of its pilots, who was later to live and work in Ipswich, shot down a Junkers 88 near the town, and then had to land damaged at Ipswich Airport, his first encounter with the soil of Suffolk. Mr Julian Kowolski, a former Wing Commander, the holder of the D.F.C., Virtuti Military and 4 K.Ws (Polish decorations), a pre-war Polish Air Force pilot, refuses to be regarded as a "Battle" hero and says, "The pilots who flew in the Battle were no better than those who flew in the rest of the war. We were just lucky to be flying during those crucial seven weeks when Britain finally beat back the German air offensive". Such is a man who flew with the Polish Air Force, was captured by the Russians, escaped to France, flew with the French Air Force, and finally came to Britain and joined the Royal Air Force.

All through September and October, 1940, the Luftwaffe continued to pound the cities and towns of Britain, with the fighters taking off to intercept, often with success. As the autumn approached the assault turned to night bomber attacks and several hastily improvised schemes were put into operation to deal with the new threat. No. 264 Squadron with its Defiants returned to Rochford and operated as a night fighter unit.

The people of Great Britain rose to meet the need for more fighter aircraft and so under a scheme inaugurated by Lord Beaverbrook, towns and cities made collections to buy aircraft for the R.A.F. The Colchester Spitfire Fund which had opened during August, 1940, closed during January 1941, with a total figure of £7,206 and as a result Supermarine Spitfire P.8677 was named "Colchester and District". During later years this area raised sufficient funds to provide a further 26 fighters, nine bombers and three flying boats, a total of £469,212. This was only one of the many collections made in the region, and many aircraft were named after towns and firms in East Anglia.

The partner in the Axis Powers, Italy, made a small contribution to the attacks on the British Isles by basing in Belgium some 100 Fiat Cr.42 biplane fighters, 75 Fiat Br.20 twin-engined monoplane bombers and a few assorted fighter and reconnaissance machines, under command of the Luftwaffe and attached to Luftflotte 2.

On 25th October, 16 of the Br.20 bombers set out to attack Harwich without success, following up with further nuisance raids during the next three months on the East Anglian towns of Ipswich, Lowestoft and Great Yarmouth. They tried on 11th November to mount a raid on Harwich with 40 Cr.42 fighters and 10 Br.20 bombers*. Two squadrons of Hurricanes intercepted the raiders, No. 257 from Martlesham Heath and No. 46 from an Essex airfield. The Italians lost three

*Details of this action are to be found in *Orfordness — Secret Site*, by Gordon Kinsey, published by Terence Dalton, 1981.

A sleek Supermarine Spitfire IX RX. 889 "Edmonton II", a presentation aircraft, is prepared in readiness to join a squadron. Many aircraft were bought by public subscription and these carried the names or places of the donors.   *Vickers*

bombers and three fighters, whilst 10 fighters made forced landings on both sides of the Channel. This set the seal on the Regia Aeronautica's operations over Great Britain and they withdrew from Belgium to warmer climes.

A local "One of the Few" was the late Wing Commander W. Guy Bruce-Lockhart, who lived in Athelstan Road, Colchester. A sergeant in the R.A.F.V.R. serving as a pilot, he was commissioned during 1941 and was awarded the Czechoslovakian Flying Medal, followed during May, 1942, by the D.F.C. Reported missing on a flight over France during May, 1941, he turned up again later in the year. During 1942 he was awarded the D.S.O. and then a Bar to his D.F.C. before failing to return from a flight over Germany during 1944.

After a spell in the London area, No. 257 Squadron returned to East Anglia, arriving at Coltishall on 17th December, 1940. The off duty pilots soon sought out the local public houses, two of the favourites being the *Kings Arms* at North Walsham and the *Ferry Inn* at Horning. One evening some of the pilots were drinking at the *Ferry Inn* when the Commanding Officer, Squadron Leader Stanford-Tuck, had an uneasy feeling that all was not well, and drinking up they left the premises. A little later in the evening a lone German bomber scored a direct hit on the public house and several of the customers were killed in the blast, including some members of No. 257 Squadron who had not heeded their C.O's warning.

During the night attacks of late 1940 and early 1941, German aircraft crossing East Anglia to raid London and the Midlands were engaged by night fighters from regional bases. Two pilots who made the news were Flight Lieutenant, later Group Captain, John Cunningham, D.S.O. and two bars and Flight Lieutenant, later Wing Commander, J. R. D. Braham, D.S.O. and two bars, D.F.C. and bars. The former pilot's usual navigator/observer was Sergeant, later Flight Lieutenant, C. F. Rawnsley, D.S.O., D.F.C. and D.F.M. and bar, and this two-man team, using the Bristol Beaufighter and later the De Havilland Mosquito, destroyed twenty enemy night bombers. 19th March, 1941, was a particularly busy night when large numbers of enemy aircraft crossed the region when making for London to attack the docks.

We hear a great deal of the pilots, but the ground crews played a major role in the air battles, as theirs were the skills which kept the aircraft flying. Some journeyed great distances to perform this function, like Charles Novak, an apprentice at the Skoda Engineering Works in Czechoslovakia during the pre-war years. When the German Army invaded his country he crossed to France, joined the Foreign Legion and served briefly with the French Air Force at Bordeaux. The invader strode in again, and still on the run Novak, accompanied by four companions, rowed across the English Channel in the dark until they were picked up by a motor torpedo boat near the English coast. After a spell in a Falmouth hospital, he joined the R.A.F. and after training was posted to Duxford when No. 310 (Czech) Squadron was formed on 10th July, 1940.

Sleeping on the job and working long hours to maintain the aircraft, the ground crews enabled a high degree of aircraft availability to be kept. During June, 1941, the Czech Squadron moved to Martlesham Heath, where they stayed for some time, eventually being disbanded at Manston on 31st August, 1945.

Scourge of the Luftwaffe night bombers, the Bristol Beaufighter all-black night fighter with its secret radio-location gear was the mount of Group-Captain John Cunningham and his observer Flight Lieutenant Rawnsley. The aerials can be seen protruding from the nose and wing leading edge.

B.A.C.

On 28th January, 1941, King George VI visited Bircham Newton, Norfolk, and held an investiture at which Squadron Leader Stanford-Tuck received the D.S.O. and a previously awarded bar to his D.F.C. Another Coltishall pilot, Flight Lieutenant Van Mentz, of No. 222 Squadron received the D.F.C. from His Majesty, but was killed shortly afterwards.

The first Hurricane fighter-bomber squadron was formed at Martlesham Heath during March, 1941, when No. 607 (County of Durham) Squadron worked up with the Hurricane IIB fitted either with eight 40lb. or two 250lb. bombs. Their early sorties were sweeps over the Low Countries escorting light bomber squadrons, at the same time throwing their weight into the attack.

Enemy attacks continued during the summer of 1941 and one in particular calls for mention, the night raid of 10th/11th May, when 1,212 people were killed and 1,769 seriously injured in the London area.

An unusual incident occurred at Ipswich Airport during June when a Spitfire taking off behind a similar machine lost visibility in the dust caused by the first aircraft's slipstream and crashed, but fortunately the pilot was not badly injured.

On 28th July, the night fighters had another success, when a German bomber was intercepted over Colchester and shot down, crashing in Wivenhoe Park. At this time, the first of the American built Bell P.39 Airacobra fighters to enter R.A.F. service were allotted to the Air Fighting Development Unit at Duxford. When more

King George VI awards a fighter pilot at Bircham Newton, Norfolk, during 1940. The station personnel are drawn up on parade in a hangar for the ceremony.

Hawker Hurricane armed with four cannon banks to display its deadly armament. Too late for the Battle of Britain, this version was used mainly in the ground attack role. *Hawker Siddeley*

aircraft became available, they were formed into a squadron, No. 601, also at Duxford, but the unit had only a short life, as the aircraft encountered numerous mechanical troubles and were not greatly liked by the pilots. The squadron later re-equipped with Spitfire V's.

Non-operational mishaps still occurred, as when a Hawker Hector exercising on 11th July, 1941, with the Royal Navy off Felixstowe crashed into the sea 2½ miles off shore. Its occupants were duly rescued. On the same day a Hurricane crashed at Thorpe Hall, near Walton-on-the-Naze, but the pilot once again was not badly injured.

Further success came the way of Wing Commander John Cunningham, now commanding No. 604 Squadron at Coltishall, when on the 10th August, 1941, he shot down a Heinkel 111 and damaged another, finishing up by making a difficult single-engined landing at night in his Beaufighter.

During September, Nos. 56 and 609 Squadrons at Duxford and its satellite at Snailwell, and Coltishall with its Matlaske "second field" were equipped with a mixed batch of Hawker Typhoon Mk.1s and Mk.1.Bs under Squadron Leader R. P. Beamont, the Wing being under the command of Wing Commander Gillian. The first units to receive this new type of aircraft, the squadrons took some time to become operational owing to the unreliability of the Napier Sabre motor. The airframe was also suspect, with a structural weakness at the rear fuselage which had cased several fatal crashes.

When the Luftwaffe decided to send high altitude reconnaissance aircraft over the British Isles, Nos. 124 and 616 Squadrons were stationed at Debden and Great Sampford with the new Spitfire Mk.VI high altitude interceptor. On 5th September one of these aircraft stalled at 36,500 feet whilst trying to reach a Junkers Ju.86 and a few days later two Mark VIs had to give best to another Ju.86 which was "topping" them at 38,500 feet over Clacton, Essex.

It is interesting to note that at this period of the War, the biplane Gloster Gladiator was still in limited service. On 23rd December one force-landed in a field at Bradwell, near Great Yarmouth, without damage to the pilot or aircraft.

During January 1942, the Typhoon's troubles were gradually being cured, although it still suffered from the occasional undercarriage failure, the cannons sometimes fired themselves and the engines frequently caught fire when starting up. The main trouble was the weakness in the tail section of the fuselage, and several Typhoons still crashed as a result of losing their tailplanes.

When the German battle ships *Scharnhorst* and *Gneisenau* passed up the Channel from the French Atlantic coast on 12th May, 1942, many of the attacking aircraft flew over the district, and one of these, a Spitfire, crashed in Goring Road, Ipswich.

In the region, Nos. 247, 266 (Rhodesia's second squadron) and 609 were at Duxford and No. 182 at Martlesham Heath, all with the Typhoon. Another new type which made its appearance in our skies was the De Havilland Mosquito II

The big and heavier brother of the Hurricane, the Hawker Typhoon with its four 20 mm cannons and later bombs under the wings was feared by German troops and train drivers alike. This is the Mk. IB version with a high visibility cockpit cover as opposed to the earlier metal framed type.

Hawker Siddeley

night fighter which equipped No. 157 Squadron at Castle Camps, near Haverhill, Suffolk.

On 9th and 10th July, 1942, Duxford was visited by H.R.H. the Duke of Kent the Commander-in-Chief, Air Marshal Sir Sholto Douglas, and the Air Officer Commanding No. 12 Group, Air Vice Marshal Saul. It was the first time that 35 Typhoons took to the air at one time.

Heavy security measures were taken on the 22nd July, at Newmarket Heath, Suffolk, when an entirely new type of aircraft used the large space available for taxi-ing trials. It was the Gloster F.9/40 "Rampage", later named Meteor twin-engined jet fighter, serialled DG.202/G and fitted with the first two Rover W.2.B. turbines. Under early development these were "ground engines" only, not cleared or deemed safe for airborne use, but sufficiently powerful for fast taxi-ing runs. Developed engines were delayed beyond the anticipated delivery dates, and the aircraft did not in fact fly until nine months later, on 5th March, 1943, at Cranwell, Lincs.

On the day of the ill-fated Dieppe Raid, 19th August, 1942, the Duxford Typhoon Wing made three sweeps over the Continent in support of the ground forces, No. 266 (Rhodesian) Squadron from Matlaske scoring one of the first Typhoon victories when they destroyed a Junkers 88 off the East Anglian coast.

The Luftwaffe also feared the De Havilland Mosquito II night fighter which gradually replaced the Beaufighter in this role. The four 20 mm cannons are visible in the nose above the four .303 machine guns. *Hawker Siddeley*

The Luftwaffe continued to send over its high altitude "spy" aircraft, now a more developed version of the Ju.86 known as the Ju.86.P.1, and several penetrated the regional airspace. They were extremely difficult to intercept, and it is recorded that two No. 609 Squadron Typhoons reached an altitude of 34,500 feet, without being able to reach their target, still several thousand feet above them.

An unusual ceremony took place on 29th September, 1942, when the three American Eagle Squadrons, Nos. 71, 121 and 133, all of which had served at Martlesham Heath were handed over to the United States Army Air Force. During their 18 months with the R.A.F. they had destroyed 73½ enemy aircraft.

No. 1401 Met Flight at Bircham Newton, Norfolk, and No. 1403 Met Flight at Duxford were still operating the ageing Gladiator biplanes for this vital duty, aircraft at this time being at a premium. New aircraft were coming into service for these tasks, as recorded when a Spitfire of No. 1561 Met Flight of No. 416 Squadron crashed at Grange Farm, near Martlesham Heath, whilst a number of operational types were used for other purposes, like the Lysanders resplendent in black and yellow stripes of No. 1488 Fighter Gunnery Flight stationed at Martlesham and the Defiants resident at West Raynham, Norfolk, of No. 1482 Bomber Defence Training Flight. Aircraft of the same type were at Marham with No. 1483 B.D.T.F.

Throughout the remainder of 1943 the Luftwaffe visited the British Isles but in

Members of the "Eagle" Squadron pose with their mascot at Martlesham Heath. These pilots were American personnel who flew with the R.A.F. before America entered the war.　*Richard Batley*

decreasing numbers, and the aircraft of Fighter Command gradually changed from a defensive to an offensive role. In ever-increasing numbers they ranged over Europe, creating havoc wherever possible. Another duty for the new fighters with their longer range was escorting bombers on daylight raids over Europe. In this role they were joined by the fighters and fighter bombers of the American 8th and 9th Air Forces based in East Anglia which, although under separate control, co-operated fully in all aspects.

During the first months of 1944 the tempo increased daily as the population of fighter aircraft grew in the Eastern Counties. The American-built North American P.51 Mustang became the equipment of several R.A.F. squadrons, the first Wing

40

was formed at the new airfield coded "Bentwaters" near the village of Rendlesham, in Suffolk. The Wing was led by Wing Commander, later Air Commodore, H.A.C. Bird-Wilson, C.B.E., D.S.O., D.F.C. and bar, A.F.C. and bar who, later became Commanding Officer of R.A.F. Coltishall. The Wing was engaged on long-range escort duties and mass fighter sweeps over the Continent and even into the heart of Germany. These Mustangs were the new look version which had been somewhat redesigned by the R.A.F. and were quite different in both appearance and performance from the earlier version which had served at Snailwell and other aerodromes with the R.A.F. in the area in the low level Army Co-operation role. A great deal of the improvement had been brought about by replacing the American Allison motor by a Packard built Rolls-Royce Merlin.

No. 1 Squadron arrived at Martlesham Heath on 15th February, 1944, with Typhoons and carried out daily fighter-bomber raids on the French coast, sharing the airfield with the 356th Wing of the 8th U.S.A.A.F. To many of the squadron this sharing was a new and not unpleasant experience after the stringent rationing of the earlier part of the war. The goods available in the American P.X. Shop included cigarettes, rationed to 140 per week at 3d. for 20. During its stay at Martlesham, No. 1 Squadron for the first time in its career carried out bomber escort duties, shepherding the countless U.S.A.A.F. bombers to the Low Countries for their daylight operations. As a testimonial to its efficiency, it is recorded that not a single American aircraft was shot down by enemy fighters whilst the escorting Typhoons were present.

The Luftwaffe still made spasmodic raids on towns in the area and when these occurred the fighter squadrons gave chase. They usually had some success with the bombers, but the Focke-Wulf FW.190 fighter bombers, employed on hit and run raids, were more difficult to catch owing to their high speed and low altitudes.

During the first weeks of April, No. 455 (R.A.A.F.)* Squadron moved to Langham in North Norfolk and was joined later by No. 489 (R.N.Z.A.F.),† Squadron, these two units forming the Langham Beaufighter Wing. As their title suggested, they were equipped with the twin-engined Beaufighter. Their first operation was mounted on 6th May on enemy merchant shipping and eight days later two enemy merchant ships were sunk off Ameland. Later that month and in June several cargo ships were sunk in operations ranging from Denmark to France. In 1976, the wreckage of one of these aircraft came to light on the beach at Blakeney, in line with the end of the old Langham runway.

Even the lowly came to grief, like the Miles Martinet target tug from Ipswich Airport which crashed on Friday, 26th May, 1944, at Gulpher Farm, Felixstowe. The pilot, Flight Sergeant Pritchard and Leading Aircraftsman Lambourne were both injured in this mishap.

An unusual task for R.A.F. fighters was shooting down U.S.A.A.F. bombers whose occupants had baled out, leaving them flying on over the Eastern Counties under automatic control. The job required patience, as the bombers had to be

*Royal Australian Air Force.
†Royal New Zealand Air Force.

brought down in an area with a scattered population, and many incidents are recorded of fighters turning these aircraft out to sea again by using their slipstream to manoeuvre the wayward bomber. The reader may wonder why an aircraft was allowed to fly crewless under automatic control across populated districts, but it was standard procedure to engage the automatic pilot so that crew members could escape from a stricken aircraft. In many cases an aircraft which appeared to be in its death throes, would suddenly, for no apparent reason, regain its composure and fly straight and level until it eventually ran out of fuel.

A different target presented itself to the fighters after D-Day, when pilotless flying bombs, the "V.1s", made their noisy appearance, thundering across the countryside at fairly low altitudes. Shooting these missiles down was a tricky business as the attacking fighter, if approaching from the rear, sometimes flew through the ball of fire as a ton of explosives went up. Many pilots specialized in tipping the missile over with their wingtips or slipstreams, causing them to crash in sparsely populated areas. Unfortunately in many cases, although the fighters managed to divert them from their original course, the V.1s still caused considerable damage on impact with the ground. During the evening of 26th September, 1944, a V.1. diverted by a fighter crashed at Bromley, Essex, damaging the church and several houses.

The early V.1s were launched from specially built installations on the Continent, but on 1st September, 1944, the first air-launched V.1. parted company with its carrier, a Heinkel 111, over the North Sea. Standing fighter patrols were flown to deter these intruders, and many of the flying bomb carriers were shot down either before they could launch their missiles or shortly after they had despatched them. The Mosquito with its long range and heavy fire-power was particularly useful for this purpose and was used extensively in the role.

Between 16th and 18th September, fighters from airfields in the Eastern Counties were flying missions in support of the ill-fated Arnhem campaign, using their cannon to help silence A.A. guns and destroy radar installations.

During October, another Wing of R.A.F. Mustang 111s, No. 133 Wing was formed at Andrewsfield, near Braintree, Essex, and comprised seven squadrons, whilst during December another large Wing of Mustang 111s (P.51.Cs) was formed at Bentwaters, Suffolk. With over 120 aircraft between them, these two Wings comprised the R.A.F's long range fighter force with bomber escort duties as their prime task, basically with the Lancasters and Halifaxes of Bomber Command.

The end of 1944 and the beginning of 1945 saw the fighter squadrons based in the region making daily sorties to support the armies advancing through Belgium and the Low Countries. Other duties included intercepting the occasional Luftwaffe reconnaissance or bomber aircraft coming in over the North Sea and escorting the daily light bomber sorties.

A Martinet target tug crash-landed at Eastward Ho Golf Links, Felixstowe, during a blizzard on 19th January. The New Zealand pilot, Flying Officer T. W.

Smith was not hurt, nor was a Canadian pilot of another Martinet, Flying Officer Merryfield, when he force landed at Field Hall Farm, Kirton, on 9th February.

Whilst the Bentwaters Wing was escorting Lancasters on a daylight raid on Bremen on 23rd March, 1945, several of the new Messerschmitt Me. 262 jet fighters attacked the force. A Mustang of No. 126 Squadron flown by Flying Officer Yeardley shot one of them down; this was the first R.A.F. victory over an enemy jet aircraft. Another Bentwaters Mustang also scored a first on 10th April, 1945, when a Mustang 111 of No. 165 Squadron flown by Flying Officer Haslop shot down a Messerschmitt Me. 163 rocket interceptor near Leipzig, Germany.

On 16th May, the body of Flight Lieutenant Mieczyshaw Befinger, a thirty-year-old Polish Officer of No. 309 Squadron, Andrewsfield, was brought ashore at Felixstowe by an A.S.R.* launch. His Mustang collided with another aircraft of the same type over the sea, and the other pilot was seen in his dinghy, but disappeared into a sea mist, and was not seen again.

The tremendous strength of the Mustang was well shown up on 9th June, when Mustang 111, KH.521, 5J-1 of No. 126 Squadron stationed at Bentwaters, was engaged in mock combat with some U.S.A.F. Mustangs, or P.51s off the Suffolk coast. Flown by Flying Officer Wright, the fighter dived away towards its base, but

*Air Sea Rescue.

Germany's secret weapon, the Messerschmitt Me. 262 twin jet fighter which in its early encounters with the day bombers wrought considerable destruction. This is a two seater version captured by the advancing armies and bears R.A.F. markings.
Myron Burak

when some 300-350 feet above the ground, the rear fuselage fractured and the tailplane started to come adrift. As the crippled aircraft smashed into the ground at high speed, the pilot was thrown out and, his fall broken by small trees and bushes, escaped miraculously with slight injuries. The aircraft was a mangled mass of wreckage and local legend says that a piece of the wing metal skin is embedded in a large oak tree at Campsea Ashe, near Wickham Market. Another Mustang from Bentwaters crashed and burned out at Stratton Hall Farm, Levington, on Monday, 30th July, 1945, after an engine fire at 18,000 feet. The pilot, Sergeant Norman Barden, baled out and landed with only slight injuries.

The surrender of Germany brought operational flying almost to a standstill. So, after the tremendous activity of the past five years, and the almost continual roar of fighter aircraft engines thundering in and out of the many airfields in the region, the inactivity was almost like complete silence, and the now still sleek machines stood dispersed on the airfields awaiting their next orders. Many no doubt expected service in the far warmer climes of the Far East, whilst others anticipated the occupation role. Still all waited, engine and cockpit covers flapping in the wind, and the pilots and ground crews languished in the Flight Huts and Messes scanning the notice boards for the Posting Lists and later, the "demob" rolls.

Many crashed wartime aircraft of both sides lay deeply buried in East Anglian fields and woodland after the conflict, but in recent years members of aviation archaeological groups have consulted old maps and the memories of local residents in their efforts to locate crash sites. Success has been varied, in some cases quite considerable portions of wreckage having been recovered and in other cases the finds having been no more than a few scraps of twisted metal or the odd empty cartridge case. Many of these relics have found their way into museums in the region.

The Norfolk and Suffolk Aviation Museum at Flixton, on the Suffolk side of the River Waveney near Bungay, contains a remarkable collection of Second World War relics and wreckage in addition to its array of complete aircraft. Another museum, devoted in the main to the U.S.A.A.F.'s 390th Bomb Group, is housed in the old control tower of R.A.F. Framlingham at Parham, still a reminder of the days when B.17s roared off from the nearby runway.

The advent of the metal detector has greatly aided the search for buried aviation relics, though it has at times proved a mixed blessing when it gets into the hands of unscrupulous "merchants". Many crash sites will remain undisturbed, however, as they are protected by their designation as War Graves.

CHAPTER THREE

Black Wings

DURING the early 1930s it was never considered that the heavy bombers in service with the Royal Air Force would have to operate from bases in the British Isles and attack targets on the Continent of Europe. However, as the Expansion Schemes for the growth of the Royal Air Force were implemented during the mid-1930s new specifications for bomber aircraft covering this requirement were issued, and at the same time airfields to accommodate the new generation of bombers were opened, those in the Eastern Counties included Wattisham, Honington, Stradishall, Feltwell, Mildenhall and Marham, to name a few.

The old bombers, mostly single-engined aircraft with limited range and endurance, had been a marvellous sight in their silver finish but the new bombers, when they passed their acceptance trials at Martlesham Heath and had been received for squadron service, were far less conspicuous in their new brown and green camouflage, with its attendant black undersurfaces, as they stood on the newly commissioned stations in the Eastern Counties.

Bomber Command, which had been formed on 14th July 1936, with its Headquarters at Uxbridge, Middlesex, comprised four Groups, Nos. 1, 2, 3 and 6. Later on as the bombing offensive mounted towards the middle period of the War, this number was increased to five operational Groups, Nos. 1, 2, 3, 4 and 5 and one training Group, No. 6. The main aircraft types employed by the juvenile command were the Fairey Battle single-engined light bomber and the Bristol Blenheim twin-engined light bomber, with the Armstrong Whitworth Whitley, the Handley-Page Hampden and the Vickers-Armstrong Wellington representing the medium bombers.

It was with these types that Bomber Command went to war, first in France with the Advanced Air Striking Force and later, after the evacuation, from Dunkirk, from home bases in Eastern and Southern England. It was only late in 1941 that the first four-engined heavy bomber, the Short Stirling, went into action from Eastern Counties bases, followed during 1942 by the Handley-Page Halifax and the Avro Lancaster, the former operating in the main from bases in Yorkshire whilst the latter resided in Lincolnshire and the Midlands as well as a few squadrons in East Anglia.

When the new airfields constructed under the Expansion Schemes first came into operation some of them housed squadrons using aircraft which were already semi-obsolete. Thus Stradishall was the home of Nos. 9 and 148 Squadrons equipped with the R.A.F.'s last biplane bomber, the Handley-Page Heyford. The

Last of the canvas biplane bombers, a Handley-Page Heyford poses with squadron aircrew members at Stradishall during 1937.

Mrs M. Martin

latter squadron converted to the single-engined Wellesley monoplane bomber and then to the twin-engined Wellington, while No. 9 converted from Heyfords direct to the Wellington. The Heyford was also the war-horse of Nos. 38, 99 and 149 Squadrons at Mildenhall, No. 38 at Marham and No. 102 at Honington, whilst the Heyford's successor, the Handley-Page Harrow, a twin-engined high wing monoplane, equipped Nos. 37 and 214 Squadrons at Feltwell, No. 115 at Marham and No. 75 at Honington. The single-engined Vickers Wellesley equipped No. 77 at Honington and No. 148 at Stradishall.

When a party assembled at R.A.F. Mildenhall one windy day early in February, 1938, to go over to Stradishall to open the new airfield there the only aircraft on the Station strength was a Miles Magister, a two-seat trainer, intended for the personal use of the Station Commander, Group Captain Henning. It was not until early the following month that the station was ready to receive the advance parties of Nos. 9 and 148 Squadrons.

One of Stradishall's Wellesleys gave an impressive display at the opening of Ipswich Airport on 9th July, 1938, little more than ten days after more than 7,000 people had visited Stradishall to see the new aircraft on the occasion of Empire Air Day. Wellesley K.7732, also of No. 148 Squadron was not so fortunate on 29th September, 1938, when descending rapidly through low rain clouds, a wing broke off and the bomber crashed at Kedington, killing the crew of three.

The first Air Scout Troop in the country was formed at Stradishall by Pilot Officer John Shore of No. 148 Squadron, assisted by Mr Backler from nearby Haverhill. Later, as a Flight Lieutenant, John Shore was shot down while flying from Honington, but escaped from Stalag Luft One, being the second R.A.F.

One of the lesser known Expansion types, this Handley Page Harrow K.6933 belonged to No. 115 squadron and operated from Marham during 1937.

officer to return to England from a prisoner-of-war camp. He became a test-pilot and was awarded the Military Cross and the Air Force Cross, but was tragically killed after the war when his Lincoln bomber flew into a Welsh hillside.

After the two Stradishall squadrons had re-equipped with Wellingtons during January, 1939, No. 9 moved to the new aerodrome at Honington, Suffolk*. This Unit, which had a bat in its squadron badge, was known before the War as the "Ipswich Squadron". Its place at Stradishall was filled by a New Zealand squadron, No. 75, which was formed by ferry crews who had come to England to collect a squadron of Wellington bombers purchased by the Royal New Zealand Air Force. With the outbreak of war imminent it was decided to retain both men and machines in England.

As war clouds gathered, working-up exercises were carried out in earnest by the units of Bomber Command. One such practice attack was made during January, 1939 on the highly secret "radio location" station at Bawdsey Manor, on the Suffolk coast, by Blenheims of No. 104 Squadron based at Bassingbourn in Hertfordshire.

The new aerodrome at Watton, between Thetford and Swaffham in Norfolk, was commissioned on 4th February, 1939, and although scheduled to operate heavy bombers of No. 6 Group, it soon transferred to No. 2 Group and housed light bombers. Another new station in Suffolk, at Wattisham, between Ipswich and Bury St Edmunds was commissioned on 11th May and became operational when the Blenheim IV bombers of No. 110 squadron arrived and began working-up and training routines. The squadron suffered its first casualty when one of its Blenheims crashed at Barking Tye Common, near Needham Market, as a result of engine

*Two aircraft of No. 9 Squadron collided over Honington while carrying out fighter evasion exercises. Remains of one of the Wellingtons are now to be seen at the Norfolk and Suffolk Air Museum at Flixton, near Bungay.

failure soon after take-off. At this time R.A.F. Wattisham was commanded by Wing Commander O. R. Gayford, the pre-war R.A.F. long-distance record holder.

During the last warm summer days of peace, the Royal Air Force flew large formations of bombers over France to show the flag and to impress the French with our apparent air strength, and the Armée de l'Air, the French Air Force, used the bombers as targets for their fighter defence forces. These flights took place during the 10th-14th July, and those on the latter day, Bastille Day, passed over the centre of Paris. Further formations carried out the same procedures on 25th July, when the fighters again attempted interceptions.

The rumblings in Europe continued to increase and on 1st September the R.A.F. went on to a war footing. No. 82 Squadron moved to Horsham St Faiths on the outskirts of Norwich, and No. 110 to Ipswich Airport, where the latter's Blenheims stood by for take-off instructions against a target in Germany. Newly acquired American-built Lockheed Hudson patrol aircraft of No. 233 Squadron stationed at Bircham Newton in North-West Norfolk carried out extensive coastal patrols.

The first R.A.F. aircraft to pass through German air space after the declaration of war was a Blenheim IV, N.6215 from No. 139 squadron based at R.A.F. Wyton, in Huntingdonshire, which carried out a photographic reconnaissance of the German Fleet on 3rd September, 1939. The following day five Blenheim IVs of No. 110 Squadron took off from Ipswich Airport at 15.55 hours, followed at 16.00 hours by five similar aircraft of No. 107 Squadron from Wattisham. The objective of both flights, led by Flight Lieutenant Doran, was the German Fleet then in the German Bight. Hampered by low cloud and heavy rain, and flying at only 100 feet above the sea, they sought the battle fleet in the Schilling Roads and eventually located the pocket-battleship *Admiral Scheer,* on which they scored two hits. They also hit a supply vessel.

All No. 110s Blenheims returned safely, although scattered when returning from the target area. No. 107 Squadron was not so lucky, as the aircraft became temporarily lost in the atrocious weather and pushed on to the German coast in two separate groups. During the ensuing attacks, carried out by only four aircraft, the leader having disappeared en route, one of the Blenheims was destroyed by blast from its own bombs, its altitude being so low. Another returned home still carrying its bombs and the fate of the other two aircraft remains unknown. The first bombs to be dropped on German soil during the war were those from Blenheim N.6204 of No. 110 Squadron during this operation.

Later the same day six Wellingtons of No. 9 Squadron from Honington and six from No. 149 took part in a raid on Brunsbüttel and the North Sea end of the Kiel Canal. Both units suffered heavy casualties, Flight Lieutenant Grant managing to carry out a successful attack from 6,000 feet, although his aircraft, Wellington L.4278 was damaged by anti-aircraft fire.

No. 110 Squadron lost its Commanding Officer on 27th September when Wing

Commander Cameron's aircraft, on a photographic mission over the Kiel area, was shot down by fighters over the land. The Germans buried him with full military honours close to the spot where he crashed.

In spite of such losses, the squadrons based in the Eastern Counties continued their efforts against the German Navy, Throughout December, 1939, the Wellingtons carried out raids on the German Fleet in the Heligoland Bight and in North German ports, those sorties of Nos. 38, 115 and 149 Squadrons from Mildenhall and Marham on the 3rd, 14th and 18th December being the last daylight raids carried out by Wellington bombers.

A Blenheim, N.6183 of No. 107 Squadron flown by Sergeant Cunningham, scored a probable success while carrying out a reconnaissance over the German Bight on 4th March, 1940. Through a gap in the clouds the pilot spotted a U-boat on the surface, and with commendable speed he dived on the enemy vessel, which he left in a sinking condition after delivering four 250lb bombs right on target.

Such bombs could be effective against small vessels, but when used against armoured warships they were too small to do much damage. No. 107's Blenheims from Wattisham led by Wing Commander Basil Embry located their targets, the German battleships *Scharnhorst* and *Gneisenau* which were steaming off the Dutch coast on 6th April, but their 250lb bombs caused only minor damage.

Basil Embry achieved fame later in the war as an escaper and in due course rose to high rank in the R.A.F., but he was not the only Wattisham pilot to gain distinction. Flight Lieutenant G. T. B. Clayton who was later to rise to the rank of Air Vice Marshal, was awarded the Air Force Cross during April 1940, and Wing Commander Laurence Sinclair was awarded the Distinguished Service Order for his leadership of No. 110 Squadron and the George Cross for his unselfish action in trying to rescue the crew of a blazing bomb-laden Blenheim aircraft.

May was a disastrous month for the British Expeditionary Force and their allies in Europe, then withdrawing towards the French Coast. In order to stem the German advance, the locally based Blenheim squadrons flew continual sorties, bombing and strafing troop columns. No. 110 Squadron flew from Wattisham on the 10th May, led by Squadron Leader Sabine, to make sweeping attacks on air transport, especially Junkers Ju. 52 troop carriers, whilst two days later No. 107 Squadron led by Wing Commander Embry attacked bridges in the Maastricht area of Holland, losing three aircraft. Later that same day the other Wattisham unit, No. 110 again revisited the area with eleven machines, of which two were lost and three badly damaged.

On the following night, the 11th, the Wellingtons of No. 115 from Marham attacked the German-occupied airfield at Waalhaven, near Rotterdam, whilst other aircraft from the same station went to Hamburg. Later, as the attention of the Allied air forces was turned to the German war industries, the "Wimpies" from Marham bombed Duisberg and Gelsenkirchen.

Losses among the Blenheim squadrons mounted almost daily, though not all were due to enemy action. Ipswich was fortunate in February 1940, when a Blenheim IV taking-off from Ipswich Airport suffered engine failure whilst climbing-out over the town. The pilot managed with great skill to crash-land the aircraft in the narrow part of the River Orwell near Ipswich Station, although it was fully loaded with fuel and bombs. The crew escaped injury, and inflating their dinghy, paddled the few yards to the shore.

Five Wattisham Blenheims were lost on the 14th May whilst carrying out strafing operations over the Low Countries, and such was the opposition on the 17th, when No. 82 Squadron went for troop concentrations in the Glembleaux district of Belgium, only one of the twelve Blenheims returned. Later on the 17th, No. 110 Squadron tried new tactics, making late evening and moonlight attacks on targets in Belgium. Sorties such as these were badly hampered by the hordes of refugees crowding the roads, for the advancing German infantry was mingling with the civilians in the hopes that they would thus escape attack.

One Blenheim that did reach home after suffering considerable flak damage over the target area was one of No. 15 Squadron, which force-landed in a French field on 18th May. The crew did their best to patch up and repair the damage and when airworthy enough, they started up the engines and lined up for take-off. Managing to get airborne and gradually gaining height they set course as best they could for England and arrived over their home country after dark. Joyful to see airfield lights they made for them and brought off a successful landing at Martlesham Heath.

One of the less successful aircraft came to Marham during the second half of May, when No. 218 Squadron arrived with its Fairey Battles. The squadron did not keep its light bombers very long, soon re-equipping with the Wellington medium bomber.

Wing Commander Embry was on his last operation with No. 107 Squadron when he led the squadron on a mission over France on 29th May, 1940, for he had been promoted to the acting rank of Group Captain and posted to R.A.F. West Raynham, in Norfolk, that day. He was not to take up the post for some time, however, for when in the target area, Embry's Blenheim received a direct hit in the fuselage from enemy anti-aircraft fire. Corporal Lang in the gun-turret amidships was killed by the explosion, but Embry and his navigator, Pilot Officer T. Whiting, were able to bale-out, landing near the advancing German troops. Both were swiftly captured, but Embry managed to slip away from his captors and, after pursuing an adventurous and often desperate course across France, eventually reached the Spanish frontier. He arrived back in Ipswich on 2nd August and in due course resumed his duties. His remarkable exploits are related in great detail in a fine book *Winged Victory* by Anthony Richardson.

Even returning British bombers sometimes had to run the gauntlet of the British defences, which were not sufficiently versed in aircraft recognition at this time to distinguish friend from foe. An Armstrong Whitworth Whitley returning from a raid on the night of 22nd May was hotly engaged by the anti-aircraft guns at Felixstowe and Harwich but managed to carry on, whilst on the 22nd January, 1941, a Blenheim flying off the coast near Lowestoft was mistaken for a Junkers Ju.88 and shot down by naval anti-aircraft fire, the crew all perishing.

The Harwich balloon barrage was also a hazard to returning bombers. One of the first victims was a Hampden of No. 44 Squadron from Waddington, Lincolnshire, which struck a balloon cable on the night of 4th June, 1940. Three of the crew died when it crashed into the River Orwell, only the pilot, a sergeant escaping. An even worse tragedy occurred on Thursday 13th June, when another Hampden belonging to No. 144 Squadron based at Hemswell, Lincolnshire, flew into a balloon cable and crashed onto the East Anglian Flour Mills at Felixstowe Dock. Bursting into flames, destroying the bomber and part of the mill, the crew all perished and a member of the mill staff, Mr D. J. Grayling died later from his injuries. The flames reached out and set fire to four barges anchored in the Dock alongside the mill, the *Golden Grain, Phoenician, The Miller* and *Rayjohn,* as well as five railway trucks.

Many of the Eastern Counties based squadrons continued their daily forays across the Channel, bombing and machine-gunning the advancing German armies as opportunity offered. Two of the squadrons, Nos. 99 and 149, left their bases at Newmarket Heath and Mildenhall when Italy declared war on the Allies on 10th June and flew to an airfield at Salon, not far from Marseilles, to carry the war to the junior partner in the Axis. Because the French held up operations, fearing reprisal attacks by the Italians, the first raids on Italy were not made until the 15th June, and the two Wellington units returned to England on the 17th June.

About the same time the Blenheims, now with partial fighter escort, turned their attention to the Luftwaffe-occupied airfields in France, considerable damage being inflicted on parked aircraft at Merville on 14th June. When the French Government accepted the German Armistice terms on 22nd June and all fighting in France ceased, the Blenheims switched to a daylight cloud-cover offensive against oil installations, refineries and railways in north-west Germany.

The Blenheim lacked both the speed and, in spite of extra guns having been fitted since its entry into service, the armament needed to defend itself successfully against attack and losses sustained by the squadrons operating this aircraft continued to be severe. The 10th July was a black day for No. 107 at Wattisham, for only one out of six aircraft returned from an attack on a German occupied aerodrome near Amiens. The badly mauled No. 105 had been resting at Honington and became operational again on moving to Watton, but No. 82 Squadron operating from Bodney, between Swaffham and Brandon, was virtually wiped out on 13th August whilst carrying out a day-light raid on North West Germany.

After the fall of France the fear of invasion was intensified and the R.A.F. made plans for close co-operation with the Army if the Wehrmacht did mount an operation against Britain's shores. The large concentration of barges and transport being massed in the Channel ports were photographed from the air daily and the Blenheims carried out heavy attacks on them from time to time. A new alert was raised when bodies in German uniform were washed up on the beaches from Great Yarmouth southward, local rumour telling how an invasion had been attempted and had failed. Only later was it learnt that the troops had been drowned whilst carrying out exercises off the Continental coast.

The heavy Luftwaffe attacks on England seemed to indicate that preparations for the invasion were coming to a head, although intelligence reports indicated that the attempt had been postponed from 21st September to the 24th. As the chosen day for "Operation Sealion", the proposed invasion of Britain, came and passed the bomber attacks on the barge concentrations went on, and then another target presented itself to the British bombers, the long-range guns which had started to fling shells into the South Coast towns from their emplacements in the area of Cap Gris Nez. During September the attacks on the Channel Ports were mounted on a round-the-clock basis, but the daylight raids had to be cancelled owing to the heavy losses sustained by the attacking forces. The losses were tragically emphasised in the case of a Blenheim from No. 105 Squadron which had mechanical trouble when returning from Cologne and crashed into Foxley Wood as it attempted to land at Swanton Morley; all the crew were killed. So were the crew of a Wellington which crashed into the sea in flames only 150 yards from Felixstowe beach on 7th November; only two of the airmen's bodies were recovered. On 15th December the body of a German airman, Unteroffizier Karl Fritz, was washed up on Felixstowe beach, while five days later the body of an R.A.F. air gunner drifted ashore on the same spot; the sea made no distinction between friend and foe.

The biggest raid by the light bomber forces up to that time was carried out on the night of the 10th-11th February 1941, when more than 200 aircraft attacked targets in North West Germany. But again the losses were heavy, several aircraft crashing on and around their bases as they returned.

The new heavies of Bomber Command made their appearance during March and were blooded on operations. The four-engined Short Stirlings of No. 7 Squadron at Oakington, Cambridgeshire, made for the German warships *Scharnhorst* and *Gneisenau* at Brest while the new twin-engined Avro Manchesters of No. 207 Squadron bombed the important naval base at Lorient. One of the Manchesters, L.7278, was on its way home from Lorient on 21st March when the port motor caught fire. Two crew members baled out as the machine lost height, but they were too low for their parachutes to open properly and both were killed. The pilot brought the stricken aircraft in for a forced landing in a field near Wymondham, Norfolk, but it struck a large tree, spun round and broke up; two of the remaining crew members were killed, the rest were seriously injured.

The Marham based Squadrons, Nos. 115 and 218, also joined in the attacks on the warships at Brest on the 4th and 30th March and 13th, 14th and 25th April, while the Wattisham squadrons with others based in the region changed their target

First of the new four-engined heavy bombers to see service, the Short Stirling operated from many regional airfields. Owing to its somewhat limited performance it was superseded during the middle years of the war by the Halifax and Lancaster. *Shorts*

to enemy ships in the North Sea. The method of attack was to go in fast and low, drop their bombs and climb away as swiftly as possible to avoid the intense flak. This was an extremely dangerous operation, and many aircraft were lost.

In contrast with the experiences of the Blenheims, the Stirlings of No. 7 Squadron from Oakington stood up well to attacks by defending fighters when they made an unescorted daylight raid on Emden on 27th April. Meanwhile, the Bristol Blenheim IV bombers were still in the thick of the fray, with Nos. 107 and 110 Squadrons flying daily sorties from Wattisham against enemy shipping off the Dutch coast and against targets in the coastal belt of Northern Germany. One target was the liner *Europa* sealed up in her dock at Bremerhaven.

Serving with No. 107 Squadron at this time was Pilot Officer Bill Edrich, better known as a cricketer than as a bomber pilot. While operating from Great Massingham, he spent as much time as the war would allow with the local cricketers in their village games.

The bravery of the Blenheim crews, flying against heavily defended targets in aircraft which were comparatively slow and lightly armed, could never be doubted. If any proof were needed it came with the award of the Victoria Cross to Wing Commander H. I. Edwards, a Wattisham pilot, who on 4th July 1941, led No. 105 Squadron in a daylight attack on Bremen, one of Germany's most heavily defended areas. Four aircraft were lost and Wing Commander Edwards was himself wounded, but his daring leadership in an operation which required the attackers to fly at no more than 50 feet and his determination in pressing home the attack fully merited the high award.

Three days later another V.C. was won by one of the New Zealanders flying Wellingtons from Feltwell, Sergeant J. A. Ward of No. 75 R.N.Z.A.F. Squadron, for saving his aircraft while over enemy territory. Incredible as the feat must seem, Sergeant Ward wriggled out through the astro-hatch of the Wellington of which he was the second pilot and scrambled down the side of the fuselage, making hand and footholds in the structure as he went, in order to reach the wing. He then made his way along the upper surface of the mainplane and using an engine cover, smothered a fire in the rear of the engine nacelle. Having put the fire out he made his way back to the fuselage and, helped by the navigator, climbed back into the aircraft. As a result of his action the aircraft reached its base safely. The Canadian pilot, Squadron Leader Widdanson, was awarded the Distinguished Flying Cross and the rear gunner, who warded off a night fighter while Sergeant Ward was busy on the wing, the Distinguished Flying Medal. Sergeant Ward was lost on operations during September 1941, and was buried in a Hamburg cemetery.

Another man to receive the senior award for gallantry was Wing Commander H. G. Malcolm who, early in the war, was serving in East Anglia. He won the V.C. when No. 18 Squadron, after its posting to North Africa, attacked Chenigiu airfield on 4th December 1941, the entire squadron being shot down in the course of the operation.

New aircraft began to come into service with the squadrons based in Eastern England during 1941, some of them being American types supplied under "Lease-Lend". The first Boeing Fortress B17C to enter service with the R.A.F., AN.521, arrived at R.A.F. Watton, Norfolk, on 1st May 1941, after flying from America to Scotland in eight and a half hours. These four-engined monoplane bombers were destined to be used by the R.A.F. on high-flying operations against selected targets, operating at altitudes of up to 34,000 feet, but their range was not impressive. They carried seven machine-guns and a load of four 1,000 lb bombs of American design, the only type which could be used.

On 7th May, 1941, No. 90 Squadron was formed at West Raynham to use the Fortress I, as the R.A.F. designated the B17C. Owing to the special nature of the operations on which the Fortress was to be employed, air-crews were selected after very searching tests with oxygen equipment to ensure that they could stand up to the rigours of the work they would have to do; the age limit was twenty-five. In addition to the rarity of the atmosphere, crews had to endure air temperatures as low as minus fifty degrees Centigrade.

The first crew training flights were made from Massingham and Bodney, in Norfolk, though neither airfield was really suitable for such large aircraft. No. 90 Squadron suffered its first casualty on 22nd June when AN.521, the first Fortress to be received, crashed with the loss of its entire crew while on a training flight.

American built Boeing Fortress I of No. 90 Squadron, R.A.F. which flew from Marham, Norfolk. Not wholly successful these aircraft intended for extreme altitude bombing saw only limited service and were withdrawn soon after entering operations.

The Fortresses went into action for the first time on 8th July, when three of them made a high altitude raid on a target in North Germany without any great success. They were in action again on the 24th when three of No. 90 Squadron's aircraft made the long run to Brest to attack the battleship *Gneisenau* and the cruiser *Prinz Eugen* still sheltering in the French port. The Stirlings of No. 7 Squadron also ventured forth against the German capital ships about the same time, making a daylight attack on the *Scharnhorst,* which had moved from Brest to La Pallice in an attempt to escape the R.A.F. bombing.

Another new four-engined bomber, the Handley-Page Halifax, made its first raid on Italy during the night of 10th/11th September 1941 using Stradishall as a forward base from which to begin the long haul to Turin. Even so, they could carry barely enough fuel and three of the aircraft crashed on the way home when their tanks emptied prematurely. A Halifax was employed as the tug when the giant General Aircraft Hamilcar glider was towed aloft for the first time from Newmarket

The Handley-Page Halifax went through several design changes which altered its appearance considerably. This is a Mark I with pointed fins and four Rolls Royce Merlin motors. *Rolls-Royce*

Heath during February 1942. These tank-carrying gliders were later used in fairly large numbers.

The skies of the Eastern Counties were busy on 12th August when a large-scale attack was carried out on two large power stations near Cologne which were then the most powerful generating stations in Europe. 54 Blenheims from bases in the region, escorted by a squadron of Westland Whirlwind twin-engined single-seat long-range fighters temporarily based at Martlesham Heath, took part in the raid. Unfortunately a Blenheim from Martlesham Heath and one from Ipswich Airport which were to have acted as group navigators were shot down before reaching the target area, but the power stations were left in a badly damaged condition.

During October, 1941, it was decided to withdraw the ageing Blenheim from operations as the losses with this type were mounting, but the Blenheims of No. 82 Squadron at Bodney found a new lease of life when they were employed as intruders over airfields in the Low Countries. The writing was on the wall for the Blenheim when three American Douglas Boston III light bombers arrived at Wattisham on 14th October for working-up trials.

The Blenheim was not the only type to suffer losses, however, and people in Norfolk and Suffolk became somewhat used to crippled aircraft crash-landing as they returned from operations. A Wellington, obviously with engine trouble, flew along the shore off Felixstowe on 14th August and soon afterwards people ashore heard a loud explosion as it crashed in the sea. It was presumed to be that aircraft which had dropped four high-explosive bombs, only one of which exploded, at Hollesley.

When more than 400 heavy bombers visited Berlin, Mannheim and the Cologne area on the night of 7th/8th November no fewer than thirty-seven of them were lost, including several Stirlings from bases in the area. Two days after Christmas Avro Manchester L.7483 of No. 207 Squadron, returning from Germany with failing motors, made a heavy landing at Martlesham Heath and ran off the end of the runway and through the boundary fence, but it was luckier than a Whitley from Croft in Yorkshire which fell foul of the balloon barrage at Harwich during the night of 28th January, 1942. The crew of five were all killed when it crashed in flames near the Cork Lightship; two dead crew members were picked up, Sergeant Campbell was buried at sea and the body of Sergeant Dobson was brought ashore.

One unit which had more than its share of ill-fortune was No. 1 Anti-Aircraft Co-operation Unit, based at Langham, in North Norfolk. The Hawker Henley Mk.III target tugs with which this unit was equipped were prone to engine over-heating owing to their slow progress while towing a large sleeve target, and several of them crashed or force-landed in various parts of North Norfolk, one of them at Nelson's birthplace, Burnham Thorpe. One wonders what the admiral's reaction would have been to the mine-laying operations carried out by the Stirlings of No. 218 Squadron, which moved to Marham in January 1942. These "Gardening" operations, as they were known, doubtless had their effect on enemy coastal traffic but the R.A.F.'s work did not prevent the German major warships from breaking out of their French bases and making a run for north Germany through the English Channel and the North Sea in February.

There was feverish activity on many of the Eastern Counties' airfields on 12th February, a wet and windy day, when it became known that the battleships had put to sea. No. 88 Squadron at Attlebridge, north-west of Norwich, sought the enemy warships without success in their newly acquired Bostons, while the Blenheims of Wattisham's No. 110 and West Raynham's No. 114 also attempted to stop the ships, but with no more success than the suicidal attacks mounted by the "Stringbags"* of the Fleet Air Arm in the Channel. No. 82 Squadron from Watton made a final attempt to locate the enemy force, but in terrible weather conditions the ships eluded their would-be attackers and ploughed through the grey North Sea to the relative safety of their home bases.

The skies throbbed throughout the night of 30th/31st May 1942 when Bomber Command mounted "Operation Millenium", the first thousand-bomber raid of the war. No fewer than 1,046 bombers were dispatched to Cologne, and the sound of their engines had hardly died away when a new note was heard as the De Havilland Mosquitos of No. 105 Squadron roared away from Horsham St Faiths to make their

*Fairey Swordfish, biplane torpedo bombers of the Fleet Air Arm.

first operational sortie, an early morning attack on the still-smoking ruins of Cologne, devastated by the heavies earlier. The Mosquitos, unarmed bombers which depended on the speed given by their twin Rolls-Royce Merlin engines to give them relative immunity from fighter attack, were a new and important concept in aerial warfare. They were to have a considerable effect on the course of the war and were to take part in several spectacular operations during 1942.

Another new type made its appearance on the last day of May when No. 21 Squadron at Bodney received its first American-built Lockheed Ventura, an enlarged version of the already well-known Hudson. Dogged by mechanical troubles, this aircraft did not fulfil expectations; later it was said that the Ventura could do anything that the Hudson could do, and burn more fuel doing it.

There was still work for the war-weary Blenheims from Wattisham and West Raynham, however. They joined in the offensive against German war industry on 30th May and then spent the next few days attacking Luftwaffe bases in Holland, hitting those at Venlo, Twente, Schiphol and Vechta.

During mid 1942, Stirling N.3703 coded MG-F of No. 7 Squadron, based at Oakington, Cambridgeshire, was shot down over Holland and made a forced landing near Gorkum. The crew were made prisoner-of-war, but the bomber which had not suffered a great deal of damage was salvaged and repaired by the Luftwaffe and was flown in German markings for some time by a Luftwaffe Test Group.

We are able to survive wars by our ability to submerge the horror and terror of it all and to remember happy and humorous moments. This is an unfortunate trait in that we tend to give the impression, to younger generations, that war is a glamorous and happy occasion; something that is very far from the truth. Mrs Ruby Robertson of Halesworth, who joined the W.A.A.F.* in 1939, gained little impression from seeing her first bomber but vividly remembers the first Station dance at Mildenhall. At this dance, to which local army units were invited, she danced with a handsome Army officer "no other than Richard Green, the famous screen hero of 'Robin Hood'." Mr Wigg of Saxmundham smiles when he recalled that during his early Service days the drill instructor stood the squad at ease on the parade square and pointing to the airman alongside him said, "I'll bet you come from Suffolk, don't you." "Yes Sergeant," replied the man. "I knew it, I knew it! You swing that rifle of yours like a ruddy muck fork!"

The development of new types of aircraft was not the only work going on behind the scenes, for new navigational aids and new methods of bomb aiming, new types of radio and more advanced radar sets were being worked on by the backroom boys. So it was that on the night of 11th/12th August 1942, two "Gee"-equipped aircraft from Marham made the first operational trip using the new radar navigational and bombing aid. Munchen Gladbach was the target that night, and on their return the bomber crews reported that they had been able to locate the target area without difficulty.

Though in Britain there might be a feeling that the tide was about to turn, in

*Women's Auxiliary Air Force, now Women's Royal Air Force (W.R.A.F.)

Occupied France morale was at a low ebb. The Germans were apprehensive and maintained constant patrols in the streets, which did nothing to encourage French morale, and matters were not improved by the sudden disappearance of many Frenchmen who were considered by the forces of occupation as being a hindrance to their rule. It was necessary for the Allies to remedy this situation by boosting French morale in some way.

The French Resistance movement reported that at noon each day the Germans put on a show of force in the Champs Elysées, parading a column of infantry led by a military band, the parade being guarded by a string of armoured cars with guns manned ready for any attack. The troops kept well away from the tree-lined sides where danger might lurk and were dismissed in front of the former French Ministry of Marine, which had become the Paris Headquarters of the dreaded Geheimat-staatspolizei, the Gestapo. A daring scheme was devised by the Air Officer Commanding Coastal Command, Sir Phillip Joubert de la Ferté, to let the French know that they did not stand alone during these dark days. The red, white and blue tricolor has always been dear to the heart of the Frenchman, and Sir Phillip reckoned that if such a flag could be dropped in full view of the assembled crowds, to the embarrassment of the occupying Germans, the message would be plain to the French.

Accordingly Flight Lieutenant A. K. Gatward and Sergeant G. F Fern, who were serving with No. 236 Squadron flying the twin-engined Bristol Beaufighter VIC from Wattisham, were summoned to Coastal Command headquarters and told of the secret plan, then code-named "Operation Squabble". When they returned to Suffolk, the word was put round that "They had been posted on a course," taking their aircraft with them. In fact Beaufighter ND-C was flown down to Thorney Island, Hampshire, where the two-man crew practised "real low-level flying both over land and sea" and also made intensive study of the landmarks of central Paris until they knew them by heart. In preparation for the event a new tricolour was obtained from the Royal Navy's dockyard stores at Portsmouth: after it had been halved a flat iron bar was sewn into the short edge of each piece so that it would make the greatest possible visual impact when it was dropped.

When all was ready, ND-C took off on its mission on 13th May but over France the crew found clear skies and the mission had to be aborted as were further attempts on the 15th, 21st and 26th May. On 12th June however, the forecast was good cloud cover along the route the Beaufighter would have to take, and once more ND-C set out with its unusual load. Flying extremely low over the Channel and hedge-hopping across the French countryside, the Beaufighter made good time to Paris. At exactly the right moment the pilot sighted the Eiffel Tower and climbed for the "performance".

Even the best laid schemes can fail and for the first time for many weeks there was no parade, so the disappointed crew took the Beaufighter the length of the Champs Elysées below rooftop level, roared up over the Arc de Triomphe, dropping the tricolour at that spot and then shot up the Gestapo Headquarters at top floor level. ND-C raced for home at between 100 feet and a mere 30 feet, on the way hurtling low over a German airfield. The Beaufighter arrived safely at Northolt, its only damage, an oil radiator dented by a low flying crow.

Reports from France confirmed that the operation had had the desired effect on French morale, though the German forces in the Paris area were told by official sources that the Beaufighter was "a Luftwaffe aircraft out of control". This rather extraordinary statement did nothing to spoil the satisfaction of Flight Lieutenant Gatward, who was later promoted to Wing Commander and in the course of further operations gained the Distinguished Service Order (D.S.O.) and the Distinguished Flying Cross (D.F.C.) and bar. Sergeant Fern, the navigator, who gained the Distinguished Flying Medal (D.F.M.) for the "flag-showing" operation, was later commissioned and attained the rank of Squadron Leader.

The arrival in service of the Mosquito presented the R.A.F. with an excellent small bomber and an ideal aircraft for special operations which were in the same tradition as that carried out by Beaufighter ND-C. It was six Mosquitos of No. 105 Squadron from Marham that carried out the first R.A.F. daylight raid on Berlin on 19th September 1942, though this attack, carried out in bad weather, was largely unsuccessful. Only one aircraft dropped its bombs on Berlin while the one flown by Squadron Leader Messervy, D.F.C. was shot down by a German Fighter.

No. 105 Squadron had received its Mosquito IV bombers during April and its first operation was the Cologne raid already described. At that stage the graceful twin-engined aircraft carried as its main bomb load four 500lb. high explosive bombs, but in later versions this load was considerably increased. This first Mosquito squadron, which caused the Germans great concern, carried the unit

Deadly and feared by the enemy, the De Havilland Mosquito bomber turned up at the most unexpected times for the opposition. The example illustrated, a Mark IX, was the unarmed bomber version. *Hawker Siddeley*

code GB, one of the first aircraft to enter service being DZ.360, coded GB-A. The squadron was at first commanded by Wing Commander Peter Simmons, but Wing Commander Hughie Edwards, V.C. from Wattisham took over command in August 1942 at which time the light bomber squadrons left Wattisham to make way for engineers who moved in to lengthen the runways in preparation for the arrival of the 10th Air Depot Group, United States Army Air Force.

The Mosquitos from Marham first came into the public eye when, on 25th September 1942, No. 105 Squadron made a daylight raid on the Gestapo headquarters in Oslo which was timed to coincide with a large rally of Quislings, Norwegians co-operating with the Nazis. The bombers left their Norfolk base and flew to an aerodrome in Scotland, where they topped up their fuel tanks before making their way at low altitude across the North Sea. Arriving over the target exactly on time, they carried out the attack with creditable accuracy, not only inflicting a severe shock on the Germans and their collaborators but boosting the morale of Norwegian patriots.

Three days after the raid, R.A.F. Marham was transferred from No. 3 Group to No. 2 Group, No. 218 Squadron leaving the station for Downham Market and the long-serving No. 115 going to Mildenhall. With its newly installed Mosquito squadrons, Nos. 105 and 139, Marham became a light bomber station, and remained as such for the rest of the war.

Throughout October the light bombers, the Bostons, Venturas and Mosquitos, ranged daily from their East Anglian bases over Occupied Europe, hitting at military objectives of all kinds. Air activity over the region became more noticeable the following month, when quite large formations of Bostons, Venturas, Mitchells and Mosquitos were to be seen flying fast and low over the countryside.

It all led up to a raid on 6th December that has gone down in the annals of aerial warfare. Code-named "Operation Oyster", this raid had as its target the huge radio valve and electrical components factory of Philips at Eindhoven in Holland. The attack on the main plant was made by Nos. 105, 107, 139, 464 and 487 Squadrons, while Nos. 88, 226 and 21 Squadrons bombed the valve works, the targets being well covered with bombs and machine-gun fire and very severe damage being inflicted on the two vital factories.

Mrs Lena Smith of Witnesham, Suffolk, whose home was at Eindhoven, recalls running out of her house and seeing aircraft appear just over the rooftops. Vivid in her memory is the sight of a flak tower with gun and crew on top which must have received a direct hit at its base; it seemed suspended in mid-air for a time before settling down in a cloud of smoke and dust. She speaks of the accuracy of the bombing, which left the surrounding properties relatively undamaged while destroying large parts of the factory buildings. Although to many Dutch people the raid meant the end of their place of work, they took it philosophically as a sign that the R.A.F. were preparing to free them from the oppressor's yoke.

On the debit side, however, four Bostons, one Mosquito and no fewer than nine

Venturas were lost or went missing, though Ventura AE.697 managed to struggle across the North Sea and ditch off Bawdsey, on the Suffolk coast.

The Venturas from Methwold, Norfolk, led by Squadron Leader L. H. Trent were particularly unlucky. First they ran into intense flak as they flew low over the Dutch countryside, and then the arrival of large numbers of enemy fighters drew the attention of the Spitfire escort. One by one the bombers crashed, until Squadron Leader Trent's aircraft and one other Ventura were the only survivors of the formation. As they dropped their bombs on the target the other Ventura took a direct hit and blew up in the air.

The lone survivor turned for home after dropping his bombs, but the grim story was not over. The Ventura was hit again and again and began breaking up in the air. Squadron Leader Trent and the navigator survived, being thrown clear as the plane crashed, but the rest of the crew perished; it was only when they and other survivors of the raid were released from prisoner-of-war camps in 1945 that the story of the Methwold Venturas came to light, and Squadron Leader Trent was awarded the Victoria Cross for the gallantry he displayed in pressing home the attack.

Another V.C. was won by an East Anglian bomber pilot, Flight Sergeant G. H. Middleton on the night of 28th November. Middleton was the pilot of Stirling BF372 of No. 149 Squadron, which had taken off from Mildenhall to bomb the Fiat Works at Turin. While over the target he was badly hurt when an A.A. shell struck his aircraft, his injuries included the loss of an eye, but as he collapsed, the co-pilot, Flight Sergeant Hyder, took over and carried on the attack.

The pilot regained consciousness a little later and in spite of his severe injuries insisted on taking over the controls to fly the Stirling back to its home airfield. The aircraft was practically out of fuel by the time it crossed the English coast, so Flight Sergeant Middleton ordered the crew to jump to safety, but before they could all get away the Stirling crashed into the sea, taking with it not only the gallant pilot but Sergeant Mackie, the front gunner, and Sergeant Jeffrey the flight engineer both who had stayed behind to assist the pilot.

It was also in an attack on Turin that another Stirling pilot, Flight Sergeant A. L. Aaran of No. 218 Squadron based at Downham Market, on the edge of the Fens, won the Victoria Cross on 12th August 1943. Aaran's aircraft, EF.452 was badly damaged and the pilot grievously wounded in the face and arms. Like Flight Sergeant Middleton, he lost consciousness as a result of his wounds but insisted on taking over the controls again when he came round, though the Stirling was then flying on three engines.

He endeavoured to make a landing in Sicily, but owing to the damage done to the instruments and the state of the crew they overflew the island and crossed the Mediterranean to make landfall over North Africa. Putting the bomber down for a crash-landing, Flight Sergeant Aaran managed to get it down in one piece, thus saving the lives of his crew. He himself was carried from the aircraft, but he died the next day from his terrible injuries.

With such a large number of Short Stirling bombers operating in the region, Short Brothers set up a large repair depot at Madingley, a few miles west of Cambridge. Named "Selvos Limited", it not only dealt with local repairs to Stirlings but also carried out modifications as these became necessary.

A strange visitor to the area was the half-scale flying research model of the Short Stirling, the Short S.31. This miniature aircraft, powered by four Pobjoy Niagaria 90 h.p. motors, carried a crew of two and was the aerodynamic proving design for the full size bomber. Arriving at Stradishall, a Stirling base, it was damaged on landing, but after languishing in a hangar for several months, it was finally repaired and flown out again.

New crews arriving at the station and eager to take a first look at their new mounts were confronted with the S.31, a gift for the practical jokers. Taken along to the hangar in question, they came face to face with a bomber not a great deal larger than a Hurricane fighter!

On 5th May 1943, No. 7 Squadron at Oakington exchanged its Stirlings for Avro Lancaster B.III's and started operations with their new aircraft. Life on a bomber station at this time is recalled by Mr L. Patient of Chelmsford, who was posted to East Wretham, near Thetford, which was then the home of a Czech bomber squadron, No. 311, flying Wellington ICs.

"During my stay they converted to Lancasters, and there was one incident I vividly recall. A group of us were standing on the other side of the 'drome on parade when a Lancaster, on a training flight with an instructor and four pilots aboard, banked very steeply in front of the control tower, narrowly missing it. In so doing the wingtip touched the concrete apron in front of the tower. We stood there as the big plane just crumpled into the ground. By the time we'd reached it nothing remained but four charred and smoking engines lying on the concrete.

One Lancaster always occupied the same 'frying-pan'* dispersal when she was at home. This was 'Q for Queenie', and we grew to love the sight of her. One morning however, the dispersal was empty, and it remained so for several days until one morning there was Queenie again. But wait, this was not our Queenie. It was an intruder, a brand new one; it could never be the same as the old one. We never did learn what happened to her.

Our next adventure was a move to a new aerodrome at Tuddenham near Mildenhall, to prepare for the advance party of thirty men, but for the time being we were three only and we dined extremely well until the arrival of the cooks three weeks later."

The part played by the heavy bombers in hammering at the enemy homeland night after night was of great importance to the war effort, but it was the light bombers that made some of the more spectacular raids of 1943. On 27th January, for instance, nine Mosquitos of Nos. 105 and 139 Squadrons made a 1,400 mile round flight from their Norfolk bases to carry out a daylight raid on the Burmeister and Wain shipbuilding yards in Copenhagen, one of the main producers of diesel

*Hardstanding shaped in plan view like a frying pan.

engines for the German U-boats and therefore of great significance. Two aircraft were lost on this operation, in which the Mosquitos were led by Wing Commander Hughie Edwards, V.C.

Five days later, Berlin again heard the smooth roar of Merlin motors as the Mosquitos of No. 105 Squadron from Marham broke up a large parade about to be addressed by Field Marshal Hermann Goering. More importantly, perhaps, the roar of their exploding bombs was heard all over Germany as radio listeners waited to hear a broadcast of Goering's speech, which was delayed for half an hour. Those first three Mosquitos, led by Squadron Leader Reynolds, with Pilot Officer Lismore as his navigator, returned safely after completing their task but three other Mosquitos which left Marham later that day, led by Squadron Leader Darling of No. 139 Squadron, found the defences on the alert. The leader was lost as they headed for Berlin, the remaining aircraft flown by Sergeant Mansey and Flight Sergeant McGeehan returning safely after bombing the German capital, forcing the Propaganda Minister, Joseph Goebbels, to dive for cover.

One of the Marham Mosquitos, a BIV, failed to make its home base on 20th March. Circling on the approach to Martlesham Heath, it crashed into Foxborrow Wood at Brightwell, the pilot being killed instantly and the observer, Flying Officer Clear, dying later of his injuries.

The Mosquitos of Nos. 105 and 139 Squadrons were out again on 27th March when they attacked the Zeiss and Schatt optical works at Jena in daylight. Another force consisting of twelve Venturas of No. 487 R.N.Z.A.F. Squadron and six Bostons of No. 107 with fighter escort which two days before attacked the large Amsterdam power station and the Royal Dutch Steel Works at Ijmuiden met such fierce opposition that only one Ventura reached the target; its bombs missed. The lone Ventura was eventually shot down, crashing in Holland, so No. 487 Squadron was entirely lost. On 26th May, King George VI visited the squadron to pay his respects to the depleted unit and to have a word with those who were even then endeavouring to rebuild the squadron.

Norfolk had by this time become the home of several light bomber units mainly employing the North American Mitchell twin-engined bomber, and flying from Foulsham, Attlebridge and West Raynham. Several of these squadrons consisted of personnel of the Allied forces in exile, the Free French, Norwegian, the Polish Air Forces and the Royal Netherlands Navy. One of the Dutch squadrons, No. 320, flying Mitchells from Attlebridge, made their first sortie on 17th August against targets in Northern France. Later that month they were operating over their own country.

The same day that No. 320 Squadron made its first operational flight the skies over the Eastern Counties vibrated to the massed throbbing of bomber engines as the R.A.F. despatched 600 "heavies" to Peenemunde, the German experimental establishment on the Baltic coast which was even then developing the rocket weapons with which Hitler hoped to turn the course of the war back in his favour. 40

of the bombers were lost on this operation, and a further 15 crashed on their return from the raid.

The region's airfields saw the completion of many epic flights by the bombers, one of the most gallant of them all being that of a No. 61 Squadron Lancaster LM360, which had set off for Dusseldorf on the night of the 3rd/4th November 1943. The pilot, Flight Lieutenant W. Reid, was badly wounded when the bomber was attacked by a Messerschmitt night fighter, but he carried on towards the target. Then he was again wounded in an attack in which the navigator, Flight Sergeant Jefferies, was killed and the wireless operator, Sergeant Norris, mortally wounded. He was still three-quarters of an hour's flying time from the target, but Flight Lieutenant Reid decided to carry on and eventually bombed his objective before turning for home. With all his navigational instruments smashed and his navigator dead, he set course by the stars, successfully crossing the North Sea and bringing the badly damaged bomber in to land at Shipdham, in Norfolk, though on the way he became helpless through loss of blood. For his gallantry he was awarded the Victoria Cross.

The difficulties facing pilots returning from operations were increased greatly when fog hid their home airfields. During the last weeks of September 1943 experiments were carried out with a device intended to assist aircraft which returned to a fogbound countryside, the initial trials being conducted at Lakenheath. Code named "FIDO" which stood for Fog Investigation Dispersal Operation, the device consisted of two large pipelines running on the surface of the ground alongside the runway. Petrol was pumped under pressure through these pipes and then ignited in burner units, the intense heat of the burning petrol causing the fog to disperse in the vicinity of the runway.

The system was extremely costly to operate, and several aircrews who used it have related to the author how perturbed they were as they approached to two leaping lines of flame and contemplated the effect of a swing off the runway. The "crash strip" at Woodbridge (Sutton Heath) was equipped with the device, which was used there on many occasions*.

The glare in the sky created by "FIDO" was parallelled on the other side of the North Sea by the marker flares employed by the Pathfinders which provided target-marking facilities for the main bomber forces. The Pathfinder Force, No. 8 Group, was formed in August 1942 and was to play an important part in spearheading the bomber attacks on Germany, though the Commander-in-Chief disapproved of its formation because he feared that the posting of experienced crews from other Bomber Command units to the pathfinder force would drain the command of its best crews.

During July 1943, Marham became a part of the Pathfinder Force. The station's versatile Mosquitos, equipped with "Oboe", the blind bombing radar device, sought out their targets in all weathers, placing their scintillating flares and markers "on the spot" for the heavies to follow. No. 109 Squadron was the first unit

*The history of R.A.F. Woodbridge is told in full in *Bawdsey — Birth of the Beam*, by Gordon Kinsey, published by Terence Dalton, 1983.

to use "Oboe" operationally, during a raid on Dusseldorf on New Year's Day 1943.

The ability of the new force was shown on the night of 25th/26th July, 1943, when Mosquitos of No. 109 Squadron marked the target, the Krupps armament works at Essen, for the following force of 600 bombers. Even the German radio, not renowned for its frankness on such matters, admitted that the factories had suffered severe damage. Another example of the "Mossies" work was seen on the night of 12th October 1943 when the marking of the Pathfinders and the bombing of the main force combined to such good effect that a direct hit was made on the lock gates at Dusseldorf — from 29,000 feet in darkness.

The Pathfinders were not the only aircraft to go out ahead of the main bomber force, for during December 1943, No. 2 Group Mosquitos were given a new role in support of the heavies of Bomber Command. Mosquito bombers and Mosquito long-range intruder fighters were both involved in the operation, code-named "FLOWER" the former going out ahead of the main bomber force and attacking the Luftwaffe night fighter bases while the latter roamed the skies over the same area in an attempt to keep the German fighters grounded. Two bases usually employed for these operations were Bradwell Bay, on the southern shore of the Blackwater in Essex, and Coltishall in Norfolk.

There was no let-up even at Christmas. On Christmas Day 1943 some 1,300 aircraft attacked installations near Calais, on the Channel Coast of France, the majority of the attacking force coming from the Eastern Counties and Lincolnshire.

As the attacks mounted, so did the enemy's defences become more efficient and better prepared. With the German coastal early warning radar chain now fully established it was possible for the defence system to get its fighters up in advance to meet the incoming R.A.F. bombers. Many schemes were experimented with in order to confuse the German defences; bombers flew a zig-zag course towards their target or were routed so as to arrive over their target from the opposite direction to that from which they were expected; and attempts were made to swamp the radar screens with interference.

Efforts had been made throughout the course of the war to develop radio counter-measures to defeat German fighter control and radar systems. In 1942 No. 109 Squadron had been operating from Stradishall as a trials radio counter-measures unit and at that time it had on its strength two unusual aircraft, the Wellington Mk VI pressurised high-altitude version of the bomber. Their stay at Stradishall was brief, however, as there were numerous breakdowns with this pioneer aeroplane.

The final outcome of this line of development was the fitting of several bombers with radio interference gear and the formation of a special group, No. 100 Group, which operated from several north Norfolk airfields such as Foulsham, North Creake, Little Snoring and Great Massingham. This group was commanded by Air Vice Marshal E. B. Addison, a very experienced officer in radio and allied subjects, and its aircrews were selected from the more experienced crews. Later long-range fighters were also equipped for this work and carried out their duties actually over enemy territory.

So important was this radio counter-measure work that at the end of the war there were no fewer than 14 squadrons engaged in such operations. The same group carried out the broadcasting of fake operational information to the German night fighter forces from high over the North Sea. A new phase began in February 1944 when No. 214 Squadron operating from Sculthorpe began using the Boeing Fortress III, the R.A.F. equivalent of the U.S.A.A.F.'s B17G for radio counter-measures and radio jamming duties.

In the spring of 1944 the Mosquitos carried out further special operations in the same conditions as the Oslo raid of September, 1942. Information had been received from Holland that in the Gestapo headquarters in the Hague the German secret service held files containing the names of Dutch patriots and lists of those selected for internment and worse. It was essential that those files should be destroyed and the job was given to No. 613 Squadron from Swanton Morley, in Norfolk.

Led by Wing Commander Bateson, the squadron's eleven Mosquitos took off on a warm April day to fly across the North Sea at an altitude of 50 feet or less. If the operation was to be successful pinpoint bombing was necessary, for the bombs had to fall on the Kunstzaal-Kleiskamp Art Gallery, then used as Gestapo headquarters, and not on the Peace Palace next door. The bomb-aimers did not miss, and after the raid further confusion was created for the Germans by Dutch underground workers who were able to introduce thousands of false documents into the debris of the art gallery; utter chaos resulted when the Germans tried to reassemble the secret files.

Active preparations were being made for the coming invasion of Europe and to this end exercises were carried out in the Thetford area. Residents were mystified by aircraft dropping large flares at night, those involved being the Mitchells of No. 98 Squadron which were making simulated attacks on road transport in the vicinity. Witnesses said that the flares turned night into day and seemed to light up the best part of Norfolk and Suffolk.

Early on 6th June, 1944 much consternation was caused by the large numbers of aircraft passing over the region and the fleets of bombers flying towards the Continent, followed by tugs and their gliders. This was "D Day" and all the air activity was in support of the Allied landings. One incident, as a result of this operation, was that British civilian employees on the American bases were all detained on the aerodromes as a precautionary security measure, and not allowed home until the last plane had returned home. One workman stated that he was treated with great kindness and that their "hosts" were full of apologies for their enforced stay.

During 16th-18th September, armadas of gliders and their tugs set out from

Eastern Counties airfields, and gaining altitude, set course for Arnhem, Holland on a massive airborne landing attempt. The fleet, which was in two sections, took almost two and a half hours to pass over, and consisted in the main of twin-engined D.C.3s and Albemarle tugs with Horsa gliders, whilst the large tank carrying Hamilcar gliders were towed by the four engined Stirlings and Halifaxes. The Brightlingsea Observer Corp Post reported 1,500 aircraft in the air at one time with 129 planes passing overhead in a seven minute period. One and a half hours later the tugs appeared coming in from the sea again with the odd one still towing its charge which for some reason or other had failed to disengage. Many of the returning tugs were also in trouble themselves with smoking engines, feathered airscrews and metal and fabric streaming aft from rent wings and tail units.

A Lancaster from Mepal, Cambridgeshire, developed engine trouble over Felixstowe on 7th December, 1944, and turning inland crashed into the River Orwell, near Shotley. The crew launched their dinghy, hoisted sail and landed near Stratton Hall, Levington, and then walked over the fields to Trimley St Martin. Previously another bomber returning to Feltwell, Norfolk, had crashed into the sea just off Felixstowe Pier, and burst into flames with its crew of seven, comprising: —

424063 Flying Officer C. B. Oxenham (New Zealand); 2208026 Sergeant J. Corell; 1825324 Sergeant A. Craig (washed up 1st September); 128907 Flying Officer D. C. Haggis (washed up 1st September); 139976 Sergeant Dyer (washed up 2nd September); 639500 Flight Sergeant Murrey. The seventh crew member was never recovered.

As the Allies advanced towards Germany, so the bombers concentrated on the German war industry, but the still struggling Luftwaffe managed to send its intruders over to harass the bombers when they returned to their bases, waiting for them and attempting to shoot them down as they prepared to land.

Mosquitos of Nos. 21, 464 and 487 Squadrons made a spectacular attack on the Gestapo Headquarters at Shell House, Copenhagen on the 26th March, 1945. The purpose of the raid was to destroy the German records of Danish patriots and because of the situation of the target, called for precision bombing of the finest nature. Flying from local bases, they were escorted by Mustangs of No. 64 and 126 Squadrons, also from the region and led by Wing Commander Donnet, the Belgian ace.

Flying in the formation of Mosquitos was a "Wing Commander Smith", in reality, Air Marshal Basil Embry, the Air Officer Commanding No. 2 Group, who had looked at the other side of the sheet of instructions forbidding officers of Air-Rank taking part in operations over enemy territory. In an operation of this nature, casualties were bound to happen and none so tragic as Wing Commander Kleboe. Leading the second formation his low-flying Mosquito struck a signal post and, losing a wing, hurtled into a building and exploded. Unfortunately two other bombers mistook the blazing aircraft as their target, and their bombs fell near a convent where 87 children and 28 adults were tragically killed. The Gestapo

Headquarters was hit fairly and squarely and destroyed; the remainder of the Mosquitos led by Wing Commander Bateson returning home.

During April, Lancasters of No. 186 Squadron, stationed at Stradishall, took part in "Operation Manna", which consisted of dropping food supplies to the ex-occupied countries. On one such operation to Waalhaven, near Rotterdam, NF. 995 flown by Pilot Officer Rose was hit by small arms fire and the dropping mechanism was damaged, so the pilot returned to his base without delivering his containers of food. On arrival back at Stradishall, it was discovered that the undercarriage was also inoperative and so the usual cure of jerking the aircraft was resorted to. This also proved the undoing of the cargo, and subsequently the district around the aerodrome was showered with "groceries". Pilot Officer Rose eventually landed NF.995 safely at the emergency airfield at Sutton Heath, near Woodbridge.

Avro Lancaster R.5868 of No. 467 Squadron, coded PO-S for Sugar, toured U.S.A.A.F. bomber bases in the Eastern Counties on goodwill and inspection visits. Having survived 125 missions, this veteran aircraft created considerable interest among our Allies. It still lives on, as after being preserved at R.A.F. Scampton, Lincs, for many years, it has now been refurbished and is resident in the Royal Air Force Museum at Hendon, London.

9th May, 1945, V.E. (Victory in Europe) Day and Germany surrendered, bringing to an end the daily and nightly excursions of the bombers from the region out across the North Sea to targets almost beyond their range, with so many of their numbers never returning to their home shores.

During V.E. Day celebrations, R.A.F. Mosquitos and U.S.A.A.F. B.24s dropped coloured flares over the region and all flew with their navigation and landing lights switched on, whilst searchlights formed giant V-signs in the night skies.

In order to illustrate that the ground crews who had supported the bombers in their offensive over Germany could see what had happened on the other side, plane loads of them were flown over the target areas so they could see from the air the destruction which had been wrought on the enemy.

Although the offensive was now dead, several jobs had still to be done, and as a result Nos. 301 and 304 (Polish) Squadrons operated from Chedburgh, Suffolk, in the transport role, flying Handley-Page Halifax C.VIIIs. Their duties included parachute training and supply dropping, whilst No. 299 Squadron at Shepherds Grove, near Stanton, Suffolk, performed the same duties with Stirling Vs.

With demobilisation eating into the air and ground crews, many of the wartime built airfields were closing down, whilst the remaining squadrons settled in what was to be the permanent stations of the post-war Royal Air Force.

An unusual award for bravery was made to a member of the R.A.F. when the Station Padre at Stradishall, Squadron Leader the Reverend S. W. Harrison, was decorated with the George Medal for his courage in attempting to rescue the crew of a burning aircraft.

During the war years, 677 R.A.F. aircraft were known to have crashed in Norfolk alone, the majority of them belonging to Bomber Command.

In order to provide emergency landing facilities for stricken aircraft approaching the Eastern Counties, a large landing strip was constructed on Sutton Heath, near Woodbridge, during the middle years of the war. This strip, much wider than the normal runway, served as the main diversionary airfield for the region, and many brave deeds were carried out by crews making for this haven.

On 23rd October, 1944, a Lancaster, ME.787 of No. 619 Squadron arrived over the airfield after an extremely eventful journey from Germany. Squadron Leader Purnell was the sole occupant, having ordered the rest of the crew to bale out over Holland, so badly was the aircraft damaged, the flight-engineer and navigator being the last to leave. Burning well from a flak hit in the lower fuselage, the Lancaster with its one-man crew struggled across the North Sea, losing height all the while, until it eventually crash-landed at Sutton Heath with only one of its Rolls-Royce Merlin motors running.

A little earlier on 19th October, 1944, a Lancaster ND.453 of No. 635 Squadron made for Sutton Heath with the majority of its tailplane missing and only two motors running. Crossing the coast at almost zero feet, it passed low over Ipswich, when a third motor decided to stop and the pilot was forced to make a fast belly landing in the dark only six miles from his destination. The Lancaster burst into flames, but all the crew with the exception of the wireless operator escaped, the latter unfortunately being trapped in the inferno.

Others like Lancaster ND.806 of No.166 Squadron crashed and burned after struggling as far as the airfield, having been engaged in a series of fights all the way home over the North Sea on 27th April, 1944. On the other side of the coin, a No. 100 Squadron Lancaster, having safely reached the strip, was refuelled and made ready to go back to its home base. Unfortunately while taking-off it lost power, struck a building, exploded and burned out, all the crew being lost.

A feature of the extra wide runway was that it was divided into three lanes marked Red for priority One, Yellow for Priority Two and Green for Priority Three landings. Ex-Flight Lieutenant Whatling of Ipswich recalls a hair-raising experience as he was making an emergency approach. He was about to touch-down when another aircraft landing alongside him veered across in front of him. Slamming the throttles of his Halifax "up through the gate"* he managed to claw enough height and speed to pass over the top of the other aircraft and then pushed the bomber down again in order to get down before he ran out of runway.

Squadron Leader Holmes from Bradford also recalled a frightening wheels-up landing on the strip in a Stirling after being badly damaged over Eastern Europe whilst engaged on a S.O.E.† mission from East Anglia.

Mr Donald Smith of Ipswich remembers a visit to the site on Christmas Eve, 1944 and the intense activity taking place. He witnessed 43 emergency landings in one afternoon, including Lancasters, Halifaxes, Mosquitos, Fortresses and

*Into the full power emergency position.
†Special Operations Executive.

Liberators. Many made wheels-up landings and a group of cranes stood by to hoist the wreckage off the runway so that landings could continue. It gave a fantastic impression of the efficient manner in which serious emergencies could be handled and all assistance given to troubled crews. Bulldozers also cleared the wreckage away and two steadily mounting stacks of twisted metal grew daily, one R.A.F. and the other U.S.A.A.F.

The cost of war is recorded in the picturesque village church of St Peter, Westleton, Suffolk, where a fine stained glass window perpetrates the memory of these R.A.F.V.R. officers, Pilot Officer James Frederick Deck. 12.11.14. Killed 1.11.41. Flying Officer Harold Frederick Deck. 14.01.13. Killed 26.7.42. Flight Lieutenant Charles George Frederick Deck. 24.5.18. Killed 14.4.45.

Badly damaged Wellington at Marham showing geodectic construction of airframe where the fabric covering has been burned off. *Mrs M. Martin*

Armoured train as used by the L.N.E.R. and similar to the one which was based at Westerfield Junction, near Ipswich and operated on the Ipswich-Felixstowe branch line.

CHAPTER FOUR

Raiders Overhead

IN THE late 1930's towns and villages in the Eastern Counties, like others throughout the land, were preparing for the long awaited conflict, and had formed embryo Air Raid Precaution organisations as early as 1936. The Observer Corps, later to be granted the prefix Royal, had preceded the A.R.P. by several years, although the Corps had worked semi-secretly.

After the Munich Crisis, the Government issued to every home and business in the British Isles a buff coloured 36-page booklet entitled "The Protection of your Home against Air Raids", which gave instructions to enable the householder to carry out certain works. This was followed up a few months later by a further two booklets entitled "Masking your Windows" and "Your Gas Masks".

July 1939 saw the introduction of a new Civil Defence Act which gave local authorities more power and allocation of finance to push A.R.P. measures further. It also laid down that firms with 30 or more staff had to organise A.R.P. training classes, and if they employed 50 or more employees they were compelled to provide air raid shelters. All A.R.P. activities were in charge of the Lord Privy Seal, Sir John Anderson.

A stern measure followed on 24th August 1939, when Parliament passed the Emergency Powers (Defence) Act 1939, which covered all aspects of civilian defence.

As the tension grew, further preparations were made and on the 23rd August, street lamps were dimmed for the first time and sand-bag filling began. Blackout precautions were instigated, and trials carried out after dark. Searchlight units which had arrived in the area exercised together with their attendant anti-aircraft batteries. During the blackout trial at Ipswich some embarrassment was caused by the fact that the Town Hall clock light was forgotten and it shone out brightly over the darkened borough.

Blackout enforcement was rigid, cars being fitted with slatted metal screens over their headlights, whilst cyclists were required by law to carry an illuminated red rear light. The shortage of batteries caused concern, and Suffolk Court records tell of a young lady who was summoned for failing to display a rear light. The battery shortage was offered as an excuse, but she was fined eightpence.

On the 1st September, 1939, the Germans marched into Poland and that was it. Plans which had been formulated earlier to evacuate school children from London were implemented and train loads of children, mainly from the East End of London, arrived at Eastern County towns. Engaged on the same task were several paddle steamers, carrying children from the Gravesend and Dartford region, which arrived at the piers of Walton-on-Naze, Felixstowe and Great Yarmouth. Transported inland by buses, the children settled down in holiday camps, schools, public halls, hostels and places of amusement where they stayed for a while before departing inland to more permanent billets. In Great Yarmouth an appeal was made for 12,000 blankets for use by the evacuees, and this appeal was met by the local inhabitants. School children from North Kent travelled by bus and coach to Sudbury, Suffolk and by train from Ilford to Ipswich, while children from Birmingham were evacuated to the Saxmundham district of Suffolk. All these children were re-evacuated on Sunday, 19th May, 1940 to Wales.

At 19.47 hours on Friday, 1st September, 1939, the blackout regulations came into force and lasted for the duration of the war.

At 11.15 hours on 3rd September, Mr. Neville Chamberlain, the seventy-year old Prime Minister of Great Britain, made his famous statement. "I am speaking to you from the Cabinet Room of No. 10 Downing Street. This morning the British Ambassador in Berlin handed the German Government a final note stating that unless we heard from them by eleven o'clock that they were prepared at once to withdraw their troops from Poland, a state of war would exist between us. I have to tell you that no such undertaking has been received and that subsequently this country is now at war with Germany."

Fifteen minutes after the announcement the A.R.P. sirens sounded and aircraft of Fighter Command were "scrambled" to intercept reported enemy bombers, but these turned out to be R.A.F. bombers crossing the coast near Felixstowe, Suffolk. That Sunday people were busy digging trenches, erecting shelters, filling sand bags and generally hurrying around with a purposeful air. France followed Great Britain later in the day by declaring war on Germany at 17.00 hours.

The following night, the sirens at Colchester, Essex, sounded at 03.30 hours, a full moon and clear starlit sky not helping to allay the fears of the residents.

Another precaution taken at this time was to place gas detector boards in prominent places, and the tops of postal pillar boxes were painted with gas detector paint.

The war came closer to the Eastern Counties during the early days of November when Heinkel float planes from the Köstenfliegerstaffel 3/906 (Coastal Reconnaissance Squadron) laid magnetic mines in the Thames Estuary and off Harwich, the first such operation being on the 20th November. They returned the next night and the following night, but were not detected until the 22nd when coast watchers observed an object in shallow water off Southend. This turned out to be a parachute magnetic mine, and was successfully made inoperative by a bomb disposal squad from H.M.S. *Vernon* led by Lieutenant Commander J. G. D. Ouvry. The mine was taken away for examination and thus the Navy were able to glean at first hand what they would be up against. The mines, however, took their toll with the loss of the Dutch liner *Simon Bolivar,* bound for the East Indies with refugees from Holland, a Japanese merchantman, s.s. *Torchbearer,* a collier, s.s. *Sheaf Crest,* a merchantman and in Harwich Harbour itself, the destroyer H.M.S. *Gipsy.* Leaving harbour in company with H.M.S. *Boadicea,* and the Polish destroyer *Burza,* the *Gipsy* struck a mine and sank rapidly with considerable loss of life, the other two vessels fortunately not being damaged. It is of interest that a magnetic mine of this batch was dredged up in the Orwell Estuary on 7th August 1974, and detonated with still violent results out at sea.

On Thursday, 7th December 1939 an enemy seaplane flew low along the shore off Felixstowe and was illuminated by searchlights which the plane attempted to machine-gun. The coastal defences fired at the aircraft which was apparently on a mining mission.

The New Year came with bitter wintery weather, even the salt water of Ipswich Docks freezing over, and still no notable enemy air activity until the 9th January 1940 when a savage attack was made by the Luftwaffe on unarmed ships. The Trinity House lightship tender *Reculver* was machine-gunned and bombed off the Norfolk coast near Great Yarmouth. Commanded by Captain W. J. Lees, who was wounded in the knee, the ship with a complement of 40 men on board, of whom 2 were killed and 30 wounded, reached harbour a "floating wreck". Several lightships were also attacked off the East Coast and one of the lightship men described the action. "We were horrified when the aeroplane came for us. It was always reckoned that lightships were immune from war actions and we had got used to seeing German aircraft passing overhead and low alongisde over the water. We were taken by surprise when they attacked and when they found out that we did not have an answer they flew round and bombed us. The plane circled us four or five times and then came straight across and dropped four bombs. This was followed by machine gun attacks until the lantern was extinguished and the lightship started to list. We took to the boats where we were further machine gunned."

On 29th January 1940, German aircraft attacked the East Dudgeon light vessel stationed off Wells, Norfolk. People listening to the radio heard its S.O.S. and the lifeboat was launched to go to her aid. On arrival at the scene the lifeboatmen found no one on board and the ship's boats gone. Of the crew of eight, only one survived, Mr. John Sanders of Great Yarmouth, who was washed ashore the following day. The crew had managed to make the shore, but when beaching the boat capsized and they were thrown into the water.

Enemy air attacks were confined to ships at sea during the spring of 1940 and as a result of these attacks an unusual decision was taken when it was decided to arm the East Coast lifeboats with a machine gun apiece. The Gorleston and Great Yarmouth boat, the *Louis Stevens* new at the outbreak of hostilities, and the Cromer boat were the first to be equipped. The Royal Air Force also flew protective patrols to cover the movements of fishing boats which became nicknamed "Kipper Patrols".

First of the modern maritime patrol aircraft, the Avro Anson, almost outmoded at the outbreak of war, was called upon to fly the "Kipper Patrols" from Bircham Newton to protect fishing vessels. This example L.9151 is seen in typical surroundings. *Mrs M. Martin*

One of the first enemy actions over the region occurred during the night of 30th April, 1940, when a mine laying Heinkel 111 twin-engined bomber crashed with its load near the junction of Skelmersdale and Victoria Roads, Clacton, Essex. The explosion created a great deal of damage and resulted in the deaths of two local residents and the four German airmen, whilst 34 were severely injured and 122 more slightly injured.

Belgium fell to the advancing German armies on 28th May, 1940, and the first anti-invasion measures were carried out by removing roadside signposts, railway station nameboards, and route indicators from buses. Tall posts were erected in open fields of any size with trip wires to ensnare and damage enemy aircraft should they attempt any landings. As a result of the new threat, all Great Yarmouth schoolchildren were evacuated, leaving in special trains from Vauxhall Station en route to the Midlands. This was a large operation and the organisation fell on the shoulders of the Clerk of the Education Committee, Mr G. Wraighton, and his staff. The elderly and infirm inhabitants followed, leaving only essential personnel in the borough. A town with a normal population of some 54,000 people now carried on with a mere 20,000 inhabitants, the children being conspicuous by their absence. Other East Anglian coastal resorts became almost "ghost towns", with a majority of the shops shut, and in some instances grass growing in the streets.

During the night of 7th June 1940, the village of Eyke near Woodbridge, Suffolk, was rocked by a tremendous explosion, when a twin-engined Heinkel 115 floatplane crashed with the magnetic mines it was carrying. Two of the three man crew were killed instantly, and the pilot died later in hospital. As the aircraft had not been engaged by fighters or gunfire it is mysterious how this marine aircraft, obviously on a mining mission, should come to grief several miles inland. Two days earlier a parachute mine had claimed the Ipswich Corporation Sewage boat *Sweep II*, which sank in about three minutes, with two crew lost and two missing, one mile off Landguard Point.

With the fear of invasion imminent, all sign-posts and direction boards were removed and stored for the duration of hostilities.

An enemy bomber was shot down at Cley-next-the-Sea, Norfolk on 19th June 1940 and the crew of four taken prisoner of war, whilst that night two aircraft were heard engaging each other about midnight off the shore at Felixstowe. At dawn, a British parachute was picked up in the sea, presumably from a Blenheim which was missing and believed to have been shot down by a Heinkel 111. The next day, arrangements were made for the evacuation of Felixstowe, Trimley St Mary and Trimley St Martin and the village of Nacton, near Ipswich, in view of the invasion threat.

During the following night Ipswich suffered its first casualties when a large whistling bomb dropped on a house in Dale Hall Lane, killing Mr and Mrs R. Anderson and their maid. The whistle from this bomb was found later and measured 14 in. long by 1.5/8 in. diameter. Colchester also received its first bombs during the night when they fell on the Mersea Golf Course whilst on the 29th incendiary bombs at Ardleigh, Essex set fire to fields and hedgerows.

Activity worsened on 3rd July when a warehouse was burned out at Mistley, Essex, and a Dornier dropped 20 high explosive bombs in the Cliff Lane district of Ipswich, killing one lady. Lowestoft received heavier treatment, four people being killed and 23 injured when shops in the town were hit. It was the turn of the Ipswich dock area on 8th July 1940, when the flour mills were hit and later an unexploded bomb was found under the choir stalls of nearby Saint Mary at the Quay church. Two high explosive bombs entered the four mills of Messrs R. & W. Pauls and passed right through the building to the ground floor. Later that day a Heinkel 111 crashed into the sea about ten miles off Felixstowe.

King George VI visited Felixstowe on the 11th July, 1940, crossing over from Harwich by boat to inspect the coastal defences from Landguard Point to Felixstowe Ferry, later leaving by road. The same day Norwich had its first raid when two enemy aircraft bombed Barnard's Mousehold Factory at 17.00 hours and then turned their attention to Messrs. Colman's Carrow Works, where the workers were hurrying through the gates on their way home. When the bombs dropped amongst them, many were left dead and dying in the street. The same aircraft then attacked Boulton and Pauls Riverside Works and the London and North Eastern Railway Locomotive Depot. As a result of this raid 27 people died and many were injured.

The next day, a military target was attacked when a lone raider made a dawn attack on R.A.F. West Raynham, Norfolk, hitting a hangar and destroying four aircraft, whilst on the 11th, Great Yarmouth experienced its first raid when a single enemy aircraft dropped seven 50 kilo bombs on residential districts and killed four people. Another raider the same day dropped 18 H.E. bombs in the Nacton Road area of Ipswich, hitting the South Eastern Senior School and bursting a sewer in the road.

Norwich was hit again on the 19th with homes and businesses destroyed and the buildings of the Norfolk and Norwich Aero Club at Mousehold Aerodrome badly damaged. In the restricted reporting style of the period, an East Coast newspaper described an incident on 13th July 1940. "An enemy raider believed to be a Heinkel bomber raided an East Coast town,* and dropped a salvo of bombs, killing two people and a man and woman later died in hospital. After hitting the homes, the bomber machine-gunned cattle on a nearby marsh, some of which were killed and others had to be destroyed later. Watchers saw the Heinkel making out to sea, whilst at the same time an R.A.F. bomber, apparently returning from a raid over enemy territory, altered course and engaged the German aircraft. In a few seconds two Spitfires appeared and the R.A.F. bomber left them to it. The Spitfires darted about like gnats above and below the twisting enemy bomber, and shortly afterwards, the two fighters returned in close company and in a cockiness that suggested victory."

*Great Yarmouth.

Bomb damage at Ipswich showing Anderson shelters in garden sites and the considerable destruction wrought on closely situated rows of houses.   *Mrs G. Wilton*

Further preparations were made for the anticipated invasion with the Local Defence Volunteers* in active mood. Typical of the state of readiness was an East Anglian church notice-board giving guarded information to the parishioners that the bells would now only ring in the event of an invasion.

PARISH CHURCH OF ALL SAINTS

THE CHURCH BELL. IN FUTURE THE BELL WILL NOT RING EXCEPT FOR ——————————— WELL YOU KNOW. *BUT* THE SERVICES WILL STILL GO ON AS USUAL. EVENSONG WILL BE HELD AT 3.00 P.M. SO AS NOT TO USE THE ELECTRIC LIGHTS.

The month closed with the Luftwaffe increasing their daylight attacks on coastal towns, naval installations and coastal convoys.

August, 1940, was one of those summer months that people remember but on this occasion it was not the weather which immediately sprang to mind, but activity in the skies over Southern England. Residents of the region woke on the 1st to find their gardens and streets littered with leaflets which had been dropped by German aircraft during the night, urging the British people to ask for a peace with Germany. Later in the day, a solitary Junkers Ju88 bombed the canteen of Boulton and Paul's Riverside Works at Norwich and the business area of the city. Great Yarmouth also suffered several raids by single aircraft.

During the next few days a pause took place whilst the Luftwaffe regrouped its units along the Channel Coast, but on the 8th attacks were resumed on airfields and coastal shipping, including a very heavy attack on a convoy off Felixstowe which was defended by fighters and anti-aircraft fire from escorting ships. On the 15th many very heavy attacks were pressed home on R.A.F. airfields, one such raid being levelled at R.A.F. Martlesham Heath, Suffolk, when 20 Messerschmitt Me 110's carrying 250kg. bombs escorted by a Staffel of Me 109s caused considerable damage. During the day the R.A.F. lost 29 fighters and 17 bombers. On this Thursday many aerial battles took place very high over the Suffolk coast in the Felixstowe area, one aircraft and two parachutes falling into the sea about two miles off shore. Some time later a dinghy containing a pilot was seen in the sea about half a mile off shore from the Fludgers Arms Hotel. Eight H.E. bombs were dropped near the Martlesham Heath Wireless Station at Vanderlight Wood, Foxhall, whilst a Hurricane from the nearby airfield crash landed on the Felixstowe Ferry Golf Course, the pilot Flight Lieutenant Harper being only slightly injured.

On the following day more than 90 H.E. bombs fell in the Boxted and Langham districts of Essex, whilst on the 19th a daylight attack on the Hythe district of Colchester was followed at intervals by single aircraft attacks. The Luftwaffe put in over 1,500 sorties on the next day, whilst on the 21st a Dornier Do 17Z bombed R.A.F. Watton, Norfolk, making itself a nuisance. The same day at 17.25 hours a Dornier Do 17Z serialled U5 + CS of the 8.KG.2., had set out to bomb an

---

*L.D.V., forerunner of the Home Guard.

aerodrome in the Newmarket area but was shot down over Ipswich by Flying Officer R. E. P. Brooker of No. 56 Squadron. Mr Donald Smith of Ipswich watched the action as the bomber with its port engine on fire and three Hurricanes on its tail, crashed in a corner of Gippeswyck Park after the crew of four had baled out. Landing on the roof of an engineering works, some of the crew were threatened by the local womenfolk and remained aloft until the arrival of the Fire Service with their scaling ladders. Mr Smith is the proud possessor of the manufacturer's plate for this aircraft. At 16.20 hours the same day Harvey Wilson and Osborne's Shipyard and Jewson's Timber Yard at Lowestoft were bombed and six people killed.

On the 25th August, the residents of Abberton, near Colchester, saw a raider fall in flames near the village, whilst further to the north R.A.F. Debden was heavily attacked but not seriously damaged. The next day people at Colchester noted 15 parachutes descending at one time as pilots on both sides baled out to safety. It was the turn of R.A.F. Rochford, Southend on the 31st, considerable damage being inflicted, and later in the day the Sewer Outfall Works at Colchester came under fire, with damage to the filter beds and to a 32 in. water main. Another R.A.F. airfield, Debden, was the target later in the day, but again it escaped any great damage.

September came in bright and hot but no let-up in German activity. On the 1st Little Horkesley Church, in North Essex was reduced to a heap of rubble with the lead sheets from the roof being thrown some 300 feet into the fields. The bells were destroyed, but volunteers managed to retrieve the altar vessels and memorial brasses for safe keeping. The R.A.F. suffered again on the 4th when R.A.F. Bradwell Bay on the Essex coast was attacked.

Tension mounted on the 7th when the Local Defence Volunteers were called out and troops put on standby as unconfirmed reports of intended invasion grew and non-essential personnel were advised to leave the area. At 20.07 hours the signal coded "Cromwell" was sent out to all Army units putting them on full alert, as conditions were deemed right for invasion, but many units though that it had already stared. Several bridges were blown up, and church bells rung to alert the population.

Four people were killed on the 9th, when bombs were dropped in Battery Green Road, Lowestoft, whilst on the next day evacuation notices were posted at Ipswich, the inmates of the local Heathfields Hospital being evacuated. On a sunny Saturday afternoon, a Junkers Ju88 dropped four H.E. and one oil bomb at Saint Margaret's Green, Ipswich, whilst later in the day the local Airport received attention.

Coggeshall Church, Essex, was totally destroyed by two heavy H.E. bombs dropped by a single raider on 16th September and on the 22nd two parachute mines were released over Ipswich during the evening, one of them floating down over the town and exploding behind a house on the edge of Rushmere Golf Links. The

Chaos caused at Ipswich by an aerial mine which failed to explode on impact and was partially emptied and then exploded.   *Mrs G. Wilton*

other, dropping on a partially opened parachute, landed in a stonemason's yard in Cemetery Road, caught up on a crane and did not detonate. After intense work by a Bomb Disposal Squad who emptied a great deal of the explosive, the mine was blown up on the evening of Sunday, the 22nd, when it still destroyed a number of houses.

By September, 1940, over 2,300,000 Anderson metal shelters had been distributed for householders' protection, thus covering approximately one quarter of the population. The shelter was supplied free to people in danger zones and earning less than £250 a year. If one wished to purchase a shelter it cost £7 plus installation. The directions for erection directed one "to dig a hole seven feet six inches long by six feet wide and four feet deep" into which were inserted six curved corrugated steel sheets, bolted together at the top. End plates with a hole at ground level for entrance and exit and an emergency plate in the opposite end completed the structure. Fifteen inches of soil all over the top completed the protection, and to this day (1976) many Anderson shelter sections still exist above ground as sheds, garages and the like. After the war, large numbers of the galvanised shelter sections were purchased by the National Coal Board for use in the mines.

The Home Secretary, Mr Herbert Morrison, after repeated appeals by a large section of the population who were reluctant to go outside into an Anderson shelter at night, had designed and issued an indoor shelter. Named the Morrison shelter, it resembled a steel table six feet six inches by four feet nine inches with steel mesh sides and capable of supporting the weight of a fallen ceiling. Issued free to persons earning less than £350, they could also be purchased for seven pounds.

Enemy aircraft attacking Great Yarmouth on the 1st October were engaged by No. 74 Squadron and a Heinkel 111 was damaged, whilst next day a Dornier 17 which was strafing the streets of Colchester was intercepted by Hurricanes and shot down at Earl Stonham, Suffolk, the crew of four being captured by members of a searchlight unit. Colchester was the target again on the 3rd when bombs hit the Old Heath Laundry, killing three lady workers. Later a Junkers Ju88 crash-landed on the marshes at Brightlingsea, Essex, during the afternoon, and the crew of four were captured.

On Saturday, 12th October, about 8 o'clock in the evening, a Junkers Ju88 caught in searchlights at the entrance to Harwich Harbour, dived and crashed into the sea off Landguard Point, the wreckage being found the next morning. The Luftwaffe suffered another casualty about 23.20 hours on 16th October, when a Heinkel 111K flew into the balloon barrage at Harwich and crashed on the foreshore at Shotley, where it caught fire, although the two parachute mines aboard did not explode. The crew of six perished in the crash.

A new terror weapon appeared on the 27th October, when many anti-personnel "butterfly bombs" were scattered over Ipswich their deadly trip-wires causing the death of Police Constable Doyland and severe injuries to Police Sergeant Coe and Station Sergeant Revett. An enemy aircraft machine gunning the streets of Felixstowe was hit by defensive fire and crashed into the sea, whilst two days later many more "butterfly bombs" were scattered over the West Mersea district of Essex. Perhaps it was the aircraft which had dropped these missiles which that day crashed into the River Stour off Shotley, one of the crew being captured.

King George VI visited Colchester on 30th and 31st October to inspect troops in the town. He also went to the Headquarters of the No. 18 Group, Observer Corps, besides visiting observer posts in the area.

November, 1940, came and the short days and longer nights brought no respite as on the 1st just after dawn a lone low flying Dornier 17Z eluded the defences, appearing over R.A.F. Wattisham and dropping its bombs on the barrack blocks and airmen's married quarters, killing ten airmen and injuring nineteen. A Heinkel 111K bombed Ipswich later in the day, its sixteen bombs falling on the Eastern district of the borough. R.A.F. Wattisham was visited again on 4th November but this time at dusk when two Junkers 88s and a Dornier 17Z hit a hangar which was soon a blazing inferno with several aircraft inside. Next day a Heinkel 111 had another "go" at R.A.F. Wattisham, but in poor visibility its bombs fell in nearby fields. Whilst this raid was in process, the Blenheims of No. 110 Squadron based at Wattisham were attacking the raiders bases in Northern France.

In order to boost the ego of the Italian Air Force, the Corpo Aereo Italiano, Mussolini asked the Luftwaffe to be allowed to join them in the destruction of the British Isles, and to this end, some fighters and bombers were despatched to bases in Belgium. The aircraft were semi-obsolete Fiat CR42s, single seat radial engined biplanes in the Gloster Gladiator class, and twin-engined monoplane Fiat BR20s which were in the Armstrong Whitworth Whitley category. On 25th October, 1940, some 15 aircraft set out for a night attack on Harwich, but without reaching their target. November the 5th saw them after the same target again, and with the same result, but on the 11th a bold daylight attack was mounted by ten bombers and forty fighters, which set out for Harwich. This action ended with three bombers and three fighters being lost to R.A.F. fighters, a BR20 crashing at Bromeswell near Woodbridge, and two CR.42s force-landing, one on the beach at Orfordness and the other in a field at Corton.

The Italian formation was engaged by Hurricanes of No. 46 and No. 257 Squadrons, the latter flying from Martlesham Heath and led by Flight Lieutenant H. P. Blatchford, in the absence of Squadron Leader R. R. Stanford-Tuck. The preserved A.R.P. report for the day states "Following enemy aircraft reported to have crashed at about 14.10 hours — one in sea off Orford, one Italian fighter on beach at Orford, one Italian bomber at Bromeswell, east of Woodbridge and at 14.17 hours one Italian fighter at Corton, north of Lowestoft".

On 17th November another night raid was directed at Harwich, but without result, followed again by night attacks on Harwich, Ipswich, Lowestoft, and Great Yarmouth, the last being on 2nd January 1941. The majority of these raids did not reach their targets, but one interesting item does arise from these intrusions. Superintendent D. G. Foster writing in *Constable's Country,* the official magazine of the Suffolk County Constabulary, says in the Spring 1971 edition, "On Saturday, 21st December, 1940, Ipswich appears to have had a visit from the Italian Air Force. An aircraft was heard flying in the vicinity of Ipswich for about half an hour at 5.50 p.m. and while flying in a Northward direction across the eastern side of the town, seven large incendiary bombs and four high explosive bombs were dropped. They fell in Bixley Road, Princethorpe Road, Chilton Road, the playing fields of

The railways of the region were prone to enemy attack, but the staff in all sections of the London and North Eastern Railway managed to make good and keep the trains running.

Copleston Road Schools, the Borough General Hospital, now Heath Road Wing hospital, and near the nurses quarters. One of the bombs which fell in Princethorpe Road did not explode, being recovered from the kitchen of a dwelling. This was later identified as an incendiary bomb of Italian origin. The high explosive bombs were of a 100kg semi-armour piercing type and apart from causing some damage, there were no casualties".

The L.N.E.R. main railway line was bombed between Colchester North Station and Parsons Heath on 12th November, resulting in single line working for rail traffic, whilst on the night of the 14th/15th the night skies of East Anglia throbbed with the unsynchronised beat of Luftwaffe bomber motors as 435 Luftwaffe bombers "blitzed" the city of Coventry, killing 380 civilians and severely injuring 860. Two people were killed on 18th November when Royal Avenue, Lowestoft was bombed, and on the 29th three more were killed when the Cooperative Wholesale Society Factory in Waveney Drive, Lowestoft, was hit.

The night fighter forces of the R.A.F. combating the night bombers on 25th November comprised No. 25 Squadron at Debden, Essex with Blenheims and Beaufighters, No. 73 Squadron at Castle Camps, Cambs, with Hurricanes and No. 264 Squadron with its Defiants at Rochford, Essex.

Heavy bombs dropped on Norwich on 2nd December fell near the Cathedral, causing considerable damage in the precincts, whilst on the 9th a multiple incendiary bomb, "Molotov Bread Basket", dropped over the Lexden district of Colchester set fire to many houses, but quick work by the Auxiliary Fire Service (A.F.S.) prevented more serious spread of fire.

Low cloud and bad weather prevented a great deal of air activity during the early part of January, 1941, but on the 7th a Heinkel 111 dropping down through the murk, released a massive bomb directed at Ipswich Gas Works. Fortunately it overshot and buried itself deep in soft ground in nearby Holywells Park. This monster was dug out and on 14th February, after the explosive had been steamed out, it was put on display in Ipswich where it raised a considerable amount of money towards the war effort. In the same conditions another bomber picked out the railway station at Halesworth, Suffolk, where a bomb fell on the station building, killing the Stationmaster, Mr Holland, his wife Hannah and a young lady, Miss Joan Clarke, aged eighteen, who was with them at the time. The three victims are buried side by side in a corner of Halesworth Cemetery. Brightlingsea, Essex was bombed on the night of the 10th.

On the 18th a train from London was approaching Lexden, near Colchester, in a snowstorm, when a Heinkel 111 emerged over the train, strafing it and dropping six bombs. Turning, it made another attack and six passengers and the guard were severely wounded. A lady passenger and the guard, Mr Arthur Pyke, of Ipswich, died from their injuries. Several raids were made on factories and the harbour at Great Yarmouth, but on the 30th a raider was shot down and crashed on the saltings at St Osyth, Essex, all the crew perishing.

Several ex-R.A.F. servicemen remembered that whilst doing their "Square bashing"* at Great Yarmouth, one of the first orders they were taught to obey was "disperse". This was due to the frequent hit and run raids which occurred, evidence of this being clearly seen on the local buses which bore traces of machine gun bullets.

March with its longer days and shorter nights brought relief to the people of England, but it gave no respite from the raiders. A new ruse was tried by the enemy when they bombed Great Yarmouth on the 1st, flying round with their navigation lights on to give the impression of friendly aircraft. These raids did considerable damage to public buildings and the gas works, whilst a little further inland, Norwich received several visits with Barnard's factory, the aerodrome and dwelling areas bearing the brunt of the vengeance. At 09.30 hours on the 4th March a Dornier bombed the N.A.A.F.I. Canteen and several roads in Lowestoft, the aircraft being eventually shot down, whilst three days later another Dornier bombed the Yacht Basin, Swingbridge and Harbour at 13.20 hours killing ten people and injuring 37. Throughout the rest of the month, attacks were made on Ipswich, Norwich, Great Yarmouth, Lowestoft, King's Lynn, Colchester, Chelmsford, Harwich and Clacton, and although fortunately the casualties were not high, damage to property was considerable.

On 24th March three Heinkel 111s and two Messerschmitt 109s, flying as a unit, attacked Ipswich Airport with H.E. bombs and machine gun fire.

Great Yarmouth experienced its worst raid just after midnight on the 8th April, following the fire-bomb attack of the 4th, when a number of bombers dropped H.E. bombs, incendiary bombs and parachute mines. The premises of Marks and Spencers, Rose's Fashions, Boots, Hills Restaurant, Johnson's Clothing Factory, and the Education Offices were all gutted by fire. 68 persons died including five Special Constables in one Police Post. The late Mr Douglas Pettit of Ipswich, who was in the R.A.F. and billeted in one of the sea-front hotels stated that "with the burning buildings, crashing bombs, and intense heat which seemed to gush out in waves, it was a miracle that the A.F.S. performed to contain the fires. Access to the scene of the conflagration was hampered by falling buildings and wreckage and we only just managed to get into several buildings in time to save some of the inmates. In the hotel where we lived, the kitchen in the basement lost its side wall and a pan full of hot fat, ready for frying chips, exploded all over the lower building."

The next two days saw renewed attacks on the town, as well as a night attack on Lowestoft, when 16 civilians and six Servicemen were killed. Ipswich was not neglected on the 8th, when two 250kg bombs hit Holy Trinity Vicarage and the Gas Works Repair Shop, killing a Senior A.R.P. Warden and a young lady. On the 10th 15 fighter bombers again attacked the Ipswich Dock area, inflicting casualties on the auxiliary services.

Royalty visited Ipswich on 17th April when the Duke of Gloucester came to inspect the Services, followed on the 24th by the Duke of Kent who, during his tour of inspection, visited Warden's Post M6 and signed the Report Book, later

*Marching rifle drill etc. on the square or Parade Ground.

continuing on to Great Yarmouth to inspect the Services there the next day.

With the shorter nights of May 1941 people hoped for relief from the night bombers, but they continued their onslaught with a heavy attack on Ipswich on the 4th, hits being made on Crane's Factory and round the Christchurch Park district. People at West Mersea, Essex, still recall the freak bouncing bomb which fell on the 6th. Dropped by a fast low flying bomber, it hit a mudflat, ricochetted off the slime, passed through a house-boat, taking away part of the cabin, and exploded as it re-entered the sea. The explosion caused the seams of a local fishing smack, the *Water Lily*, to open and she sank at her moorings. Colchester Sewage Works were hit the following day, but little damage resulted, which was surprising as one of the craters was 40-feet in diameter.

Fison's acid plant at Ipswich received a direct hit by a large H.E. bomb on the 9th, whilst the railway line to Felixstowe was breached on the 12th. On the same day Felixstowe Dock had a lucky escape when a H.E. bomb exploded against the wall of a building containing seven tons of explosive which did not detonate. On Monday, 19th May, a Junkers 88 flying low along the sea front at Felixstowe was hit by machine gun fire from the paddle steamer (mine-sweeper) *Princess Elizabeth* and caught fire and crashed. Next day the body of the pilot, Sergeant Pilot Herbert Lindemann was landed at Harwich by the minesweeper.

June did show a falling-off in raids, but 14 Naval personnel were killed at Lowestoft on 13th June, when a blockship in the harbour was sunk. July saw the resumption of raids on East Anglian towns when on the 9th a heavy bomb dropped in Cecil Road, Ipswich causing considerable damage when it exploded twelve hours later and Great Yarmouth experienced 21 attacks between 01.05 and 03.45 hours on the same day.

On 2nd August, compulsory fire watching was instituted with civilians of both sexes between the ages of eighteen and thirty-five years having to register for duty, the duty period being 12 hours, paid at the rate of three shillings a duty. A new target was sought by the Luftwaffe when on the 6th a determined attack was carried out on electricity high tension pylons at Ardleigh, Essex, heavy land mines being used, but, as they missed no damage resulted.

A metal cylinder found at Russell's Farm, Falkenham, near Felixstowe on Sunday 17th August caused a lot of concern, but eventually the label asking for it to be returned to the Superintendent of the National Physical Laboratory at Teddington, Middlesex, diagnosed it as a weather recording device.

A Dornier 17Z came to grief at Burnham, Norfolk, on the 21st when it was shot down by Spitfires of No. 611 Squadron.

In Norwich, an Air Raid Spotters Club was formed in order to increase the efficiency of spotters engaged in identifying aircraft. As a by-product of the London "Blitz" over 750,000 tons of rubble from the bombed areas was conveyed by some 1,700 freight trains to East Anglia, where it was utilized in making runways for the new aerodromes being constructed.

The lack of raids during September and October brought much needed relief to East Anglia, although on 12th October raiders at Ipswich caused some damage and on Saturday 25th four H.E. bombs were dropped on the sea-front at Felixstowe, one scoring a direct hit on the Spa Pavilion, the German radio the next day reported that "A large warehouse near Harwich had been bombed."

The lull at the end of 1941 did not continue, as on 13th January, Lowestoft experienced a bad raid, when a Dornier dropped four H.E. bombs which killed 51 civilians and 18 servicemen. Boots, Wallers, Bonsalls, Freeman Hardy and Willis and Fifty Shilling Tailors were all destroyed in London Road North, whilst ten days later fifteen people were killed in another early morning raid on the town. A lone raider over Great Yarmouth at 12.50 hours on the 18th February caught workers going home and left eight dying in the streets. March was comparatively quiet, but on the 27th, 28th, 29th and 30th April "Baedeker Raids" were carried out on the City of Norwich. Such cities as Norwich were deliberately bombed by the Luftwaffe in retaliation for the R.A.F.'s raids in Germany, the raids being named after the famous German tourist guide book. The Monday night raid killed 162 citizens and injured 600, whilst the Wednesday night attack killed 69 and injured 89. A.R.P. workers from all over the area were drafted into the City to assist in reclamation and salvage work. One German airman who did not reach home was N.4325/40 Heinrich Fischer whose body was taken from the water in Harwich Harbour on 8th May 1942.

The Chief Controller at Ipswich issued a statement on 5th May that contrary to strong rumours there was no intention of evacuating the town, and on that night the Fire Watchers did their first night duty. A new phase of attacks began on the 12th, when two low level fighter bomber attacks were made on Lowestoft at 08.40 and 09.00 hours, killing 18 civilians and 14 Servicemen. The raiders also attacked several patrol vessels just off shore while another group attacked Southwold and Felixstowe. A decoy site at Nacton, near Ipswich, was bombed on 2nd June but some of the bombs fell in Ipswich, five people being killed, including an A.R.P. Warden.

Over 1,500 incendiary bombs were dropped on Great Yarmouth during the night of the 25th and heavy damage resulted, the Parish Church of St Nicholas being almost burned out, though fortunately only three people were killed. Norwich escaped with low casualties the following night.

Mr Robert Malster of Ipswich recalls his memories of the Luftwaffe visits to his home city, Norwich. "We suffered severely from bombing during the war, both the local industries and housing areas being devastated. One night I particularly remember was that on which Colman's Carrow Works was hit: the flames from the burning mills along the river lit the Cathedral spire in a rosy glow. The beauty of the sight was by no means equalled by the spectacle of the spire lit by searchlights brought into the Close on V.E. night, through the latter certainly gave us much more satisfaction.

The Cathedral itself was hit by incendiary bombs one Friday night, and I well remember the sight of the Precentor, Gilbert Thurlow, now the Very Rev. Gilbert Thurlow, Dean of Gloucester, on the roof of the Cathedral using a stirrup pump to fight the fires started by the bombs. The building was saved on that occasion by the stone vaulting built after the destruction of the Cathedral by fire in the thirteenth century".

Colchester was lucky on 30th July when a cannon-firing fighter attacked the centre of the town without causing casualties, but on the 11th August, Severalls Mental Hospital just outside Colchester was bombed, four H.E.'s hitting the buildings, killing 38 patients and leaving 23 injured, including four nurses. On the 25th the eastern area of Ipswich suffered with 12 civilians dead, nine of them in an Anderson shelter in Nacton Road which received a direct hit. On the same night many incendiaries fell in the Suffolk village of East Bergholt, the German radio the next day announcing that Colchester had been heavily bombed. More new tactics were employed during August when the enemy attempted to set fire to the ripening crops. Stirrup pumps were issued to farmers in order to combat the fires in the fields.

September was relatively free from attacks but there were spasmodic raids on several towns. A Dornier bombed the centre of Colchester on the 28th with a repeat attack two days later. King George VI visited Norwich on 13th October to inspect the A.R.P. and C.D. workers. Colchester was hit again on the 19th when a Dornier attacked the Arclight Works of E. N. Mason and Sons Limited, but as the majority of the workers were in their shelters, casualties were light. The flour mills of Cranfield Brothers at Ipswich were hit by another Dornier, or perhaps the same one, on the same day. Smaller places like Orford and Aldeburgh in Suffolk were also coming under fire mainly by fighter bombers of the Focke-Wulf FW 190 type.

The first two months of 1943 saw scattered raids, mainly by single fighter aircraft, but on 21st January the Luftwaffe embarked on its "Baby Blitz" and many enemy bombers crossed and recrossed the region on their way to targets in London and the Midlands, these raids continuing until the 18th May. Electricity pylons were the target again on 5th February when several fell to the raiders, disrupting supplies of power and light. The activity increased as the days lengthened. On 12th March the barge *Alaric* owned by Messrs. Francis and Gilders of Colchester was attacked off the Essex coast by six fighter bombers. Machine gun fire wounded the skipper who died shortly afterwards.

Great Yarmouth was attacked again at 06.28 on 18th March when several large houses, used as billets by W.R.N.S., were hit and nine killed. However, two Dorniers were shot down over Essex, one at Colchester and one off Clacton. Chelmsford was at the receiving end of a heavy raid on 14th April in which the Luftwaffe lost six bombers, but the raiders managed to hit the Hoffman ball bearing factory and damaged a large amount of finished goods awaiting despatch. Next day an enemy bomber was brought down at Layer Breton, near Colchester, one of the crew being

Most of the low level hit and run raids were carried out by the sleek radial-engined Focke-Wulf F.W.190 which was capable of carrying a large bomb externally at high speed. The example illustrated is a captured aircraft under evaluation by the R.A.F.

killed and the other three captured, while five days later a high-flying Junkers 88 was intercepted by R.A.F. fighters over Colchester, crashing near Clacton, Essex.

This was the period when the Focke-Wulf FW190s stepped up their activities, ten of the type approaching Great Yarmouth almost at sea level and then gaining height to drop their 500kg bombs in the centre of the town on 7th May. Four days later a repeat performance by eighteen FW190s, again with 500kg bombs, killed 49 people and injured 41, several A.T.S.* Servicewomen being among the casualties when their billets were hit. The same day another group attacked Felixstowe Ferry, one of this group being seen to fall into the sea near the Cork lightvessel.

A new ruse was adopted earlier in the month, when on the night of 4th/5th May intruders mingled with returning R.A.F. bombers. As the defences were not firing owing to the presence of friendly aircraft, the raiders freely bombed Norwich, causing a great deal of damage by fire bombs.

On 2nd June 1943, at 05.21, nine FW190s swept over Ipswich at roof top height dropping bombs in the Felixstowe Road area and machine gunning the Gas Works. 11 people were killed, but one of the raiders, flying into the blast of a previous raider's bombs, hit a dockside crane jib and crashed into the dock near the lock gates, the young pilot being killed instantly. This raid was spectacular as shrapnel penetrated a gasholder on the dockside and set fire to the contents. As there was no explosion danger, the Fire Service concentrated on playing their hoses on the structure and letting the fire burn itself out. Later on in the day, 12 FW190s attacked Felixstowe Ferry again, and then went on to strafe the nearby villages of Alderton, Hollesley and Bawdsey.

*Auxiliary Territorial Service.

Wednesday, 14th July was the last flight day for a bomber which was shot down at midnight, five miles off Aldeburgh by an R.A.F. night fighter and on Saturday 31st July the body of a German airman, Feldwebel Franz Zweszler, was washed ashore at Felixstowe, followed the next day by that of Warrant Officer Roggenbrick.

An aircraft of a new type, a Messerschmitt 410, flying at 18,000 feet west of Felixstowe was shot down by a Mosquito night fighter on 23rd August, and it crashed at Chelmondiston, near Ipswich, with one of the crew dead. The other crew member, Obergefreiter Michael Heurer, aged twenty-two, baled out and landed at Stratton Hall, Levington, where he was detained to await the police. The next day two German maps of Western Europe were found in a field at Kirton, and it was assumed that they originated from this aircraft.

On Tuesday, 28th September Ipswich was again attacked by daylight with Crane's and Wrinch's factories as the target, the airport coming under fire as well, an Air Sea Rescue Walrus amphibian being destroyed as a result.

The largest number of enemy aircraft to pass over the area for several months made their way to London on 7th October and many bombs were jettisoned by returning bombers while a small force attacked Norwich. On Friday, 15th October, another new German aircraft type came to grief in Suffolk, when a Junkers 188 was shot down by a night fighter and blew up on impact at Church Farm, Hemley. The crew of four all descended by parachute, two dead and two alive, the survivors being captured by local forces.

Heavy attacks on the night of Wednesday 3rd November, 1943, caused damage at Ipswich when bombs demolished Brook House Nursing Home, but of the 40 patients and staff only one patient was killed and one injured although 64 tame rabbits died. During this raid Mrs Janice Dale (neé Lowe) of Bramford, near Ipswich who, only a young girl at the time, was in the kitchen with her mother who was ironing. Around 19.00 hours the sirens sounded and they heard planes in the vicinity. On hearing the whistle of a bomb they rushed into the hall of their home, as there was no time to get to the Anderson shelter next door. The bomb exploded near the back door step and the back of the bungalow disappeared, the bathroom door falling across Janice and her mother, saving their lives. Two hours later they were dug out by neighbours but great fears were felt for the mother as she was one mass of sticky red liquid, presumed to be blood. On deeper investigation it was found to be the contents of several broken jars of strawberry jam which had been stored on top of the wardrobe. Janice remembers her dolls being scattered in the road, from where she retrieved them in pieces. Another aspect of the raid was the widespread use of radar blanketing, "Window", dropped by the raiders.

Consternation was caused at Norwich two nights later when during a raid carried out in a thunderstorm, 15 barrage balloons were struck by lightning and fell blazing around the city.

The people of Colchester were startled on the night of 30th November by a tremendous aerial explosion, which turned out to be an R.A.F. four-engined bomber which blew up over the town, the main portion of the blazing wreckage crashing just outside the town. One of the crew escaped and landed by parachute in the grounds of the Military Hospital, where his injuries were promptly dealt with. Chelmsford bore the brunt of a heavy attack on 10th December, but apart from this raid enemy activity tailed off during the remainder of the month.

January, 1944, was comparatively free from incidents and this gave a feeling that perhaps the worst was over, but on 13th February, Clacton, Essex, suffered a bad raid, Marks and Spencers Store being hit and badly damaged, together with several other shops. Five enemy bombers were brought down in the district. Ten days later, oil bombs and incendiaries rained down on Colchester as a massive fire bomb attack was mounted on the St Botolph's district, quickly setting fire to the clothing factories of Leaming and Company and Hollington Brothers, Griffin's furniture depository and the furniture store of Bloomfield and Company, together with the ironmongery shop on the other side of the road. Several other premises were soon caught up in the inferno. St Botolph's Church had an extremely lucky escape when fire bombs fell on the roof, but were removed before they could inflict too much damage. Witnesses reported that the blaze could be seen as far away as Bury St Edmunds, some 30 miles distant. The estimated 1,400 incendiary bombs destroyed 14 premises, badly damaged 5 and severely damaged 94. Colchester had its last manned aircraft raid on 22nd March 1944, when incendiaries again showered down on the town, but three bombers were brought down over the Thames Estuary and two more over the Eastern Counties.

The odd bomber appeared over the region during the next few months, and one such was a Junkers 88 which was shot down in flames and crashed at Wantisden Heath, near Orford, Suffolk. On a photographic flight, the bomber was loaded with flash bombs, and of the crew of four there was only one survivor, Willi Scheel.

One of the exercises which may have helped to save life and property during the German manned bomber assault was the system of dummy airfields and airstrips dotted in open country around the East Coast. Plans were originally drawn up during 1939 for decoy sites using visually acceptable full size aircraft mockups, buildings and installations positioned in authentic surroundings near existing known airfields. Their purpose was to draw off attacks from the actual airfields and for this reason the decoy sites had to stand up to enemy photography.

Whenever possible obsolete or unserviceable aircraft were used for the deception, but as they only contributed a small proportion of the number required, steps were taken to provide further "residents". With the majority of industry fully engaged on war work, search was made for possible manufacturers of the "dummies" and finally those masters of deception, the film industry property men, came to the rescue. Appearing most realistic from aerial and low level observation, the dummies were turned out in quantity, Hurricanes, Blenheims, Battles, Spitfires and Defiants all appearing in correct markup on the decoy airfields. The deception was so good, in fact, that personnel had to be stationed at these sites to warn off

R.A.F. pilots intent on landing on the "new" airfields. Many of the sites were also equipped with flare paths to carry on the work at night, the flares being spaced closer than usual to give an illusion of greater height. The decoy aerodromes were code-named "K Sites", whilst those equipped with flare paths were known as "Q Sites". A further innovation was a site designed to give the illusion of a built up area, code-named "SD Site" for small areas and "Starfish" for the large area. One such site was on the heathland near Ipswich, adjacent to the Felixstowe Road, where the surface was lined out with tarred strips to represent roads, and fires were lit together with smoke units to decoy raiders away from the town.

Many of the Eastern Counties aerodromes had their dummy satellites, which served their purpose, as many of them were bombed on several occasions. When the enemy raids slackened off, the need for the sites was no longer there, and so towards the end of 1942, they closed down having, no doubt, saved many lives and much property.

Even in these dark days, humour still prevailed as Mr Howlett of Trimley remembers: —

"During 1940 I was stationed in Suffolk at a decoy airfield, complete with dummy aircraft, bomb dumps etc. the main object being to draw enemy aircraft away from the main aerodrome at Mildenhall. At the first sign of enemy activity, the dummy flare-path was lit, the warning signal given and all personnel made for the shelters.

On one particular night, we were all in the shelter, with the enemy aircraft overhead and the crash of falling bombs near at hand. Suddenly the tension was relieved by an unconscious humorous remark by a fellow airman from Stowmarket who was playing draughts in the corner. Above all the nearby bomb explosions and general disorder he pleaded, 'Try and keep a bit quiet chaps, I can't concentrate on my game'."

Listed below are the "K" and "Q" Sites in the area:

"K" Site with flare path lighting and dummy aircraft

Airfield	Decoy
Wattisham	Boxford
Mildenhall	Cavenham
Bircham Newton	Coxford Heath
West Raynham	Fulmodestone
Martlesham Heath	Hollesley Heath
Duxford	Horseheath
Feltwell	Lakenheath
Watton	North Tuddenham
Marham	Swaffham
Honington	Thetford

AVIATION

"K" Site only. No flarepath
Wittering   Alwalton
Wyton   Haddenham

"Q" Site. Flarepath only
Stradishall   Ashfield Green
Bircham Newton   Sedgeford
Sutton Bridge   Terrington Marsh

Great Yarmouth was somewhat different from the other large towns in the region in that it housed a large number of service men and women and two incidents, within a couple of months, involved heavy loss of life among members of the A.T.S. and W.R.N.'s who were billeted in the town. Being in the front line, the town was visited by the enemy every other day during 1941.

A feature of the bombing of Great Yarmouth was the number of large bombs dropped which failed to explode and the valuable and dangerous tasks performed by the Army and Royal Naval Bomb Disposal Units. One example was on 7th May 1942, when a FW190 dropped a 500kg bomb which hit the Southtown Railway Station, but failing to explode finished up lying on the track alongside the platform. A Naval Bomb Disposal Officer, standing on the platform awaiting a train, immediately jumped down onto the tracks and defused the bomb, rendering it safe, a fine example of cool thinking and action.

Firemen, including those of the Orwell Works Fire Brigade, fight a fire in an Ipswich Gasworks gasholder early on Wednesday, 2nd June, 1943, after an attack by enemy fighter bombers. A bomb dropped on nearby houses and killed eleven people.

CHAPTER FIVE

Pilotless Raiders

DURING the early 1940s the Allies were aware that the Luftwaffe was preparing a campaign against the British Isles, utilising, what at that time were considered unconventional weapons. Many massive structures were being built along the occupied Channel coast of France, and these had the attention of both the British and American bomber forces. The Royal Air Force carried out a massive raid on the secret establishment at Peenemunde on the Baltic in order to stem the development of these weapons.

The first to see service was the V.1 (Vergeltungswaffe 1 — Reprisal Weapon) or FZG 76 pilotless aeroplane, which carried a warhead of 2,000 lbs. (907kgs) of high explosive compared with the largest air lifted German bomb dropped of 5,000 lbs. (2,268kgs).

One of the first of these V.1's fell at Baker's Hall Farm, Bures, Essex. Although the farm buildings were damaged, there were no casualties. As this weapon was unknown at the time of the incident it was thought that an aircraft had crashed at high speed. Weeley, Essex then had a "visitation" and once again it was assumed that an aircraft had come to grief in a local potato field. The first V.1 to descend in East Suffolk exploded in a field at Peasenhall, near Saxmundham, on Friday 16th June 1944, followed by another later in the day at Woolverstone near Ipswich. On the 26th of June 1944, the first V.1 to pass over Norwich spluttered its way over the city, eventually crashing in open country to the north.

Ipswich actually saw its first V.1 on the morning of 18th July, this one fortunately passing over the town and crashing in open country. Another of these weapons crashed into a field at Boxted in late July causing a large crater and setting fire to a row of cottages.

With the new noises in the sky, more eyes were cast upwards when sounds appeared that did not sound normal, and this was the case on a fine summer's day in late August. People in South East Essex looked up after a large explosion at height, which turned out to be a B.24 Liberator of the 8th Air Force which had run into trouble, the crew baling out at high altitude. Taking some time to descend, the parachuting crew were widely spread over the district, one landing in the grounds of the Wilson Marriage School at Colchester, whilst the aircraft dinghy, which had become released and inflated, dropped into a field of pea-pickers near Fingringhoe near the Essex coast.

At last the secret of the V.1 was discovered and during the months of August and September considerable numbers of pilotless flying bombs passed over or crashed in the district, one causing death and destruction when it plunged down into Maryon Road, Ipswich on the 1st September. 15 "doodle-bugs", as they were nicknamed passed through the Colchester sector on the 16th September, one crashing at Langham, one at Aldham, and one at Wakes Colne, whilst two days later one flew into the hill in the town of Maldon, Essex and destroyed a number of houses. Another caused similar destruction in Manningtree, Essex.

It was fortunate that on Sunday 17th September, a very few V.1's put in an appearance when from noon for two hours masses of glider tugs and gliders passed over Ipswich and district on their way to Arnhem.

Four people died when a V.1 crashed into a row of cottages at Ardleigh, Essex during the night of 27th September and two days later another roared down at Sudbury, Suffolk. Anti-aircraft fire damaged a "doodle-bug" over Colchester on 6th October and the robot then turned over and hurtled down to explode in open ground near Reed Hall. A remarkable escape was recorded by soldiers who were in a hut which was in the direct line of flight of the weapon but a tree interrupted its career. Nayland, received another V.1 on 15th October, but as it landed in meadowland, only a large amount of turf was disturbed.

Halton Crescent, Ipswich, was unfortunate on Wednesday 18th October and four people died and twenty-eight were seriously injured when houses were hit.

The Essex villages of Marks Tey and Ardleigh were rapidly becoming the most V.1 bombed sites in the Eastern Counties, as for some unknown reason they seemed to attract these unpleasant visitors.

November saw no respite from the "doodle-bugs" which continued to crash down in the area. Residents in a house at West Mersea, Essex had a remarkable escape on 7th December, when one landed in the garden. As the Observer Corps became more acquainted with the low-flying miniature aircraft with the flame pulsing from the stove-pipe motor on top, they were able to direct fighters to intercept them and many were the witnesses' stories of R.A.F. fighters flying alongside and tipping the pilotless craft over with their wing tips, or disturbing the robots' flight by using the fighter's slipstream, anti-aircraft guns being used when the fighters were not present.

A little earlier in the month, it seemed a coincidence that the Fire Watchers' Night Duties should be brought to an end on Guy Fawkes Night, 5th November 1944.

At this time the flying bomb launching sites in the Pas de Calais were being overrun by the advancing Allied armies, so the Germans took to launching their V.1's from mother aircraft over the North Sea. Heinkel 111 bombers were adapted for the purpose, fitted with a launching ramp on the fuselage, and the necessary gear for igniting and starting the pulse-motor. It is reported that heavy casualties were suffered by the launching aircraft, as this was an extremely hazardous operation, the risk not greatly increased by the numbers of Mosquito night fighters awaiting their arrival off the East coast.

Large numbers of anti-aircraft guns were moved up to counter this new menace and the roads were crowded as the guns moved along them into position on the coastlands.

The notorious "doodle-bug buzz-bomb" or officially the V.1. flying bomb. This is an experimental piloted version used by the Luftwaffe for flight testing in what must have been an extremely hazardous occupation. *Myron Burak*

As the V.1's made their almost regular visits a new weapon arrived at Weeley, Essex. After a terrific explosion, a long rumble was heard in the sky. The rumble in fact was the actual arrival sound of a supersonic A.4 or V.2 rocket. The missile fortunately fell on open ground and only dug a large hole. On 25th September another V.2 made its silent arrival in a field at Hoxne, Suffolk, followed the next day by another at Ranworth, eight miles from Norwich. During the next two days six more exploded in open country around Norwich and another detonated whilst descending over the Norfolk coast. A V.2 fell into the sea off Orfordness lighthouse on Monday 9th October followed the next day by another which exploded about 8,000 feet over Harwich Harbour. Playford, Suffolk, received a "visitor" the following day, whilst V.1's still continued to buzz over the district, the cessation of their pulse-motor noise causing people to take immediate shelter.

When a rocket landed in Norfolk during the evening of 12th October it was the last one of 36 which had been aimed at Norwich and again it fortunately came to earth off-target. German records show that in this small campaign, V.2 rockets were launched from Staveren in Friesland, Eastern Holland, by the Lehrund Versuchs Artillerie Batteri 444 with 36 of the weapons being directed towards Norwich and 8 towards Ipswich. The nearest V.2 to reach its target was one which fell on the outskirts of Norwich on 3rd October.

Spasmodic V.1's still flew over the area, mainly of the air-launched variety, the last of these weapons to approach the British Isles being shot down off Orfordness by A.A. guns on 29th March 1945. The gun platform erected some 12 miles off Felixstowe, nicknamed the "Churchill Fort" but correctly known as the Roughs Tower, played a considerable part in destroying several of these weapons with its guns manned by members of the Royal Marines.

The V.2s were still coming over during the early months of 1945 as on Thursday 22nd March 1945 a very clear vortex trail of a V.2 was seen from Felixstowe as it was launched in Holland. About five minutes later, a loud explosion in the area was presumed to be the detonation of this weapon. The next day, a light as opposed to the vortex trail, was seen ascending in the same direction followed by a mid-air explosion some four minutes later. The V.2 rocket employed a very thin light skin for its hull construction and as the propellant tanks emptied, combined with the pressure charges as the rocket soared into the sub-stratosphere and then fell back into the higher density of the atmosphere, the tanks caused many of the missiles to detonate on re-entry.

Signs of better times were evident on 23rd February 1945, when Ipswich Corporation workmen replaced the electrical light bulbs in the town's street lamps. Shortly afterwards the blackout turned to a "dimout", with the relaxation of the blackout regulation, except for a five mile coastal strip, on 23rd April 1945.

Ipswich sirens sounded for the last time at 12.45 hours on 29th March 1945, though Great Yarmouth had to wait a little longer until 13.23 hours on 30th April 1945.

The following flying bombs and rockets fell in the region: —

	V.1	V.2
Essex	412	378
Suffolk	93	13
Norfolk	13	29
Cambs.	—	1

The following incident demonstrates the danger involved in dealing with these missiles and the unsung heroes who dealt with them.

On Sunday morning 12th January 1945 at 06.15 hours a V.1 flying bomb landed near the front door of Capel Green Farm at Capel St Andrews, near Woodbridge, Suffolk, the residence of Mr Gladwin. Fortunately the warhead did not explode. Winged by anti-aircraft fire from the 7th City of London Regiment stationed locally, this bomb turned out to be the most perfect specimen of the seven which landed undetonated.

The Bomb Disposal people made tracks for the site, the officer in charge of defusing being Captain H. J. Hunt, assisted by Captain G. Tyson and Captain C. Horsfall, an expert in X-ray photography. The first person on the scene was Mr W. Meadows, the bailiff from nearby Home Farm, and the Gladwin family were immediately evacuated to the latter farm. When the Bomb Disposal convoy arrived at the spot, they found that the V.1 had made a smooth landing, burying its nose in deep muddy land, which had no doubt saved the farmhouse.

Captain Hunt, stated, "Our instructions were that before defusing, the bomb was to be X-rayed to ascertain the type of fuse, also to find out if it had an attachment or was 'booby trapped'. None of us had operated in this way on a flying bomb and naturally we were none too happy. True we had intelligence reports but we also knew the very small numbers of flying bombs which did not explode, so perfect were the German fuses."

The explosive contents was a charge of about 850 kgs (1,870 lbs.). Fuses included a highly sensitive electric impact fuse connected to switches in the nose, in all-way mechanical impact fuse and sometimes a clock fuse. The third was designed to destroy the bomb should the other two fuses fail to function. We wondered why the bomb had failed to explode and afterwards came to the conclusion that it had not by reason of the soft earth it had fallen into. The bomb was almost 28½ feet (8.6 m) long with a wing wpan of 17½ feet (5.2 m) and the propulsion unit was 11 feet 3 inches (3.4 m) long.

Setting about X-raying the fuses, the squad encountered great difficulties as they stood almost up to their waists in the ooze, and keeping a footing was a feat. After deciding that the nose fuse had smashed, it became imperative to remove the missile from the mud. Assistance was requested from the nearby R.A.F. Station at Sutton Heath. During the hours that we had to wait for the tractor, we were troubled by aircraft, some flying very low, circling the emergency landing strip.

The noise and vibration did not help the position, as we did not know the type of fuse in the bomb and wondered if the vibration overhead could set them working.

The R.A.F. tractor arrived and a steel cable was passed round a tree so that the tractor and its driver were at the back of the farmhouse and would have a little protection from the blast if the bomb detonated. The mud sucked hard at the bomb casing and it would not budge, so it was decided to take the extremely risky course of giving it a quick tug. Had the "doodle bug" exploded it would have cleared an area of 400 yards completely. The strain was taken — the cable snapped, but a heavier cable did the trick. After X-raying the fuses they were removed but not without further drama. Captain Hunt had to send to Ipswich, nearly 20 miles away, for a glass fountain pen filler. This was needed so that a liquid solution of plaster of paris could be placed, drop by drop into the mechanism where it quickly set and rendered the fuse inoperative.

The bomb was a fine specimen, and the casing was sent to the United States of America and Captain Hunt at a later date, then Major, was able to obtain the fuses and now proudly has them at his Halesworth home.

During 1968, Major Hunt made a nostalgic journey back to the site of his hazardous operation, and met Mr Meadows who still clearly recalls that eventful January morning, after which he had the Gladwins as visitors for ten days.

On 24th September 1956, The Duke of Gloucester, President of the Imperial War Graves Commission, handed over to the Dean and Chapter of Westminster for custody in Westminster Abbey, the Roll of Honour of civilians killed by enemy action in the United Kingdom during the Second World War. This comprises six finely printed volumes listing 60,000 names and includes 340 people of Norwich, 216 from Great Yarmouth, 54 from Colchester, 37 from Clacton, Walton and Frinton, and 40 from Ipswich.

The volumes are placed on a Memorial base situated close to the West Door near the Unknown Warrior's Tomb and outside the entrance to the Chapel of St George, where the volumes recording the Service are housed.

Thirty years after it was launched, the motor section of a V.2 rocket serves as a flower garden against the entrance gate to Walnut Tree Farm, Stowupland, Suffolk. The missile in its headlong plunge back to earth, exploded in mid-air, and the rear section fell into a ploughed field on the farm. The farmer, Mr Robert Allard, pushed the one ton motor section into a ditch, and it remained there over the years, until Mr Allard's daughter and son-in-law, Mr and Mrs Cyril Bloom, unearthed it and put it in the present position. A few months later, during 1974, several more V.2 relics, some of them quite large portions, came to light off West Mersea, and in the Brightlingsea area of Essex, local air historians being kept busy assisting in unearthing these seemingly long lost relics. The majority of the work was carried out by a Naval Mine Disposal Unit from Portsmouth, the work being hazardous by virtue of the fact that mines could still exist in the sea-bed, and there was the possibility of an unexploded V.2 nose section.

CHAPTER SIX

Cousins in Arms

U.S.A.A.F. Eighth and Ninth Air Forces

ALTHOUGH formed initially in the United States during January, 1942, the first elements of the American Air Force took up residence in the Eastern Counties much later, when the Second Wing of the Eighth United States Army Air Force was established at Old Catton, on the outskirts of Norwich.

In order to gain operational experience, the 15th Bomb Squadron joined forces with No. 226 Squadron of the Royal Air Force, which at that time was flying an American-built aircraft, the Douglas Boston III, and operating from Swanton Morley, Norfolk.

A beginning was made on 29th June, 1942, when an all-American crew, flying a "borrowed" R.A.F. Boston, made a sortie against the railway yards at Hazebrouck, from which they returned safely. They made history as being the first United States Army Air Force personnel to bomb Europe in the Second World War. This operation was followed on the 4th July, American Independence Day, by a low level sweep over the Low Countries, made by six crews still flying "borrowed" Bostons, to strafe and attack enemy airfields. One Boston, piloted by Second Lieutenant Loehri, was hit by anti-aircraft fire and, too low for recovery, hurtled into the ground, its crew being the first to die whilst engaged in operations over Europe. Another crew were extremely lucky in that, after their aircraft had been severely damaged, suffering the loss of one airscrew and resultant engine fire, the pilot, Captain Kegelman, managed by skilled airmanship to bring the smoking bomber home across the North Sea to its Norfolk base. The awards made to the United States Army Air Force crews included three American Distinguished Flying Crosses and the American Distinguished Service Cross to Captain Kegelman, the awards being the first made in Europe.

The fighter element of the Eighth Air Force came into being in the region when the 350th Group was formed during the autumn of 1942 at Duxford, Cambridgeshire, and equipped with the Bell P.39 Airacobra, an unorthodox and not too popular aircraft. The Observation side of the force was represented by two Squadrons of the 68th Observation Group based at Wattisham, Suffolk, also flying the Bell Airacobra.

By this time, autumn 1942, more two-engined light bomber units were being based in the Eastern Counties, some being based at newly constructed airfields and others sharing existing Royal Air Force aerodromes. The aircraft comprised North American B.25 Mitchells, Douglas A.20 Havocs and Martin B.26 Marauders. At a

Drab finished Douglas A.20 rests on the airfield at Rougham, Suffolk. The star design on the wheel cover is unique, and the lack of unit markings is also obvious by their absence.   *Mr and Mrs Hall*

later stage the B.26s were mainly transferred to the Ninth Air Force, which operated basically to the south of the region.

Winter 1942 saw the arrival of the four-engined Boeing B.17 Fortress. On 27th January, 1943, B.17s from Shipdham, Norfolk, were among a force of 64 aircraft of this type which bombed the North German ports of Wilhelmshaven and Emden. In this, the first raid of Germany proper by United States Army Air Force aircraft, only one B.17 was lost, whilst seven enemy fighters were claimed by the Fortress gunners.

Several operations were mounted during early spring of 1943 against targets in north-west Germany, but after flying across the North Sea the bombers usually arrived to find the target area completely obscured by cloud and so had to return home, frustrated, to try again another day. Often these sorties were marred by the loss of aircraft and crews due to weather and mechanical failure over the North Sea. Local records contain a note that on the 13th February, 1943, the body of 0-885396 Second Lieutenant Jap A. Powell, aged twenty-six, flying from Saffron Walden, Essex, was brought ashore at Felixstowe.

In order to counteract the cloud hazard, some B.24s of the 329th Bomb Squadron were fitted with the R.A.F.'s "Gee" blind bombing equipment. Flying from Bungay, Suffolk, they made several runs to Germany during the early months of 1943, but without any great success. The Royal Air Force was apprehensive of this secret equipment, already installed in its night bomber force, falling into the hands of the enemy, so only the worst possible weather was deemed suitable for these operations, which were called off during the last week in March. After the equipment had been removed from the B.24 Liberators they returned to their normal bombing duties.

Consolidated Liberator B.24.D of the 93rd Bomb Group comes in to land at Hardwick, Norfolk, during late 1943.   *U.S.A.F.*

In other earlier operations over Germany and Occupied Europe both the B.17s and the B.24s ran into numerous difficulties due to the altitudes at which they flew. Extreme cold caused guns to freeze up, ammunition belts to go stiff, cameras to freeze and there was the ever-present fear of oxygen failure and subsequent loss of consciousness and even death.

With the new units of the United States Army Air Force arriving almost daily, the construction of new airfields all over the Eastern Counties went ahead at a terrific pace. An American Staff Sergeant engaged on the construction of the runways at Debach airfield near Ipswich describes vividly the day-by-day life in his wonderfully local book, *Here we are together* published by Longman Green & Co. In this book Robert S. Arbib Junior has painted a colourful scene of the trials and tribulations caused by the weather, and remembers the wartime restrictions.

In Suffolk alone as many as ten new airfields were being constructed at about the same time in order to accommodate the hosts of American aircraft due to arrive later in the year. When the airfield at Raydon, Suffolk, was constructed it was estimated that the cost to the British taxpayers was £750,000.

The fighter side of the Eighth Air Force came into operational being when the Republic P.47 Thunderbolts of the 78th Fighter Squadron arrived at Duxford, Cambridgeshire, on the 3rd April, 1943, whilst the 56th Fighter Squadron moved into Horsham St Faiths, Norfolk, two days later. Aircraft of this type had been at Debden, Essex, for some time previously, working up and solving problems which had arisen in both the airframe and engines, as well as the radio installations.

During the following weeks, high-level sorties were flown over Northern France with the Thunderbolts, and a few losses were sustained for the claiming of several Luftwaffe machines, mainly Focke Wulf FW.190s. It was unfortunate for the newly arrived United States Army Air Force squadrons operating over Europe that the German High Command had at this time reinforced the fighter strength in this area, in order to combat the increasing day raids by the bombers from the Eastern Counties. This reinforcement, of course, included the newly introduced FW.190, a radial engined monoplane of slimmer lines than the P.47 and, at altitudes of 20,000 feet or below, definitely superior in performance. Casualties amongst the P.47s still persisted, many caused by engine failure, and a few by inexperienced pilots being "jumped" by the FW.190s and of course, pure battle losses. One pilot, First Lieutenant Johnson, had his aircraft's hydraulic system damaged when attacked resulting in only one undercarriage leg dropping into the down position. At Horsham St Faiths, his Squadron Commanding Officer took off and, flying close to the luckless Johnson, surveyed the damage, and made suggestions to either get the down leg up or the up leg down. Nothing worked so Johnson flew out to sea, baled out off Great Yarmouth, and was promptly rescued by an Air Sea Rescue launch.

The late spring of 1943 saw an ever-increasing number of B.17s and B.24s rising almost daily from regional bases like Earls Colne and Andrewsfield in Essex, Framlingham and Mendlesham in Suffolk, and numerous others in Norfolk.

The Martin B.26 Marauder twin-engined medium bombers which had been based mainly in the northern part of the area were moved down to Essex and placed

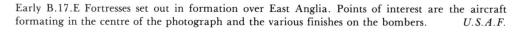

Early B.17.E Fortresses set out in formation over East Anglia. Points of interest are the aircraft formating in the centre of the photograph and the various finishes on the bombers.   *U.S.A.F.*

Liberator B.24.H 29567 "Bambi" of the 34th Bomb Group undergoes inspection at Mendlesham, Suffolk. The cat-walk across the bomb-bay is clearly visible when the bomb-doors are open.

U.S.A.F.

under the command of the Ninth Air Force, whilst the Fortress Wings had their Headquarters at Elveden Hall, on the Suffolk/Norfolk border.

13th June, 1943, was a day never to be forgotten by the Eighth Air Force. That day the 94th Bomb Group took off from their base at Earls Colne, Essex, and on their return were to land at their new base at Rougham near Bury St Edmunds, Suffolk. In all 18 aircraft from this Group took part and among the crews was Brigadier General Forrest, flying as an observer. When approaching their north German target of Kiel, the bombers were intercepted by fighters and several were lost, including that of Brigadier General Forrest. Badly mauled, the surviving B.17s struggled back over the North Sea. As they approached the Norfolk coast, the crews began to prepare for landing, in many cases removing the gun barrels for cleaning. At this stage, they encountered a formation of Junkers 88s which promptly shot down another nine bombers. Only a pitiful handful of B.17s were able to make their new base.

During early summer, ever-increasing numbers of bombers were meeting heavy opposition over Occupied Europe and Germany and losses mounted, especially among the newer and less experienced crews. The German fighter pilots seemed to "sense" the newcomers and made them their special target. These B.17 operations, with up to 300 aircraft taking part, presented a large target for the

Martin B.26 Marauder twin engined medium bomber at Rougham. The heavy forward armament can be seen in the fuselage mounted pods and of interest are the large four-bladed airscrews.

Mr and Mrs Hall

high-level anti-aircraft guns of the defences, and in certain atmospheric conditions their presence was betrayed by the long condensation trails stretching out behind them in the sub-stratosphere.

Many local people were surprised to see the exotic mascots adopted by some American units, but learned to expect almost anything from their Allied friends. The 390th Bomb Group at Framlingham had a honey bear, whilst other Groups brought in all types and kinds of pets and, because it was feared that the situation might get out of hand, rules were imposed in order to prevent units from overstepping the mark.

The twin-engined bomber was not generally associated with the Eighth Air Force, but in the early days of 1943 some did serve with this formation. They were mainly B.26 Marauders, a heavily loaded fast twin radial-engined monoplane which was at first not greatly liked by its crews, who had a variety of disparaging names for it. Not accustomed to its high landing speed, heavy controls and tricky handling characteristics, the crews quickly formed a bad impression of the new bomber, but as they grew more confident with it they learnt to use it to good advantage.

Residents in the Bury St Edmunds district were somewhat perturbed by the low-flying tactics employed by these aircraft, sweeping low round hillocks, dodging under high tension cables and occasionally bringing down telegraph wires. All this practice was for their first operation, carried out during May, 1943, when the unit attacked installations in Holland and the twelve bombers met stiff opposition. Several had the frightening experience of having to recross the North Sea, badly damaged, to crash or make forced landings in Suffolk.

17th May, 1943, was another black day when only one aircraft from a force of twelve returned to base. The two flights, each of six B.26's, led by Lieutenant Colonel Stillman and Lieutenant Colonel Purinton attacked targets at Ijmuiden and Haarlem respectively. Flying very low over the North Sea, when approaching the Dutch coast one B.26 lost a motor and climbed up above the non-radar level, where it was quickly spotted, the alert given and all the defences manned. One Marauder was hit by anti-aircraft fire and swung to port, ramming the aircraft alongside it, whilst the other flight member was engulfed in airborne wreckage and crashed. The aircraft flown by Stillman was also hit and, losing control, made a high-speed crash, but he and one other crew member survived the impact. The second flight of six aircraft fared no better, and were no match for the flak and fighters and succumbed to the defences, only one crew making home.

To overcome these losses, the Marauder units converted to medium altitude bombing, but as their targets were usually of the strongly protected variety many aircraft still failed to return to their bases. However, on 9th September 1943, one of the Marauders' busiest days when 219 aircraft were despatched, only three were lost, giving the crews greater confidence.

In midsummer, 1943, the bombing forces of the Eighth Air Force went for new targets and flew further than they had ever travelled before. Large numbers participated in attacks on installations in Norway with targets ranging from 600 to 1,000 miles from home, and it is remarkable that on these daylight flights, although upwards of 325 machines took part, only very few were lost. Daily during the late morning the bombers, mainly B.17s, made their circling manoeuvres over the local countryside, packing themselves into tight formations before flying out across the sea to do battle with the full fury of the Luftwaffe and the anti-aircraft guns of the Wehrmacht. To illustrate this point, records show that in one week approximately 100 Fortresses were lost, and almost the same number of crews were posted as killed, wounded or missing. The loss of aircraft during these operations caused grave concern, production barely keeping pace with the losses. As the B.17s and B.24s were manufactured in the U.S.A. it took some time to deliver them to the British Isles, where they still had to be modified and brought up to operational standards.

The American troops in the district were fortunate in being entertained by well-known entertainers who usually flew over from the U.S.A. for this purpose. Duxford was especially blessed, as this base saw the appearance of Bob Hope and Bing Crosby. One such show staged during July, 1943, went on with only a handful of troops in the audience, as all available aircraft were airborne searching the North Sea for the Group Commanding Officer who had been reported missing.

August, 1943, saw the B.17s and B.24s off to pastures new when on the 17th they took off after the thick morning mist had cleared, and climbing up, massed and passed out over the Suffolk coast, gaining altitude over the North Sea. Their target was Regensburg, the home factories of the Messerschmitt Me.109, and one of its main production centres. Although initially protected by P.47 Thunderbolts, the bombers had to fend for themselves when the fighters, finding the range too great for them, had to turn for home. Waves of Luftwaffe fighters assailed the straggling bombers as they flew over the Fatherland at between 17,000 and 18,000 feet, from which height the works were bombed. Carrying on in a southerly direction, the survivors crossed the Alps and, passing over Italy, dropped altitude and made the North African coast, eleven hours after take-off from Framlingham, Snetterton Heath and other much cooler airfields. 24 Fortresses had fallen along the route. Not all were lost to enemy fighters, as some had failed to make the Mediterranean crossing, having to "ditch" through lack of fuel.

At the same time as the B.17s had been assaulting the aircraft works, a diversionary attack was mounted on the main production centre for ball-bearings at Schweinfurt, also deep in fighter-protected air space, where stiff opposition was also encountered. Instead of the tight formations which had passed over the Suffolk coastline some hours previously, scattered flights now came home with many smoking and semi-wrecked bombers crawling low over the sea, making for the first available landing ground. Of some 230 bombers which had set out on the diversionary raid in bright morning sunshine, 36 never returned to their bases, leaving more than 370 crewmen to be replaced.

Later in the week those B.17s which were airworthy enough to do so returned from their North African airfields, bombing French airfields on the way. Of the 60 which came home by this route, most made it safely.

The Ninth Bombardment Group (H) stationed at Snetterton Heath, Norfolk, were involved in the Regensburg raid and the onward run to North Africa. Being in need of a mascot, some of the crew managed to persuade a hard-up Arab to part with his somewhat bedraggled donkey for 400 francs. Suitably wrapped in blankets and with an electrically heated flying suit wrapped round her, she was loaded into the unpressurized B.17 with an oxygen mask fitted on her nose. Flying at high altitude and temperatures of 60 degrees below zero, the aircraft bombed Bordeaux, France, on the way home; the B.17, "Miracle Tribe" flown by Captain Andy Miracle, finally made base. The mascot was named "Lady Moe" and after a hectic two years on and off the base, "Lady Moe" was killed in the autumn of 1945 when she wandered off the base on to a nearby railway line and was struck by a passing train.

One of the big raids of the Second World War was staged by aircraft of the Eighth Air Force, not operating from their familiar Eastern Counties bases but from the North African desert. This was the attack on the Ploesti oilfields in Rumania carried out by the B.24 Liberators of the 93rd Bomb Group from Hardwick, Norfolk, the 44th Bomb Group from Shipdham, Norfolk, and the 389th from Hethel, Norfolk, on 1st August, 1943. The aircraft taking part flew back to their North African bases on completing this mission and after further raids in this region returned to the United Kingdom late in August. Not as numerous as the B.17, the B.24 however carried out a large part of the daylight bombing campaign against the fortress of Europe and operated from a number of Eastern Counties airfields.

The cost of daylight bombing steadily increased, the operations of 3rd September, 1943, bearing out the point. 400 B17s and B.24s formed up for a mass attack on an instrument factory at Stuttgart, but en route they encountered thick cloud, making formation-keeping very difficult. This was followed by the expected assault by the Luftwaffe and many bombers fell before the target was reached. The Knettishall-based 388th Bomb Group lost 11 of its twenty-one B.17s on the run-in, and afterwards the 563rd Bomb Squadron of this Group was annihilated. To add further to the disarray, only one Wing managed to locate the target, the others bombing alternative targets on the way home. 45 bombers never made their home bases, five made for Switzerland where they crash-landed, 12 ditched in the North Sea and English Channel, where the Royal Air Force rescue launches picked up over 110 airmen, and many more were scattered round the south and east coasts as wrecks which had only just managed to crawl back.

Master Sergeant Charles Sige with B.17. "Friday 13th" of the 332 Squadron, 94th Bomb Group, Rougham. The gun barrels on the chin turret have been fitted with extensions and the cyclist is well armed too.

Mr and Mrs Hall

On dispersal at Leiston, Suffolk, during March 1944, Mustang G4-P "Joan". Note the long-range fuel tanks beneath the wings and also the fully tracked vehicle necessary for the Leiston mud.

W/O P. Barker

Luck smiled on the 8th and 16th September, when 21 B.17s of the 94th Bomb Group made a 1,600 mile round trip to raid Cognac, the longest run to date. They arrived back at Rougham in darkness, having to make night landings, to which they were unaccustomed, without loss.

It was estimated at this time that if a Fortress could survive ten missions it was doing extremely well whilst the average life of a Liberator was 11.

There was no respite for the weary crews in October, when the Eighth continued to suffer heavy casualties on its daylight raids on Germany. The 381st Bomb Group from Ridgewell, Essex, lost seven of its 18 aircraft and was left with all the survivors damaged, whilst the 100th Bomb Group at Thorpe Abbots, Norfolk, lost another seven, one of this Group's survivors crossing the North Sea with only one of the four motors running.

Losses continued to mount in spite of the increasing use of the P.47 Thunderbolt fighter for the protection of the bomber formations. With the aid of newly-installed long-range tanks these fighters were able to escort the heavies further along their way yet the 95th Bomb Group from Horsham St Faiths, Norfolk, in one operation against Bremen lost five bombers from 19, the 390th from Framlingham eight from 18, and the 100th from Thorpe Abbots, 12 out of 13, the latter unit having lost 20 aircraft and 200 men in one week. On the other hand, a week later, 14th October, when 291 aircraft took part in a massive raid on the ball-bearing centre at Schweinfurt and sixty bombers were lost with 600 men, five crashed on reaching home, and 120 were so badly damaged as to be of no further immediate use, the 100th Bomb Group was the only Unit not to sustain losses. During the running battles over the Continent that day the bomber's gunners and the escorting fighters claimed 186 German fighters shot down.

The role of the fighter in the Eighth Air Force was quite different from that of its Royal Air Force equivalent, as the American aircraft were used in the main as bomber escorts and for this duty flew to the limit of their endurance. As the P.47s became more readily available they occupied the new airfields still being built in the Eastern Counties. One of the first of these formations was at Metfield, near Halesworth, Suffolk, where the 353rd Fighter group settled down. These escort duties paid off, as on 27th September, 1943, the P.47s were able to shepherd the bombers all the way to Emden and to see them home safely, a sea crossing of 200 miles each way with the result that 21 enemy aircraft were shot down for the loss of one P.47.

A notable character among the fighter pilots was the deputy commander of the 56th Fighter Group based at Halesworth, Suffolk, Major (later Colonel) David C. Schilling, who, later became the Commanding Officer. He and Colonel Hubert A. Zemke, Major Robert S. Johnson and Colonel Francis S. Gabreski were all fighter aces. With respective scores of enemy aircraft destroyed of 22½, 17½, 28 and 28 they ranked as the leading aces of the Eighth.

Another P.47 Group to move into the fray was the 356th Fighter Group which

Republic P.47D Thunderbolt coded HV-B belonging to the 56th Fighter Group based at Halesworth, Suffolk, comes in to land. Note the machine gun barrels protruding from the wings and the large proportions of this fighter. *U.S.A.F.*

arrived at Martlesham Heath on 15th October, 1943, and after working up with sweeps over the Low Countries took up its war duties of bomber escorts.

As autumn approached, so the weather deteriorated, thick cloud hampering daylight operations. New navigational aids came to the aid of the bombers in the form of H 2 X, code-named "Mickey Mouse", and the "Oboe" set, both already in use by the Royal Air Force. Unfortunately their use did not bring the results that had been anticipated, in spite of large numbers of B.17s and B.24s which followed in the wake of the pathfinder leaders.

Ipswich had a narrow escape when the crew of a B.17.F from the 351st Bomb Group based at Polebrook, Northamptonshire, returning home in cloudy weather, were horrified to find on emerging from low cloud that they were heading for the centre of the town. Frantic efforts on the part of the "cockpit staff" pulled the bomber from its destructive course and they managed eventually to coax it down on nearby Ipswich Airport.

On the 10th October, 1943, First Lieutenant John C. Winant, Jnr, the son of the American Ambassador to Great Britain, took off from Framlingham (Parham) airfield in his B.17 of the 390th Bomb Group for a daylight raid on Munster, Germany, but failed to return from this operation.

On Guy Fawkes Day, 5th November, 1943, the crew of ten of a B.17 baled out and landed in the Newbourn area of Suffolk, the bomber turning round and flying crewless out to sea and destruction. On the same day the U.S.A.F. authorities at Braintree, Essex, informed the Felixstowe Police that a 2,000 lb bomb had been dropped 1½ miles north of the town, but the missile was never found.

Whilst standing at the end of the runway at Martlesham Heath, Mr Patient witnessed within a few minutes the undercarriage of a Lockheed P.38 Lightning collapse as it landed and a P.47 Thunderbolt fail to gain height on take-off and somersault into the rough at the runway threshold. The P.47 came to rest with the cockpit level with the ground, and from nowhere, a dozen Americans appeared and, carrying out the quickest shovelling act ever seen, retrieved the pilot who was still hanging upside down from his straps.

Towards the end of 1943, a new technique was devised by the Thunderbolt Fighter Groups. Some of the P.47s would be carrying 500lb bombs, whilst others escorted them, the whole force becoming fighters once the bombs were dropped. The Halesworth and Martlesham Heath Groups worked in close co-operation on these missions.

The English weather did not always help air operations. On the 29th November, 1943, the 356th Fighter Group took off from Martlesham Heath to escort returning B.17s home from Bremen, Germany, but they ran into bad weather and after a series of running fights with the Luftwaffe lost contact with each other. Five P.47s failed to return home, it being assumed that they had run out of fuel.

A further build-up of the Eighth Air Force Groups was made during December, when on the 13th of that month P.47s of the 359th arrived at East Wretham, Norfolk, whilst the 361st moved into Bottisham, Cambridgeshire.

Mid-December 1943 saw the first missions of more B.24 Groups from Eastern Counties bases, the 445th with its B.24s at Tibenham, Norfolk, and the 446th at Bungay, Suffolk, also with B.24.Hs. Other new groups were the 448th at Seething, Norfolk, with the same type of aircraft and a new B.17.G Group, the 447th Bomb Group which started operations from Rattlesden, Suffolk.

The end of the year saw 650 bombers on a daylight raid to Ludwigshafen but the complete cloud cover once again defeated them and very little damage was effected in the target area.

January, 1944, saw renewed on attacks on the German aircraft industry and massive formations of B.17s and B.24s going for the works in the Brunswick district. Escort was to be provided by P.38 Lightnings and one Group of the then new P.51 Mustangs, but the weather was such that they failed to make contact with their flocks and 41 bombers failed to return to their bases. Connected with these operations, a Thunderbolt crash landed at Church Farm, Waldringfield, on the 26th January but the pilot was not badly injured, whilst two days later a B.17 force-landed in the sea off Bawdsey, Suffolk.

P.51 Mustang 413316, G4-C "Mildred" at Leiston early September, 1944. The pilot of this aircraft was Lt. "Kit" Carson and the Assistant Crew Chief standing by the 'plane is Corporal Bloucett.

W/O. P. Barker

Word had reached Allied Intelligence at this time of the V.1 flying bomb and its launching sites on the French Channel coast, and in order to retard the construction of these installations, daylight sorties were mounted when the weather allowed.

The flat expanse of farmland in the village of Theberton, near Leiston, Suffolk, now had airborne visitors when the 362nd, 363rd and 364th Fighter Squadrons of the 357th Fighter Group arrived on the 31st January, 1944. Several soon fell foul of their first enemy in Suffolk — mud! As the runways were not finished until 13th February, 1944, no operations were possible and the mechanics used the time to service and modify their charges. Named after the wild horse of the prairies, the Mustang lived up to its name and from this, the nearest base to the Continent, were able to range as far as the enemy's capital. Strong as an ox, the Mustang was able to survive terrible punishment as when First Lieutenant Brown got into a terrific dive over Regensburg, his speed being over 600 knots, and he managed gradually to pull out and make it home to base. The Groups' first operational Commanding Officer, Colonel Henry R. Spicers was lost early in the Group's life when his cooling system was punctured and his Mustang dropped smoking into the English Channel. Opposing rescue units raced to pick him up: the enemy won, and so on the 5th March, 1944, the Colonel became a P.O.W.

*"Lord Haw Haw's" promise to wipe out the "Yoxford Boys" did not materialize and on 6th March, 1944, putting up 33 Mustangs, they set a record of 20 enemy aircraft destroyed, one probable and seven damaged for no loss. Led by Lieutenant Colonel Thomas L. Hayes, the unit received the award of a Distinguished Unit Citation for this action.

The 31st January saw a record number of 778 bombers forming up and flying towards Brunswick and its aircraft factories, where many hits were made in the target area.

Another incident involving Mr Patient at Martlesham Heath has a humorous ring.

"When taking the Bowser† for refilling at the pumps, and trying to negotiate the many pipes that surrounded the pumps, I caught the bowser itself on an American one, smashing in the folding doors at the rear end and nearly knocking off an American who was sitting on his towing truck reading a comic. Although he replied 'Don't worry bud, my mates'll fix it', somebody must have seen what had happened, and I was told to report to the American Commanding Officer. I went to his room in the big house by the gate and on entering saw an American officer with an enormous cigar, who said 'Siddown bud'. After explaining what I had come about, he told me not to worry, as it was my C.O. who had arranged the interview and he would have to arrange some punishment for my crime. 'What's yer name, son?' 'Patient,' I replied. 'First name?' 'Laurence,' I said. 'O.K. Larry.' 'How's this?' 'I am requesting that you lose your driving pay for two weeks.' 'But I don't get driving pay,' I said. 'That ain't good enough.' 'I'll have a word with your C.O. and

---

*William Joyce executed at the end of the war as a traitor for broadcasting anti-Allied matter in English from Germany.

†Petrol tanker.

see that you *do* get driving pay, an extra sixpence per day, but you can't get it for two weeks, O.K.?' I then got driving pay for the rest of my stay at Martlesham Heath."

Sunday, 20th February, saw the previous record well passed when 1,000 bombers set out for targets in Central Germany and only 21 failed to return, although several were wrecked in the United Kingdom. To the losses from enemy action were added accidental losses such as occurred on 21st February, 1944, when two B.17.Fs of the 285th Bomb Group from Great Ashfield, Suffolk, collided over the Norfolk coast whilst descending through cloud. They crashed into the marshes below with the loss of 21 aircrew.

Liberator B.24s from a new Group, the 458th based at Horsham St Faiths, Norfolk, flew their first mission on the 27th February as a diversion over the sea, for the main force en route to Gaha, Germany from which 49 did not return.

The 4th March saw another milestone in the bomber offensive when the United States Army Air Corps went for Berlin with the B.17.Fs of the 100th Bomb Group from Thorpe Abbots, Norfolk, and the 95th Bomb Group, Horham, Suffolk. Flying five miles up, the cold was intense with temperatures down to 55 degrees below and cloud screening the target, so bombing was carried out blind. Four B.17s from Horham and one from Thorpe Abbots were lost.

Two days later approximately 725 B.17s and B.24s made the long haul to the German capital again, escorted for part of the way by fighters of the Eighth and Ninth Air Forces and the Royal Air Force. The two Groups which had made the previous raid fared badly on the way to the target, losing 23 aircraft in 35 minutes, 15 of them from Thorpe Abbots alone. The total loss for the operation was 80 Allied aircraft; among the casualties was General Wilson, flying in a B.17 from Great Ashfield. One of the stragglers nearly made the English coast, ditching off Corton, Suffolk, and the crew were all rescued.

When 600 bombers made for Berlin on 8th March, the survivors from Thorpe Abbots were up among the leaders again, and on this occasion were the leading aircraft to cross the city. Ironically enough, the Norfolk Group only lost one aircraft, and this through mechanical failure.

Targets at one time thought safe by the enemy by virtue of their distance from the United Kingdom were now being attacked by the B.17s and B.24s, which ranged as far as Southern Germany, with as many as 800 machines taking part, in each operation.

The advent of the North American P.51 Mustang, which had gone through a radical re-design by the United States Army Air Force, enabled protection to be afforded to the heavy bombers over greater distances. One of the first units to operate this new long-range fighter was the 354th Fighter Group based at Boxted, near Colchester. Originally trained on the Bell P.39 Airacobra, this Group was part of the Ninth Air Force but, lacking operational control, it came under the wing of the Eighth Air Force Fighter Command. To aid its quick training the unit received several experienced pilots who had flown Spitfires in the United Kingdom with the R.A.F. Eagles Squadrons and the like. The Group was commanded by Lieutenant Colonel Kenneth Martin and was under control of General Brereton of the Ninth Air Force.

Several "bugs" had to be removed out of the aircraft which was at first classed as the P.51.B. but when these problems were solved the modified machines were later reclassified as P.51.D.

The Ninth Air Force's top ace, Glenn Eagleston, was one of the pioneer pilots at Boxted with a total of 18½ enemy aircraft destroyed, whilst Kenneth Martin, James Howard, George Bickell and Owen Leaman were all notable characters in the fighter role.

On the 11th February, 1944, Lieutenant Colonel Martin's Mustang was wrecked in a collision with a German fighter, but he managed to clear the machine, parachute down and was taken prisoner.

Another Ninth Air Force Group came into being on 11th February when the 357th Fighter Group made its first operational flight from Leiston, Suffolk, the Eighth Air Force taking over this Group in exchange for a P.47 Group.

In addition to its duties as an escort fighter, the Boxted P.51.B was able to carry two 250lb bombs on underwing racks, thus enhancing its destructive potential.

The Lockheed P.38 Lightnings of the 364th Fighter Group based at Honington,

The famous Eighth Air Force fighter airfield at Leiston, Suffolk. Situated in the village of Theberton, this airfield was the nearest to Europe at this time.   *W/O. P. Barker*

Lockheed Lightning P.38.J of the 55th Fighter Group taxies in during June, 1944. The armament on this unusual aircraft can be seen in the nacelle nose and also the large, roomy cockpit.   *U.S.A.F.*

Suffolk, had not really lived up to early expectations, and the twin-engined, twin-boomed fighter was now used as a long range escort over Germany. The group lost its Commanding Officer on its first operational mission, when his P.38 J's engines failed and he crashed in Holland. They were unfortunate also that in their first month of operations they lost 16 aircraft, several it was assumed due to engine malfunctions.

The 357th Fighter Group with its P.51s was one of the first fighter units to reach Berlin when on the 4th March, 1944 they escorted bombers, but owing to inclement weather conditions and inexperience some 23 fighters from the groups participating were lost. Circumstances were reversed on 6th March when 48 P.51s of the 357th from Leiston took off, and although 15 returned for one reason or another the rest carried on their escort mission to Berlin, shooting down some 20 enemy aircraft and all returning home safely. The United States Army Air Force claimed 81 enemy aircraft that day.

Second Lieutenant Charles F. Gamm from the nearby airfield at Sudbury died when his Mustang fighter 312410 GO-M crashed on the banks of the River Stour at Nayland. The pilot made desperate efforts to fly over the village but when all seemed well a wing struck a tree, and the brave pilot died in the ensuing crash.

Lieutenant Gamm's photograph hangs in Nayland Church and his name was added to the War Memorial with the local men who were lost. Second Lieutenant Gamm was the first "Merlin Mustang" ace, flying the re-engined Mustang with Rolls-Royce Merlin instead of the original Allison motor, and during his short stay in Suffolk had destroyed five enemy aircraft.

The sturdy P.47 Thunderbolt, almost superseded as a long-range fighter, took on a new lease of life when aided by new long-range drop tanks. In the role of strafer and fighter bomber the Thunderbolts began to make many profitable visits to Occupied Europe, seeking out railways, gun emplacements and military installations.

One feature of the mass formations which almost daily flew over the region was the number of tragic collisions occurring when the loaded bombers were forming up ready to set course over the North Sea. The B.24 Liberator was particularly prone to this hazard with a peculiar tendency to wallow a great deal when heavily loaded, and it proved a difficult aircraft to hold in tight formation. Cloud did not help, and a number of collisions and even more near-misses occurred when climbing and descending through the obscuring vapour.

All Fools Day, 1st April, 1944, was a disastrous day for the B.24s of the 44th Bomb Group from Shipdham, Norfolk, and the 392nd from Wendling, also in Norfolk, as having flown off course they unfortunately bombed Schaffhausen in Switzerland. The mistake was even more unfortunate by the way that the German Propaganda Office blew the story up for publication.

The base at Rackheath, Norfolk, became operational on 10th April, 1944, when the 467th Bomb Group moved in with its B.24.H Liberators and joined in subsequent daylight missions.

The first week in April saw a massive turnout of bombers against the aircraft works on the Baltic Coast, but early warning radar had picked up the oncoming host and the Luftwaffe was lying in wait. From this operation 52 B.17s, 12 B.24s and some 16 escorting fighters failed to return home. On the way out, a B.17 broke formation off Felixstowe, disintegrating and falling into the sea. Only two crew members, 748386 Leland J. Evans and 39037511 Fred A. Barnes, were rescued.

The Luftwaffe made one of its intruder visits on 12th April, 1944, when a prowling night fighter shot down a Fortress which was making a landing approach at Framlingham, Suffolk. Ten days later larger numbers of intruders were awaiting the returning bombers from the 448th Bomb Group based at Seething, Norfolk, which had set out late in the day to bomb the railway installations at Hamm, Germany. Some 15 Junkers 88s and Messerschmitt Me.410 night fighters waited over the well-lit bases at Bungay, Seething, Halesworth, Rackheath and Hardwick as the bombers returned in the dusk.

First of all a B.24 was shot down into the sea off Hopton and another similar aircraft was shot down a little later off Kessingland, Suffolk, no survivors being picked up from either machine. Five B.24s were quickly lost in the Beccles area and at Rackheath three more were shot down, but a Seething B.24.H did manage to shoot down an attacking Me.410 at Thurton. Several airfields were also bombed or strafed, and as a result of this tragic occurrence sharp look-outs were required by homebound bomber crews. It was generally reported that the bombers' gunners, in order to expedite the debriefing procedure and clearing up, had unscrewed their gun barrels and were busy cleaning them when the intruders struck.

Mr Farrow of Orford who lived on the perimeter of the airfield at Brome (Eye), Suffolk, remembers how when the bombers came home after dark the ground crews would switch on all available lights to guide the aircraft down. If intruders were still in the district the bombers then had to cope with a night landing which they were not too familiar with, as well as keep a sharp look-out for the enemy. He also recalls a cottage near the *Swan Inn* at Brome occupied by two maiden ladies who had the exceptional misfortune of having a Mustang visit them at the front of the building and a B.17 crash through the back garden, all in the course of one week. The bungalow where Mr Farrow lived was almost in the line of flight for the bombers, and he recalls that his mother was unable to hang out her washing when the aircraft were flying due to the amount of black oil which the aircraft dropped.

Memories of many pass before film star and wartime bomber pilot James Stewart as he looks through the book of Remembrance in Norwich Library.   *Eastern Daily Press*

A well-known personality served with the 445th Bomb Group at Tibenham, Norfolk, the Hollywood film star James Stewart, playing a real life role as the captain of a B.24 Liberator.

It was the turn of Berlin again on the 16th April when 745 bombers headed for this now favourite target, escorted by Mustangs, but the enemy's eyes had seen the advancing armada and the Luftwaffe claimed 31 bombers.

Another daylight attack on Berlin on 29th May, 1944 provided an unhappy experience for the 447th Bomb Group at Rattlesden, Suffolk. They lost 11 of their B.17s whilst the 385th from nearby Great Ashfield, lost another seven.

As the spring of 1944 turned to summer, so the impending invasion of Europe called for softening up Northern France and massed air attacks were made on military and railway installations in this area. Two new B.24 units from Suffolk shared in this task during the first week in May, the 486th Bomb Group from Sudbury and the 487th Bomb Group at Lavenham, with the newly formed 492nd Bomb Group from North Pickenham, Norfolk, coming into action on the 11th May, 1944.

The Luftwaffe visited Suffolk again on 22nd May, bombing the home base of the 385th Bomb Group at Great Ashfield, which lost a B.17 when a hangar was hit.

The Eighth Air Force set a record for outgoing traffic on 28th May, when 1,280 heavies set out for the synthetic oil plants in north-west Germany and received only slight losses.

In advanced preparation for "D-Day", the invasion of Europe by Allied Forces, the American Ninth Air Force moved to the South of England and more Mustang units took up residence in the Eastern Counties, including the 55th Fighter Group at Wormingford, Essex, and the 353rd Fighter Group at Raydon Wood, Suffolk. With its range of almost 1,500 miles, the Mustang was now capable of the longest bomber escort missions as well as deep strafing and disruption operations.

P.51 Mustang lands at Bottisham on D-Day. Belonging to the 361st Fighter Group it is watched by a group of ground crew in varying attire. The special invasion attire have been applied all the way round the fuselage.   *U.S.A.F.*

B.17s dispersed at Lavenham, Suffolk. The complicated pattern of perimeter tracks and hard-standings is well illustrated as well as the tracks to and from the hangar.   *U.S.A.F.*

The long awaited invasion of Europe came on 6th June, 1944, accompanied by frantic activity to get the maximum aircraft ready for involvement. For identification purposes all Allied aircraft carried three white and two black bands on the rear fuselage and wings, the order for these to be painted being given only a matter of hours before the operation, causing terrific effort in order to get it carried out.

August came in bright and hot, ideal weather for the day bomber, and at this time the people of south Suffolk, now familiar with the sight of the B.24s saw a new shape when the 486th Bomb Group at Sudbury and the 487th Bomb Group at Lavenham converted to the B.17G Fortress, with its all-metal natural finish and colourful paintwork.

On the other side of the county, two events left the residents in a state of mystification. On Friday, 4th August, 1944, at about 14.35 hours on a clear afternoon an American B.17 Flying Fortress bomber was seen flying in a south-easterly direction over the parishes of Tunstall and Chillesford near Orford, Suffolk. This was not an unusual sight in 1944, when there were no fewer than 44 Heavy Bombardment Groups of the United States 8th Army Air Force, equipped with B.17 Fortresses and B.24 Liberators, based in the Eastern Counties. This was, however, a very unusual aircraft; closer examination would have revealed that this bomber carried none of the Fortress's usual ten .50 calibre machine guns and that its upper surfaces were hastily painted with high-visibility paint.

Police War Reserve Green, stationed at Orford, was instructed by Police Headquarters to keep a strict watch for this aircraft, from which men were reported to be baling out. As P.W.R. Green watched a white parachute was seen descending towards Chillesford. The Fortress then turned over and dived nose first to earth, crashing with a terrific explosion, possibly the greatest explosion ever felt on British soil; luckily the only civilian casualties were some men working in the vicinity who suffered from shock and scratches.

The Fortress crashed in Watling Wood, Sudbourne Park, near Orford, leaving a crater nearly 100 feet in diameter and destroying about two acres of forestry, sheering off 20-inch oak trees as if they had been cut with one sweep of a giant knife. Not much could be found of the Fortress, only small pieces of crumpled alloy and broken engine pieces. Of the pilot of the aircraft, who had died with his machine, there was no trace.

The crew member who had baled out, Technical Sergeant Elmer Most, aged twenty-four, was interviewed by the police officer. Most stated that he belonged to the 3rd Division Detachment, Winfarthing, and that he was the eighth of a crew of nine to bale out. In reality, Sergeant Most was the only one of a crew of two to bale out. The pilot, Lieutenant John W. Fisher, Jnr, the only other member of the Fortress's crew, was unable to bale out. Another American airman had baled out in the area but he was not, as believed at the time, from the plane that had crashed but from a similar Fortress which was at that very moment winging its way unmanned towards the German V-rocket launching sites in the Pas de Calais, where there were huge concrete bunkers at Mimoyecques, Watten, Wizernes and Siracourt. The police were also told that the crashed Fortress was returning from a mission over enemy territory, that something had gone wrong and that the pilot was trying to send the plane to crash into the sea; this was not true.

The crashed Fortress had been one of four such machines which were the Americans' first attempt at guided weapon warfare. The project was super-secret and was known by the code name "Aphrodite". These Fortresses carried T.V. cameras in their plexiglass noses and were stripped of all armament, armour plating and unnecessary structural metal and the fuselages packed with ten tons of high explosives. They were known as robots or drones. The idea was for a volunteer crew of two to take off in the drone; just before reaching the English coast they had to arm the load of high explosives, switch the drone to radio remote-control and then bale out, leaving the drone to carry out its mission unmanned. The drone would be accompanied to the target by two "mother planes", usually specially adapted Fortresses, plus navigational and observer aircraft. The targets in this case, the giant concrete bunkers in the Pas de Calais, had been unaffected by conventional bombing and "Aphrodite" seemed to provide the answer. There were T.V. monitors in the mother planes and on seeing the target on the screen, the picture being transmitted from the nose camera of the drone, the bombardier would press the "dump" swith and crash the drone by radio control on to the target. Unfortunately in the case of Lieutenant Fisher's plane, something went awry, taking the plane and the pilot to destruction on English soil.

The home base of the "Aphrodite" operations, Fersfield near Winfarthing, again saw action on the 6th August, 1944 when at about 10.50 hours two more Flying Fortress drones took off with their crews and climbed into the bright summer sky. One of these drones carried a load of nine tons of Torpex, a very high explosive of British manufacture, and the other was loaded with 180 incendiary bombs and 830 gallons of napalm (jellied petrol). The idea was for the first drone, loaded with Torpex, to be crashed on to the enemy bunker, splitting it open, and then for the incendiary drone to be crashed on the damaged bunker, smothering it with a fiery inferno, suffocating the Germans underground.

After the two man crew had baled out from the incendiary drone something went wrong and the remote controlled plane did not respond to signals from the mother plane, beginning to circle the eastern outskirts of Ipswich of its own accord. The result of this fiery bomb crashing into Ipswich may well be imagined, and one can imagine the panic that might have ensued amongst the people below had they known that the "friendly" plane above was an unmanned fire bomb. Fortunately the drone veered out towards the North Sea and was crashed just off the Suffolk coast in a giant eruption of flame.

The United States Navy also took part in the Robot Aircraft Project, their code name being "Anvil". On the afternoon of Saturday, 12th August, 1944, a PB4Y four engined Liberator bomber took off from Fersfield. This Liberator was a drone loaded with ten tons of Torpex and carrying the usual crew of two. The pilot was Lieutenant Joseph Patrick Kennedy, Jnr, elder brother of the future President, John Fitzgerald Kennedy. His co-pilot was Wilford "Bud" Willy, also a lieutenant. Their target was to be the V-weapon site at Mimoyecques and the plan was to fly first over Suffolk to test the remote control of the Liberator drone and then to fly south to Clacton and from there to Manston in Kent, where Kennedy and Willy would bale out, leaving the doomed plane to fly with its mother ships to the target.

At a little before 18.20 hours on the bright clear evening. Kennedy switched the drone to remote control. It was flying at about 2,000 feet over the parish of Hinton near Blythburgh. Miss Ada Wetgate, of Blythburgh who lived in a small shepherd's cottage on a hill overlooking the Westwood Marshes, between Walberswick and Hinton, looked skywards towards Kennedy's drone and saw what she describes as vertical forked lightning where the plane had been. This quickly turned to vertical yellow, then red flame edged with black smoke. Finally a large pall of black smoke was left billowing in the bright sky. This pall of smoke appeared to Miss Westgate, from her vantage point, to be directly above the New Delight Wood, and the wood was dwarfed by the black column. Miss Westgate was struck by the terrifying force of the explosion and heard the terrific bang. Amazingly she was uninjured, although she felt as if her "brains had split" to use her own words. Her cottage was severely damaged, the front door and part of the wall being blown in and the roof collapsing. In all 147 damage reports were received, properties in Blythburgh, Walberswick, Southwold, Reydon, Wangford, Henham, Frostenden, Hinton, Thorington and Bulcamp receiving blast damage, but no civilian injuries were reported. Kennedy's drone had disappeared in two consecutive explosions, one instantly following the other. The countryside below the explosion was showered with debris from the drone and the four engines fell in a line between the Blythburgh water tower and Miss Westgate's cottage. According to several witnesses "the wreckage fell like snow". Americans were quickly on the scene and guards set up over the wreckage which was lying over a mile square area. The next day American servicemen combed the area for clues as to why the drone had exploded early killing Kennedy and Willy. There was not much to be found of the two unfortunate crewmen, though several pieces of the bomber were gathered up and transported back to Fersfield. The larger pieces of wreckage were abandoned where they lay.

Mr Farrow of Orford who was at Fersfield at this time, recalls how the war weary B.24s and B.17s were stripped out in the hangars under conditions of great security. Those who saw them wondered why the cockpit roof was removed, and also why the newly painted bombers never returned after they had taken off. It was not until a later date that they knew what was afoot so close to their place of employment, but they observed that the hangars where the work was carried out were always patrolled by armed guards and even authorised personnel like Mr Farrow were questioned regarding their business.

Some twenty-eight years later, remains of the wreckage of the Blythburgh Liberator were discovered in New Delight Woods, Blythburgh, by a team of wreck recovery experts led by Mr Stewart Evans, who had been searching for six months for traces of the aircraft. The larger parts like the engines had already disappeared. Owing to the intensity of the blast the wreckage was dispersed over a wide area, but eventually two of the bomb doors were found practically intact.[*]

Another duty for war weary bombers, especially B.24s, was the carriage of fuel and supplies to the Allied Forces advancing through Europe, three bases near Norwich, Horsham St Faiths, Rackheath and Attlebridge being the home supply depots for this operation. Many thousands of tons of fuel were carried to France either in five gallon "Jerrycans" or long bomb bay tanks.

As a kind of reverse lease-lend, a British aeroplane equipped a unit of the Eighth U.S.A.A.F., this being the De Havilland Mosquito PR XVI reconnaissance version, capable of flying unarmed with its cameras at high speed and great altitudes. It was the equipment of No. 25 (Rec) Group, commanded by Colonel Lear Gray which operated from Watton, Norfolk.

During September the retreating German Armies in Poland had drawn back as far as Warsaw and in this city were inflicting untold misery on the inhabitants. Moves were made to supply the resistance forces with arms and supplies, and it fell to the 95th Bomb Group at Horham to deliver the goods. Having made the long

*During 1983 the throttle quadrant with the four engine control levers came to light. It is now in the Martlesham Heath Aviation Museum.

daylight flight, they carried on to bases in Russian occupied territory, flying from there to bomb targets in Eastern Europe and landing in Italy, and then bombing Germany again as they returned to England.

The 27th September proved to be a black day for the 445th Bomb Group at Tibenham, Norfolk, when 37 B.24s of this Group joined forces with another 278 B.24s to attack Kassel. Set upon by masses of fighters and suffering heavy "flak", the 445th lost 25 B.24s in the space of a few minutes. Only seven made their home base, 236 aircrew were posted missing and dead, and many injured men from the seven which got back added to the number from aircraft which did not return.

The daylight raiders were meeting at this time the new Luftwaffe rocket propelled Messerschmitt Me.163 interceptor and also new intense radar controlled anti-aircraft fire. Various counter-measures were taken to try to overcome and baffle this radar detection, but these were only partially effective.

A B.24 crashed at Sutton, Suffolk, on Saturday 23rd September, 1944 after the crew had all baled out, whilst on the 27th September a B.17 from Sudbury was struck by another B.17 over Felixstowe, losing its rear fuselage. The crew of nine baled out whilst the crippled bomber crashed in the sea. The same day a P.51 from

Remains of a B.17 front fuselage after the aircraft had blown up whilst flying over Felixstowe. The control column and wheel can be clearly seen in the shattered cockpit.　　　　*Mrs G. Wilton*

Wattisham crashed at Corporation Farm, Kirton, Suffolk but the pilot, Captain C. A. P. Duffie, was unhurt.

A Liberator B.24H 294835 of the 490th Bomb Group at Eye, Suffolk, took off and climbed out on a mission. Passing over the Suffolk/Essex border at Nayland, an engine caught fire and the aircraft went into a spiral dive from which the crew were unable to extricate it, so they baled out. The bomber spiralled down until it crashed into a cornfield at Nayland. After a short while the bomb load exploded, scattering the wreckage and creating a large crater which was some time later filled in by a bulldozer. Twenty-eight years later Mr Stewart Evans and his team unearthed the remains and from the pieces recovered was able to establish the identity of the aircraft and its squadron whilst several components in a remarkably good state of preservation were collected for safe keeping.

The 6th October, 1944, saw more losses for a Suffolk unit when the Great Ashfield based 385th Bomb Group lost 11 B.17Es from its 549th Bomb Squadron when attacking Berlin, whilst the next day a nearby base suffered severe losses when 12 B.17Fs of the 94th Bomb Group from Bury St Edmunds failed to come home.

Many stories of heroism could be told of the bomber crews on these horrifying daylight raids. One worthy of mention occurred on 30th November, 1944 when a B.17G of the 487th Bomb Group, Lavenham, struggled home, mortally wounded by intense flak, and flown by Lieutenant Lauraine. With controls shot away and engines only just functioning, the weary captain eventually brought the wreckage over the English coastline, where he managed to retain partial control long enough for the crew to bale out. When it came to his turn however, he had no time to clear the aircraft as it dived out of control, carrying the brave pilot to his death. Another incident occurred on 24th November when a crippled B.24 staggered over the city of Norwich. The pilot, Second Lieutenant Ralph J. Dooley, of the 458th Bomb Group from nearby Horsham St Faiths airfield, deliberately crashed the B.24 in an open space in order to prevent casualties in a built-up area and thus saved the lives of many Norwich citizens. A plaque on a house in Heigham Street, Norwich, records this act of heroism performed by the American pilot and his crew, who died with him.

A little earlier in the month a B.17 from Thorpe Abbots, Norfolk, broke up in the air over Felixstowe and wreckage rained down over a wide area of the town. Some of the crew baled out, but were found to be dead. The fuselage shell fell on cottages occupied by the No. 3 A.A. Practice Group (R.A.F. Regiment) and 1022686 Corporal Postlewaite, 121687 Leading Aircraftsman Arran and 1304119 Leading Aircraftsman Cavard were killed whilst the second in command, Flight Lieutenant Duckworth Percy was taken to hospital with severe burns.

The Ipswich district was again shaken by a tremendous explosion on the afternoon of 12th December, 1944, when a B.17G named "Devil's Own" having taken off from its base at Debach, suffered an engine fire over the sea. Turning back, the pilot endeavoured to extinguish the fire by diving the aircraft, but this only increased the intensity of the blaze. With the collapse of the port wing imminent, the pilots put the stricken bomber down in a belly landing on the Debach runway. No sooner had the crew scrambled clear when the entire bomb load detonated, leaving a huge circle of damage on the airfield. Another B.17 ran into trouble over the coast on Saturday 30th December, 1944, and the crew baled out, two landing at Gedgrave near Orford, whilst the bomber disappeared out to sea.

A fighter pilot serving at Leiston at this time was due for fame in later years. Captain Charles "Chuck" Yeager was at Leiston with the 357th Fighter Group; on the 14th October, 1947, he flew the Bell XS-1 rocket plane "Glamorous Glennis" at a speed of Mach. 1.015 (670 m.p.h.), thus becoming the first man to make a supersonic flight. It was whilst based at Leiston that he became one of the first Allied pilots to shoot down a then new Luftwaffe type, the Messerschmitt Me.262 twin jet interceptor.

It is also recorded that he shot down five Messerschmitt 109Gs on one mission. Soon after this he was brought down in France, but by a stroke of luck managed to escape with a fellow American and with the aid of the French Underground made towards Spain. His companion succumbed to his wounds, but Yeager continued to Spain and back home. It was a rule that anyone brought down over enemy territory and "returning" was automatically taken off "ops", but this wasn't good enough for Chuck, who went around pestering authority to return to operations. Eventually, told that permission would only be given by General Dwight D. Eisenhower, who was at Teddington, Chuck applied to see the General who asked what his business was? "Killing Huns", replied Chuck, to which the General replied, "That's my business as well". Chuck was back on "ops", the first pilot to do so. Back at Leiston, he soon got back into the swing of things and finished a leading pilot; now in the U.S.A.F. he is a General himself.

Another fighter pilot who rose quickly to fame was Lieutenant Daniel, who on his first mission over Europe shot down five Focke Wulfe FW.190s before returning to his base, the 339th at Fowlmere, Cambridgeshire, making 29 in all for his Group that day. The Martlesham Heath based 356th Fighter Group claimed 23 enemy aircraft destroyed without loss to themselves on one of their first sorties with the Mustang P.51s.

Although the faster, longer ranging P.51s had partially eclipsed the plump radial-engined P.47s, the latter still played their part in the nearer combat zones, as illustrated on 17th December, 1944, when the 56th Fighter Group from Boxted, led by Colonel David Schilling, made tracks for Western Germany. In the ensuing engagements, the Luftwaffe lost 37 of its fighters, whilst all but four of the Thunderbolts returned home to Suffolk.

Christmas Eve, 1944, saw one of the largest formations ever leaving the shores of the British Isles, when over 2,000 heavy bombers of the Eighth Air Force and 500 of the Ninth Air Force and the Royal Air Force made a concentrated attack on a large number of German airfields. Such was the involvement that one of the formations was led by a Brigadier General, Fred Castle, flying a B.17 from Lavenham. Unfortunately whilst still some miles from the target area, his B.17 was hit by cannon fire, set alight, and the pilot injured. Brigadier General Castle took over the controls and ordered the crew to bale out, which they did. A wing then broke off, and the Brigadier General died in the crash, being posthumously awarded the Medal of Honour; he was the highest ranking Eighth Air Force member to receive this award. The Lavenham Group lost five aircraft that day.

Christmas Day, 1944, saw a moderate force of area based heavies over Germany, whilst Boxing Day delivered a small force to the scene of the previous engagements. The festive season was marred when a B.17F from the 390th Bomb Group, Framlingham, lost power after take-off and crashed with a tremendous explosion in the nearby village of Parham, all the crew perishing.

In the first week of January 1945, Saturday the 6th, a B.24 crashed into the sea off Landguard Point, Felixstowe, and burst into flames. The pilot was taken to Harwich Hospital, but the rest of the crew were safe. Snow and low cloud caused postponement of many missions during the first weeks of January, but on the 14th some 600 B.17s and B.24s made for the Berlin area with a strong escort of P.51s. The 390th Bomb Group from Framlingham despatched eight B.17Fs, all of which failed to return. On the last day of the month a Bungay based B.24 crashed at Tunstall, near Woodbridge, and although an extensive search was made, there was no sign of the crew. It was later stated that the crew had baled out over Cambridgeshire.

At 16.08 hours a B.24 Liberator, No. 250713 of the 446th Bomb Group, stationed at Bungay, came in very low over Snape village and made a pancake landing on the marshes adjoining the river wall at the rear of The Maltings, Snape Bridge, on 31st January 1945. The aircraft fell only 300 yards eastwards of the Maltings. The plane was searched after the crash landing but no crew could be found, they had baled out in Cambridgeshire and undoubtedly had set the aircraft to fly out to sea and crash. A lucky escape for the famous Snape Maltings.

Missions continued throughout the first two months of the year with varying fortunes, and one of the good days was 23rd February, when out of over 1,190 bombers taking part only two were lost. Not all losses were due to the enemy as on the 13th February 1945 a P.51 Mustang spun and crashed into the River Orwell near Marston Hall Farm, Trimley, and the pilot Lieutenant Baskin from Martlesham Heath was killed. B.17 43-38568 took off from the 493rd Bomb Group's base at Debach, at 09.14 hours, 20th February, 1945, and immediately upon take off the No. 3 engine caught fire. The pilot feathered the prop and extinguished the fire. Immediately afterwards, according to the pilot the engine fire resumed and the right wing also began burning. The pilot ditched in the River Deben at Ramsholt and the plane immediately sank in eighteen feet of water and completely submerged, only the tip of the tail fin remaining visible. The pilot, First Lieutenant

B.17 43-38568 in the River Deben at Ramsholt, Suffolk, after suffering an engine fire whilst flying from Debach on 21st February, 1945. Only the pilot escaped with his life from this crash.

Mr S. Evans

Frederick E. Stindt and the engineer Top Sergeant Jewel K. Haynes were thrown from the aircraft but only the pilot who swam ashore was saved. Eight crew members drowned including the co-pilot Second Lieutenant Irwin F. Roth. The aircraft was carrying a bomb load of ten 500 lb G.P. bombs plus 2 ca. M-17, and a gas load of 2,700 gallons.

Mr Stewart Evans has corresponded with a ground crewman who worked on the base at the time of this crash and he remembers the incident. He said that the investigation of the crash showed that the engine caught fire because of improper maintenance. The exhaust system was leaking because some of the brass lock nuts loosened up on the exhaust stacks.

On the night of 3rd/4th March 1945 the Luftwaffe made one of its now rare appearances over the Eastern Counties, when a force of 30 night fighters attacked the American bomber bases. Little damage was done and the same results were achieved the following night when they attempted to repeat the performance.

The cold weather of the winter and spring made servicing the aircraft out in the open a miserable task for the ground crews and the aircrews suffered the same climatic discomfort in the air. Many aircraft were lost, as a result of fog and snow, the 356th Fighter Group at Martlesham Heath losing some of the P.51s through these causes. Another unusual accident occurred in Suffolk when a Wattisham based P.51 using a L.N.E.R. train for "train busting" practice made an extremely low pass and hit the locomotive near Haughley Junction Station, writing off the aircraft, killing the pilot and badly damaging the train.

The end of March saw the bombers carrying-out bombing missions and supply dropping in support of the Rhine crossing and the low altitudes that these missions called for accounted for the considerable numbers of aircraft lost.

As April passed with its long distance runs to southern Germany and Czechoslovakia, the Eighth plodded along on large supply dropping missions to assist the Dutch people. The 385th from Great Ashfield participated in these events, and no opposition was encountered owing to previous arrangements made by the Allies and the Germans, through a neutral agency, that no armaments would be used.

Another task, but of a more pleasant nature, was the flying of ground crews over the Continent to look at the scenes of the previous years of bombing and the destruction that they had helped to bring about.

One of the last casualties occurred on Monday 21st May, 1945, when a P.51 Mustang from Leiston crashed at Red House Farm, Bucklesham, Suffolk and burnt out. The pilot No. 0-2059721 Lieutenant Alfred W. Bierweifer had been carrying out practice attacks on a B.17 just before he crashed.

The 357th Fighter Group at Leiston, almost the youngest of the Eighth Air Force Fighter Groups, were second in the European theatre of operations in the number of enemy planes destroyed in aerial combat. The score stood at 586½ enemy aircraft destroyed, 20 probables and 98 damaged, and 45 of its pilots had knocked out five or more aircraft and thus became fighter aces. On 14th January 1945 a mission led by Colonel Dregre destroyed 57½ German aircraft in the air for a loss of three of their own and as a bonus one enemy aircraft on the ground and two locomotives. Fifty-six Mustangs took part in the fray and the citation signed by General Doolittle read "For your outstanding performance in destroying 57½ enemy aircraft on January 14th mission I am recommending the 357th Fighter Group for the award of the Individual Unit Citation."

With the collapse of Germany, the bombers and fighters of the Eighth Air Force started their long trek home, and at the end of May they were moving, some via the Azores and others by way of Greenland, the last B.24 leaving on 9th July 1945. The fighters stayed on a while longer, considerable numbers taking up residence on the Continent, and the Eighth Air Force Fighter Control Headquarters moving to Honington, Suffolk. It remained there, eventually becoming the last Eighth Air Force base in the United Kingdom, until 26th February 1946 when, on a rain soaked day, the Group were handed back to the Royal Air Force and the last B.17 No. 44-83273 posed for photographs on the wet runway.

Previous to this the U.S.A.A.F. had opened its bases on 1st August 1945 to its British hosts and thousands of people had flocked to the airfields to view the aircraft, talk with the pilots and ground crews and generally see how "the yanks" lived.

During its stay in the Eastern Counties, the Eighth Air Force occupied some 112 airfields, the majority of these being of new construction. In the main the bombers were based at airfields with runways, and the fighters operated from grass or steel planked runways. One exception was Martlesham Heath, where hard runways were laid down as an experiment to accommodate the P.47s and later the P.51s based there.

The average cost of a new U.S.A.A.F. style bomber airfield constructed during 1942 was £995,000 and the total cost of airfields and other sundry installations used by the Eighth Air Force was put at approximately £645,000,000.

The Eighth lives on in many ways in East Anglia, not only in the memories of those who knew it but in memorials raised in memory of its dead. A window in Quidenham Church, Norfolk, depicting Christ with arms outstretched welcoming an American airman, was donated by personnel of the 96th Bomb Group stationed at Snetterton Heath. Sudbury Town Hall bears a plaque "To the citizens of Sudbury for their fellowship, understanding and hospitality from the officers and men of the 486th Bombardment Group. (H) 417 Air Service Group U.S.A.A.F. 1944-5." A pump house at Kesgrave bears a wonderful mural of St Christopher, painted by an American airman stationed at Martlesham Heath, whilst on the airfield still stands the first memorial erected to the American dead in Europe.

A large cemetery at Madingley, off the Cambridge-Bedford road just west of Cambridge is beautifully situated, and even more beautifully kept. Row upon row of neat white crosses record the thousands of American dead. Among those silent hosts of the departed there is one woman. A feature of this cemetery is that, once a year, an aircraft flies low over the graves and drops a sweet pea flower for each person who lost his life.

A monument on the side of the Ipswich-Norwich Road at Mendlesham, Suffolk, to commemorate the dead of the 34th Bomb Group stationed at the airfield alongside was dedicated during July 1949. Constructed of brick and concrete, it is faced with a bronze plaque designed by Mr Henry Berg, a Baltimore sculptor and depicts the open window of a bomber cockpit with the head and shoulders of the pilot, whose outstretched hand holds an olive branch. Beneath the plaque are the words "To the American airmen of the 34th who in valor gave their lives in the victory that made real the challenge for World peace and unity". The site was given by Mr George Stedman, a local resident.

During their stay in the Eastern Counties the U.S.A.A.F. lost 6,319 aircraft and 41,186 men, killed, dead and missing.

Thirty years after it all began the airfield at Parham, Suffolk, home of the 390th Bomb Group still bears memory of the U.S.A.F. with the control tower derelict but still standing, its verandah looking at the empty runway. Perimeter taxi tracks, rutted and weed lined, circle the drome, the large black hanger stands huge and erect as ever, but the sundry buildings where the fire tenders and ambulance raced forth, now stand doorless and gaunt, rusty steel window frames, paneless, and no longer opening to the hands of men long departed. The scrap of War still lingers, punched steel runway planking, but all evidence of the silver birds which roosted there has gone, only the earth and trees recalling the note of the motors, and the voices from the other side of the world.

In order to illustrate the work of these U.S.A.A.F. Squadrons, we take one at random, the 390th Bomb Group (H) U.S.A.A.F. which spent its war years at Framlingham, Suffolk.

Formed in the United States of America on 26th January 1943, it worked up with the B.17G aircraft and arrived in the United Kingdom during July 1943, becoming part and parcel of the Eighth Air Force as the 568th, 569th and 570th and 571st Squadrons. The first operation was flown on the 12th August 1943 when the B.17s attacked a factory in Bonn, Germany, and five days later it received a Distinguished Unit Citation (D.U.C.) for its sustained attacks on the Messerschmitt aircraft factory at Regensburg, deep in enemy territory. A second D.U.C. was awarded to the Group on 14th October when it carried out, in combination with other Groups, a damaging assault on the Schweinfurt ball bearing factories. Its targets in 1944 included naval targets at Bremen, communications in the Berlin district, synthetic oil plants at Zeitz, chemical plants at Ludwigshafen, the marshalling yards at Mannheim and the Cologne river bridges. Targets of a different nature included the coastline of Normandy near Caen, bombed a quarter

A P.47D of the 353rd Fighter Group at Raydon, Suffolk during the summer of 1944. Corporal R. L. Throut (centre), armament crew member explains to Airman 1st Class L. M. Hoover (on bike) and S/Sgt. L. Gamble the 20-28 lb bomb cluster installation.   *U.S.A.F.*

of an hour before the D-Day landings, and then in support of the Allied armies it made ground support attacks at St Lo, battering the Germany supply lines during the Battle of the Bulge at the end of 1944.

Its last offensive raid was carried out on the marshalling yards of Oranienburg on 20th April 1945, and in the last week of the War it was employed on food drops to the Dutch people. Returning to the United States of America during August 1945, it was disbanded at Sioux Falls, South Dakota on 28th August 1945.

On operations the Group flew 301 missions, destroyed 377 enemy aircraft, damaged 77 and claimed 57 as probables. An impressive 18,755 tons of bombs were dropped by the 275 B.17s used by the Group, and it lost 145 of its aircraft in action and 17 in England, each aircraft averaging 33 missions. An exception was 42-97093 named "I'll get By" which made 111 trips.

On the other side of the scale, the airfield at Raydon near Hadleigh, Suffolk was constructed during 1942/1943 and was initially to be used as a base for 15th U.S.A.A.F. medium bombers. These never took up residence owing to the fact that when the Italian campaign opened the 15th Air Force went to the Mediterranean theatre of operations, leaving the newly constructed airfield coded "Station 157" vacant. Then the fighter groups arrived, and made the name for themselves which earned Raydon its fame.

First to arrive was the 357th Fighter Group equipped with early versions of the

Liberator B.24.H coded 6.X-H of the 491st Bomb Group touched down at Metfield, Suffolk, during the summer of 1944. This landing is what would be described as of the "one-point variety".

U.S.A.F.

North American Mustang, and these carried out extensive training for two months before moving to another newly constructed airfield at Leiston, also in Suffolk. The Raydon district then vibrated to the radial motors of the tubby Republic Thunderbolts carrying out their daily sorties over Occupied Europe, seeking out any enemy installation to shoot-up and destroy. The P.47s belonging to the 358th Fighter Group stayed until the spring of 1944, moving then to the South Coast. Mustangs appeared again when the 353rd Fighter Group took up residence, having moved from Metfield, Suffolk, when fighter groups were brought nearer to the coast, and their former home became Liberator-equipped. Working in close co-operation with their colleagues from Leiston, the yellow and black chequered fighters roared low over Europe, destroying trains, radar installations, airfield buildings and in fact anything German. Unfortunately whilst engaged in this task, losses were fairly heavy, the low flying aircraft being subject to all kinds of ground fire. Later whilst accompanying the heavies over Europe on their large daylight raids, the P.51s were able to fly outwards to distances in excess of 1,000 miles and still return home, and many carried out daylight sorties over the heart of Berlin itself from Raydon.

October 1945 saw the last Mustangs leave, and the personnel left for the United States of America from Southampton aboard the Queen Mary; the three solid concrete runways, the black walled T.2 hangars and Nissen huts remaining, as they do to this day.

A Society named "The Friends of the Eighth" was formed during 1974 and consists of people of all walks of life who still wish to remember the days of the B.17s, B.24s, P.47s and P.51s. Ex-crews of the Eighth appear as if by magic at the meetings, and the talk and sounds, films and tapes roll on late into the night, as the exploits of over 30 years ago are relived and recounted. Duxford houses the Fortress B.17G 44-85784, the Liberator B.24J 42-50551 and the Mustang P51D 44-35253 and large gatherings can be relied on when these veteran warbirds are brought out for display.

It is believed that only one American built Martin Maryland operated from the British Isles, and that it flew with No. 1419 Flight on its moonlight journeys from Stradishall and Newmarket Heath. This example is an early model, and was later superseded by the Baltimore from the same maker.

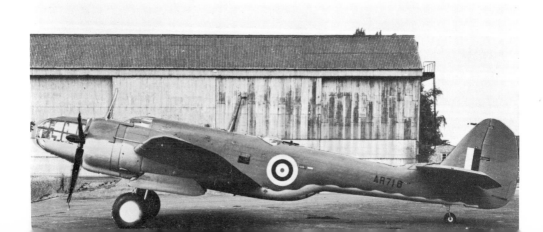

CHAPTER SEVEN

Comings and Goings

THROUGHOUT the history of warfare the main participants have always had their clandestine operations, spies, infiltrators and secret agents, and the conflict of 1939-1945 was no exception to the rule. The aerial movements of both sides fell into the two categories of the intentional and the less intentional, as the following incidents illustrate.

Considerable consternation was caused on the night of 13th-14th August, 1940, when the Luftwaffe dropped a quantity of military items over country districts including radio equipment, maps, explosives and lists of well-known people in the areas. These "Gifts" were all gathered up swiftly by the military and police authorities and it was not until some time later that the Germans admitted over the radio that this was a deception aimed to make the populace believe that a large landing had been made. The German radio continued the story by stating that the "invaders" were wearing civilian clothing and sent to disrupt British industry.

Earlier on 14th May, 1940, unusual aircraft appeared off the Air Station at Felixstowe where they landed, being expected and looked out for. They were Fokker T.VIIIW twin-engined floatplanes, ten of which had escaped from their homeland of Holland and flown to France. When this refuge was also over-run they then moved on to England, and arriving at Felixstowe were formed into a Dutch Free Air Force Squadron, No. 320, before moving on again to Pembroke Dock in South Wales. Two of the floatplanes were cannibalised for spares but the remainder were given the R.A.F. serial numbers, AV.958-AV.965. One of the survivors, AV.958 had the misfortune to crash at Middleton, near Sudbury, on 28th November, 1940, when, on a ferry flight from Wales to Felixstowe, it ran out of fuel and force-landed in a field with disastrous results.

Early in the morning of 4th July, 1940, a small biplane with a spluttering engine made a bumpy landing in a field at Thorpe-le-Soken, Essex, and two excited but weary airmen cautiously jumped out and walked across the pasture towards some houses on the edge of the field. Meeting an old gentleman, they asked him in halting English where they were and when told, expressed their great joy that it was in fact England.

For the two Belgian pilots, Michael Donnet and Leon Divoy, this was the culmination of several months clandestine and dangerous work after they had discovered a small pre-war biplane, housed in a hangar on a private estate near Terbloc, Belgium. Partially dismantled in order to comply with the German occupation regulations, the machine, a Stampe SV.4.b, almost identical to the De

Havilland Tiger Moth, and indeed, fitted with a De Havilland Gipsy engine, had been put away for the duration of the war whilst the Germans occupied a large chateau nearby as billets for nearby ammunition dumps.

Making almost nightly excursions to the hangar, dodging the sentries on the road from the town and also those posted to guard the chateau, the two Belgians gained entry to the hangar, worked on the plane by torchlight, and then dodged home again to be indoors before the 23.00 hours curfew. They toiled on for the great day, having several narrow escapes on their way to and from the hangar. The most difficult requirement for the escape was the twenty gallons of aviation fuel needed for the flight, but this was eventually procured and transported little by little to the waiting plane. Aided by willing helpers, who all stood to face the firing squad if caught, the two ex-Belgian Air Force pilots got away after a shaky start and made it to Essex.

Michael Donnet and Leon Divoy both became Spitfire pilots in the Royal Air Force, but Divoy was unfortunate to crash in Europe and become a prisoner-of-war for the second time. Donnet rose to the rank of Wing Commander and spent quite a lot of his service time in the Eastern Counties at Coltishall, Duxford, Fersfield and finally Bentwaters. Since then Michael Donnet has become Lieutenant-General Aviateur Baron Michael Donnet, C.V.O., D.F.C., F.R.A.E.S. and has held high office in N.A.T.O.

On 4th July, 1975, thirty-five years later, the two airmen made a nostalgic journey when they landed again in the same field at Thorpe-le-Soken, in the same aircraft. They intended to carry out the same procedure as previously for the benefit of the villagers and friends but unable to switch off the ageing Gipsy engine of the Stampe, after exchanging greetings they took off again.

A mysterious incident occurred at West Raynham, Norfolk, early in the War when a Bristol Blenheim bomber took off, crashed shortly afterwards on the perimeter of the aerodrome and was totally destroyed. A full check was made of all Station personnel to see who was aboard but none were found to be missing. The unauthorised flight was assumed to have been made by an escaped prisoner of war or even a spy attempting to return to Germany.

The case of Rudolf Hess is well known but there were cases of German aircraft landing in Great Britain. Personnel on the airfield at R.A.F. Oakington, Cambridgeshire, were amazed on the 9th September, 1940, to see a Junkers Ju.88D German twin-engined bomber in the landing circuit, with one engine stopped, the airscrew feathered and an undercarriage leg partially lowered. The Luftwaffe machine made a straight and level approach and touched down, whereupon the undercarriage totally collapsed and the bomber slithered along the runway on its belly. Fortunately no fire resulted, and the crew of four escaped from the aircraft and were taken prisoner by the aerodrome defence personnel. The Ju.88, which contained much valuable camera equipment, was carefully dismantled and taken away, its contents proving of great value to the R.A.F. technical departments.

To carry out a night raid on Liverpool on 21st October, 1940, the Luftwaffe despatched a twin-engined Dornier Do.17Z medium bomber from an airfield in Western France. A navigational error caused the pilot to get temporarily lost on the outward journey and instead of proceeding to the north-west of England, he arrived over mid-Wales. Then heavy thunderstorms disabled his wireless telegraphy equipment and upset the magnetic compass, the aircraft was now on a reciprocal course which brought them again over north-west France. Some time later the pilot unaware of the compass error, turned through 180 degrees, crossed the English Channel for the third time and arrived over Wiltshire. Convinced that he was completely lost, the pilot circled, ignorant of the fact that he was over Salisbury Plain, where he ran into further electrical storms. Hoping that he was over Occupied France, he decided to give the weather best, and, setting the controls to automatic, ordered the crew of four to bale out. Descending by parachute through the lightning streaked night skies, the crew all landed safely in Wiltshire, and were eventually rounded up by the Army authorities, who then set up a search for the aircraft from which the prisoners had jumped.

In the meantime the crewless bomber flew happily along on an easterly course with its automatic pilot in charge, escaping the guns of at least five counties and the London defences. Eventually, when the last of the petrol had reached the engines, the Dornier gradually lost height and in a gentle glide made a perfect wheels-up landing on the soft mud flats of the River Stour, one mile E.S.E. of Ness Creek at Erwarton near Ipswich, having covered 130 miles on its own.

Discovering the empty plane, the local police and Army authorities searched for the crew who, it was supposed had gone to ground. Being so near to the East Coast it was presumed that they would attempt to procure a boat and make a run for home.

Thus ended the fantastic episode of the bomber-less crew in Wiltshire and the crew-less bomber in Suffolk, a case which had a parallel more than three years later.

On the night of 23rd February, 1944, a Dornier 217M took off from a base in Northern France to bomb London on one of the last piloted raids of the war. With a tail wind the aircraft arrived over the target area ahead of time, and in order to kill time and await the arrival of the target marking aircraft, the pilot circled outside the area. Anti-aircraft guns opened up on the aircraft, hitting the cabin and starboard motor and starting a small fire which was soon extinguished. The crew decided to abandon the raid and they baled out over the northern suburbs of London, leaving the bomber to its fate. As standard procedure when baling out the pilot put the aircraft on automatic pilot, and the bomber flew on crewless eventually making a soft wheels-up landing in Cambridgeshire. This aircraft was a valuable gift to the R.A.F. Technical Branch, as it was the first one of its type to fall into Allied hands.

During the period of the bombing of the British Isles, the Luftwaffe had its

General purpose and dive bomber, the Dornier Do. 217E twin-engined monoplane powered by 2 BMW 1,460 h.p. 801 radial motors. With a bomb load of 6,615 lbs, it could range 1500 miles at a top speed of 309 mph.   *Flight*

secret comings and goings, as did the R.A.F. on the Continent of Europe. In Eastern England any incident, in the least out of the ordinary, was promptly reported and action taken though quite often local reticence hampered the Service and civil authorities in their enquiries. As far as can be ascertained, there were no known landings and take-offs by German aircraft in the region but their aircrews did visit and the great majority of them stayed on for the duration.

One visitor who ended his flight in this part of Eastern England was the pilot of a Messerschmitt 109 G single seat fighter, equipped with long range drop tanks, who on 15th May, 1944, took off from an airfield in Western Germany, setting out on a long-range training flight. His course set the pilot headed out across Holland and out to sea, keeping a watchful eye out for Allied fighters, now filling the skies of the area.

Approaching the English coast, he dropped to sea level, crossed the shore-line near Hopton, Suffolk and hedgehopped inland using the last of his now almost exhausted fuel supply. When this finally dried up, the pilot made a fast forced landing on Herringfleet Common, badly damaging the fighter, but escaping without serious injury and he was taken into custody by the local police. That day Mrs Kathleen Bell, of Herringfleet, was in her garden when the plane came down in a disused sandpit. She ran indoors and told her husband, who went to the wreckage and released the young pilot, while Mrs Bell cycled to Somerleyton Police Station to tell the police of the new arrival.

On the night of 13th July, 1944, a Junkers Ju.88 G night fighter, fitted with the most up-to-date radar interception gear, took off from Volkel in Holland in company with several other aircraft, engaged on a routine night bomber detection patrol. With its large fuel tanks, the Ju.88 was capable of a long endurance flight.

After flying for some time, defects showed up in the aircraft's navigational and wireless telegraphy systems, and, despite desperate efforts on the part of the crew to contact their home base, they lost their whereabouts. When fuel became a problem, the crew decided to land, and circled what they believed to be a Luftwaffe base at Venlo on the Dutch-German border. They touched down safely at about 04.00 hours*.

At the emergency landing aerodrome at Woodbridge (Sutton Heath), Suffolk, Sergeant K. E. Clifton, D.F.M., was the duty N.C.O. that night and was used to the varied types of aircraft which made use of the long "crash" runway. Something, however, struck him as being peculiar about the twin-engined aircraft which had just landed, so he guided it into a "hard standing", and then drove his Jeep in front of it when the bomber had parked. Swift recognition then gave Sergeant Clifton the answer to his doubts, and realizing that he had a Ju.88, he took steps to capture it, although by now the bomber's crew had also realized that something was wrong and made to destroy the aircraft's log and code books. Smart work by the Sergeant and the members of his duty party prevented this, and the small fire started by the Ju.88's crew was soon extinguished and the aircraft and crew secured. Mistaking Woodbridge for Venlo, the German crew had presented to the R.A.F. "Boffins" the chance to examine the latest German night interception radar, a type it was later revealed that had been developed as a result of British radar jamming "window".

Flown to R.A.F. Farnborough the next day, the Ju.88 then flew with the R.A.F. on experimental work for some time before being badly damaged in a forced landing.

The radar gear was the latest FUG.220 Lichenstein SN-2 interception radar and the FUG.227 Flensburg homing device, both designed to be unaffected by the R.A.F.'s "window" and jamming devices. As a result of this capture new R.A.F. "window" was developed which rendered the night fighters' radar ineffective, whilst a new countermeasures device called "Piperack" was fitted to the Norfolk based No. 100 Group Radio Countermeasures aircraft to put "clutter" on enemy radar screens.

---

*The full story of this event is told in *Bawdsey — Birth of the Beam.*

Before passing on from the "visitors" one most unusual one was the twin-boomed, twin-engined Fokker G-1B light bomber which escaped from Holland during the German occupation. Carrying out a test flight on 5th May, 1941, the aircraft, named "The Reaper", with illegally filled fuel tanks, managed to elude its escort, and with its crew of two crossed the English coast near Lowestoft and landed in a large field near Southwold. The bomber, coded J-8 and serialled 5567 was then flown by the R.A.F. to Martlesham Heath. On 12th May, escorted by fighters, the G-1B was flown to the Royal Aircraft Establishment, Farnborough, where after a useful life it finally went to the Woodley aerodrome of Phillips and Powis Limited of Reading.

The Royal Air Force carried out secret missions over Occupied Europe in increasing numbers. One such "job" was on 15th October, 1940, when one of the Fokker T.VIII W's which had earlier flown to Felixstowe, took-off at midnight to pick up four agents from Tjoukemeer in Friesland. On this mission, visibility deteriorated after take-off and failing to see the pre-arranged signals from the lake, it returned to Felixstowe at 04.30 hours. A second attempt was made at midnight on the 16th October, 1940, when the signal was picked up and a landing made at Tjoukemeer by moonlight. A boat headed out to the Fokker, but instead of the expected agents, it opened fire at 30 yards, and the Fokker was forced to make a rapid take-off, with the rear gunner returning fire as it did so. A safe landing was made at Felixstowe at 05.00 hours but as it landed, it was fired upon again, this time by a local Home Guard unit. A later examination revealed some 40 bullet holes from the attacks by friend and foe. The floatplane was still at Felixstowe on 22nd November, 1942, when Mr Donald Smith of Ipswich made a visit there with the A.T.C., and was informed by the staff that this one, R-25, was the sole survivor of the batch.

The first R.A.F. unit which operated in a small way was Flight No. 1419 formed at North Weald, Essex, but later moved to Stradishall, Suffolk. The Station Commander at the time was Group Captain D. A. Boyle, later Marshal of the Royal Air Force Sir Dermot Boyle, and it is reported that although not called upon to do so he consistently flew with his squadrons on operations. The unit continued its work with all-black Whitleys, dropping men and supplies in Occupied Europe.

Eventually the Flight became No. 138 Special Duties Squadron and was commanded by Wing Commander Farley, D.F.C. It moved to Newmarket Heath, using a motley collection of Whitley bombers, Lockheed Hudsons from Coastal Command, and special Westland Lysanders for short field landing work, then, in March 1942, moved to Tempsford in Bedfordshire, working from an airfield known as Gibraltar Farm. Staying there until 1944 it carried on the work of collaborating with resistance groups in Occupied Europe. Larger aircraft such as Stirlings and Halifaxes, capable of carrying larger loads over greater distances, enabled the squadron to supply the underground forces in Eastern Europe and Poland. Many and varied were the exploits of the squadron, and many will never be related.

One of the notable pilots of No. 138 Squadron was Group Captain Pickard, star of the R.A.F.'s propaganda film "Target for Tonight" with his Wellington bomber "F for Freddie".

Whilst engaged on these operations No. 138 Special Duties Squadron dropped some 995 agents, 29,000 containers, and 10,000 packages, and over the period 1942-1945 lost 70 aircraft, whilst it flew 2,500 sorties to carry out its work and it earned for itself the title "Moon Squadron".

Wing Commander John Nesbitt-Dufont, D.S.O., C. de G., a former member of the unit describes in great detail his adventures while operating from Stradishall and Newmarket Heath in his book *Black Lysander* published by Jarrolds.

In the early days this young and unnoticed outfit, equipped with an odd collection of aircraft was seemingly not wanted by other operational units. One of the unusual aircraft on the strength of No. 1419 Flight was an American-built Martin Maryland twin-engined medium bomber, probably the only one used in the British Isles; the majority of this type operated in the Western Desert.

All-black Westland Lysander as used for clandestine missions into Occupied Europe, hence the container under the fuselage and the ladder up the rear cockpit.　　　　*Westlands*

To illustrate the difficulties encountered in performing this dangerous work Wing Commander Nesbitt-Dufont describes how a Whitley of which he was co-pilot/navigator, having successfully dropped its material, clung to the cloud cover which over the Low Countries suddenly cleared and left it in clear skies. Picked up by searchlights, it then received the attention of the local anti-aircraft guns, and in order to dodge this the pilot threw the bomber around the sky, dropping from 14,000 feet to a low altitude to miss the lights. Almost above the sea, they broke clear and using the speed gained from the dive, sped home low across the North Sea. Climbing a bit to clear the Suffolk coast at 4,000 feet, they then were subjected to accurate fire by naval vessels off Harwich, and arrived at their base to find it fogbound. Directed further north, they made for Waddington in Lincolnshire, which on arrival was also fogbound. Rumbling further north they attempted to land at Driffield, Yorkshire, but the position was the same there, so they pushed on further still and as the fuel ran low landed at Leuchars on the east coast of Scotland, after over eleven hours in the air.

Although the all-black Lysanders were fitted with a large long-range tank slung under the fuselage, the distance from Newmarket Heath was too great for operational sorties into France, so the majority of the outward flights were made from south coast airfields such as Tangmere and Goodwood. Unarmed, the Lysanders ranged deep into enemy territory, circling until the recognition signal was received and then landing by the aid of torch light indicators. After the "business" had been carried out a hazardous take-off had to be made with the aircraft often grossly overloaded. The Hudsons and the occasional Anson which made the blacked-out landings in France took tremendous risks, not knowing whether the surface would bear the weight of the aircraft or whether it would "bog down" whilst sitting awaiting the take-off. Night fighters, flak, searchlight and ground troops all had to be contended with, and stories of how the pilots, when things went wrong, destroyed their aircraft and joined the Underground, taking their chance and turn to be flown home again.

Thus the Eastern Counties played their part in the not so well known war. Many of the population must have wondered what the lone aircraft was doing on a moonlight night, heading in or out in a different direction to the usual run, or been mystified by the furtive comings and goings of closed and blacked out vehicles to certain airfields in the region. As the years pass we gradually learn a little more of these days, but much will never be told.

CHAPTER EIGHT

The Invisible Eye

IN THE mid-thirties, the Annual Air Defence Exercises had year by year caused the Air Force chiefs more and more consternation, as it appeared that Royal Air Force fighters would be practically incapable of intercepting enemy bombers should they attack the capital. To try and correct the situation, an Air Defence Research Committee was set up by the Government during the autumn of 1934 with a separate committee to investigate "special methods of defence". This was instigated by two ex-Martlesham officers, Mr H. E. Wimperis, who was the Air Ministry Director of Scientific Research, and scientist Henry Tizard, later Sir Henry Tizard, who chaired the committee*.

Mr R. A. Watson-Watt, the Superintendent of Radio Research at the National Physical Laboratory, who had been investigating radio waves, was consulted by Wimperis regarding the feasibility of using them as a method of air defence.

Early experiments using the British Broadcasting Corporation's short-wave overseas transmitter, the only source of continuous beam transmission, proved promising, and as a result of this work, a section was transferred, during March 1935, to the windswept semi-deserted aerodrome on Orfordness Island. The party was led by Mr Watson-Watt and included several of his colleagues, Messrs Barren, Bainbridge-Bell, Savage, Airey, Wilkins and Muir.

This site, almost cut off from the outside world, was an ideal one for the development of a project which had to be kept from prying eyes. The experiments showed promise, although the power was weak and the range very limited.

During the latter part of 1935, two of the scientific officers went for an off-duty stroll along the shingle and seagrass beach towards Bawdsey. On their return to Orfordness they suggested to Mr Watson-Watt that the promontory at Bawdsey which stood some 70 feet above sea level, crowned by the stately mansion of the Quilter family, would make an ideal location for their work.

Up to this time the work had enjoyed moderate success, which included the tracking of aircraft flying from Orfordness to Bircham Newton on the north Norfolk coast. But a more elevated position was needed for the aerials than the Orfordness marshland.

Bawdsey Manor was purchased by the Air Ministry and the first scientists moved in during February, 1936. The higher elevation greatly increased the scope of the work, known now as Radio Direction Finding (R.D.F.), whilst the greater number of buildings available enabled more personnel to work on the project. Soon wooden and metal towers rose up well above the fir trees on the estate as the first

---

*The development of radar is fully covered in *Orfordness — Secret Site* and *Bawdsey — Birth of the Beam*, both published by Terence Dalton.

radar station in the British Isles was brought into being. It was to serve as a model for the chain shortly to be erected around the coastline of South-East and Eastern England. These towers caused a great deal of local gossip and speculation; the supposed purpose of the towers ranged from death-rays to rays for stopping aircraft engines, and tales circulated of cars which for no apparent reason stopped in the vicinity of Bawdsey, the drivers being informed by Service personnel that their trouble would cease at such and such a time. Whether with official backing or not, the stories went the rounds and maybe helped in some small way to camouflage the true purpose of the establishment. The official cover for the site was the designation of Radio Direction Finding Station, a name carried into the first years of the war.

Over the months the establishment at Bawdsey grew and a team of radio-physicists and highly-skilled technicians worked long and hard probing this new and interesting medium. Success now seemed so much nearer, the results of their experiments showing that in the main they were working along the right lines.

Bawdsey Manor sleeps again on its promontory at the mouth of the River Deben. Seen from the Felixstowe Ferry side of the river, it can be seen what an ideal site this was for experimental work of a secret nature.   *Mr A. J. R. Frost*

I hope that readers with technical knowledge will excuse me if I give a simple explanation, broadly accurate, of radio-location.

Two British Physicists gave their names to two layers of the upper atmosphere, in an area electrified by the sun and known as the ionosphere. These were the Heaviside Layer (Oliver Heaviside b. 1850) some 65 miles above the earth surface and the Appleton Layer (Sir E. Appleton b. 1892) at 140-300 miles high. These layers are used in short wave transmissions when radio signals are bounced against them thus obtaining greater distance. Experiments in the pre-war era showed that waves of certain frequencies transmitted at these layers penetrated them or were absorbed by them giving no reflected effect. Occasionally, however, freak returns of these waves occurred from distances obviously not connected with either of the two known ionosphere layers. If one knows the exact frequency one also knows its speed. Taking that the transmitted radio wave travels at 186,000 miles per second and one knows the outward and return times an impulse takes, say 1/1,000th of a second out and back, it will have travelled 186 miles placing the reflecting object at half the distance — 93 miles.

The infrequent and varying reflecting surfaces, proved not to be unknown layers but aircraft interrupting the wave and reflecting it back to a receiver. By rotating the transmitter aerials through 360°, pulsing a known frequency wave at pre-determined regular intervals and keying the receiver to know, if it received a reflection, the time between transmission of the reflected wave and its receipt back it was possible to obtain the bearing and distance of the reflecting surface. Because it was known that, with the frequencies used, no return could be expected from the atmosphere it could be assumed to be aircraft causing the return. The information obtained could be visibly shown on a cathode ray tube. Until scientists found a means of indicating height visible means, such as height finders, had to be used to pin-point the target in the sky.

John Venmore-Rowland, who attended courses at Regent Street, London, Polytechnic and Southampton University prior to going to Watchett, Somerset, on a G.L. course, tells me that early in the war they were told often enough "Don't ask why but accept that it works. We will work out the why part later.".

The Royal Air Force became officially involved with the research when a posting was made to the Experimental Station, Bawdsey, of Squadron Leader R. G. Hart as Commandant of Training, with a handful of Service and civilian personnel as his first "pupils". It is interesting to note that in these days of "Women's Lib", Mr Watson-Watt during 1937 put forward the theory that in his estimation women would make better Radio Direction Finding (R.D.F.) operators than men, and in order to prove this statement, he trained three shorthand typists stationed at Bawdsey in the new work. The ladies excelled and as a result further women were trained forming the basis of the thousands later engaged in the task.

New stations were built around the East and South-East coasts, curving along the seaboard from Bawdsey, which was the northernmost, to Great Bromley and

Canewdon in Essex and Dover and Dunkirk in Kent. Named "Chain Home" stations, abbreviated to "C.H.", these became operational during early 1938. At the same time, June 1938, Watson-Watt took up the appointment of Director of Communications at the Air Ministry, and his place at Bawdsey was taken by Mr A. P. Rowe.

In September 1938 the "C.H." stations were on continuous watch. Indeed, they plotted the Prime Minister's Lockheed airliner as he headed towards Germany. Practice for the plotters was also provided by the German Lufthansa and Dutch

Chain Home wooden receiver tower with the dipole aerials at three levels visible at the top.

John Langford

K.L.M. airliners making their daily flights into Croydon, at that time London's airport.

The "C.H." stations continued to rise around the South Coast and soon ranged as far as Ventnor in the Isle of Wight, while the chain also grew to the north with stations at Darsham High Street in Suffolk, and Stoke Holy Cross and West Beckham in Norfolk. When the more northern stations were erected experience had shown that shorter beam ranges would suffice leading to a different aerial array and lower aerial towers. These stations were prominent landmarks with their steel towers with the transmitting aerials slung between them and the four slightly smaller all-wooden receiver towers. These big towers were a hazard to low-flying aircraft and one of the steel towers at Stoke Holy Cross was decapitated by a bomber.

The next development was a major stride forward. Previously the signal had been broadcast from the transmitter towers in a broad arc, which gave a weak signal over a wide area, but now the signal was transmitted in a fairly narrow beam, allowing echoes to be obtained from low-flying aircraft or even ships at sea. This new system was known as Chain Home Low or C.H.L., and was further developed by Professor John Cockcroft.

Problems were encountered in the infancy of the C.H.L. stations as the narrow beam needed to be rotated in order to sweep or scan, and many novel methods were devised to obtain this rotary movement. One remembered by many was a mechanical device not unlike a bicycle frame, with chain wheel and pedals, which rotated the aerial by manpower. A joke among the initiated was that one could always identify one of the early Women's Auxiliary Air Force R.D.F. operators by her bulging calf muscles and unusually slim figure.

The original Chain Home stations, now operational, practised their art during the early months of 1939. Not only the local residents showed interest in the towers, for during that summer the German Air Force made a number of exploratory flights off the East Coast and up and down the English Channel, no doubt in order to glean information on the R.D.F. transmissions.

The veteran rigid airship "Graf Zeppelin", which had been fitted out as a flying laboratory, hovered off the Suffolk coast during May with its aerials tuned to pick up the signals. Sir Winston Churchill's *History of the Second World War*, Volume One, reveals the facts of these flights—stating that General Wolfgang Martini, Director of Signals in the Luftwaffe, had arranged that she carried special listening equipment to discover the existence of British radar (still radio location) transmissions, if any. The attempt failed, but had her listening equipment been working properly the "Graf Zeppelin" ought certainly to have been able to carry back to Germany the information that we had "radar", for our radar stations were not only operating at that time but also detected her movements and divined her intentions.

At the same time an unusual number of artists and bird watchers made the

Bawdsey district their "area of work", but the establishment was well placed with the sea and river on two sides of the triangle and one road leading down to the headland.

Churchill's history also records that during June, 1939, Sir Henry Tizard, Director of the Imperial College of Science and Technology, conducted him in a rather disreputable aeroplane to see the establishment which had been developed on the East Coast. Sir Henry Tizard was, of course, the first Scientific Officer at Martlesham Heath. and the establishments visited were Bawdsey Manor and Martlesham Heath. The visit is also recorded by Sir Robert Watson-Watt in his book *Three Steps to Victory* in which he states "We did our tricks for him and foolishly tried to explain to him what was inside some of our black boxes".

Another development made in those last days of peace at Bawdsey Manor was a signal system which stemmed from Watson-Watt, in which a ground signal was sent out to be picked up by a tuned receiver in a friendly aircraft. This in turn activated a transmitter in the aeroplane which sent a coded signal back to the ground receiver screen, thus giving "friendly" aircraft identification. Because of this function, named Identification Friend or Foe, (I.F.F.), recognition was established by the "Screen Blip". In the later battles this device proved itself of immense value.

When war did eventually break out in 1939, the Royal Air Force had its chain of radio location stations giving a curtain of protection from the Eastern Counties to the Isle of Wight. These gave continuous coverage of aircraft movements, our most valuable asset for the forthcoming battle and forewarning to Fighter Command to prepare their interception of approaching enemy aircraft; instead of having to fly standing patrols in order to sight the raiders, they were able to remain at readiness on the airfields until the raiders approached and then to take off and be guided to their objectives.

Mr John Langford of Ipswich served at several of the East Coast stations, and recalls details of the unit at Darsham High Street near Saxmundham, Suffolk.

The transmitting towers, 360 feet high, were constructed of steel and each carried two aerials slung between them weighing some 2¼ tons. The aerials were hoisted into position by a winch and kept taut by concrete blocks sunk into the ground about four feet and reinforced with angle iron guides at the bottom end.

Receiver towers, four in number, and lower in height at 240 feet, were constructed of creosoted timber with metal fishplates at the corners and carried copper tubes in the form of crosses serving as dipole aerials situated at three levels. The two transmitters at each station were housed in a solid brick building protected by an earth blast wall. They were of the Metropolitan Vickers Type T.1940 with air-cooled valves, the thyrators converted from Type T.1583 which used water-cooled valves supplied from a 400 gallon tank of distilled water under the floor.

Receivers were in a similar building suitably protected, situated about one third to half a mile distant, connected by land lines for synchronisation of transmitter and receiver. This was necessary so that as the transmitter was pulsed the time base of the receiver was also triggered. The receivers were of the Cossar RF.8 type, Superhet with about 400 R.F. stages, and an electrical range marker used to move up to the echo. Height, range and bearing were marked out by means of a G.P.O. calculator which looked exactly like a small telephone exchange and displayed on a screen in front of the plotting table.

The transmitter pulsed at $12\frac{1}{2}$, 25 and 50 pulses per minute with peak power at about 1.8 megawatts, the anode voltages being around 35 Kv, Grid Screen about 16 Kv and the Control Grid at 2.5 Kv.

Tuning the transmitter was delicate and it was necessary to use full power with perfect balance of current on each pair of valves. The Control Desk was situated between the Output and Drive stages and it was from here that all the fans were started and a tapping switch in the auto transformer capable of winding up the H.T. voltage was also in the desk.

With this high voltage working it was inevitable that accidents would occur from time to time and unfortunately they did with fatal results.

The experimental Filter Room constructed at Bawdsey was proved through experience and became the first pattern for the system of operational filter rooms.

Late in 1939 it was discovered by a rather tragic accident involving two squadrons of Royal Air Force fighters, resulting in the loss of aircraft, that the fixed transmitter C.H. stations released a reciprocal signal and the receivers picked up the returning signal. This represented a false impression on the screen, giving a picture of closely packed formations of aircraft, when in fact, only one was being plotted. After the incident the "inland" or back side of the aerials was "blacked out" to prevent this deception. Detection of aircraft inland of the radio detector stations was still therefore left in the hands of the Observer Corps.

The Royal Air Force was not alone in its research into electronic devices, as the Luftwaffe had been developing a system of radio beams, and produced the Lorenz method of radio guidance. Using these beams, German bombers were able to bomb targets accurately by night. They carried out guided raids on a small scale over the British Isles to prove the system operationally, but this in turn gave British scientists the chance to detect the beams and develop counter-measures.

Several of the early W.A.A.F. R.D.F. operators who attended the courses at Bawdsey Manor remembered their days at the School, and how they were billeted in the adjacent Coastguard Cottages on the cliff overlooking the sea. These were situated a good walk from the main buildings, and as the Manor grounds were laid out with thick shrubberies and areas of scenic gardens, the journey to and from the Block on dark nights was quite an experience. Daphne Griffiths, later Flight Officer Garne, described those early days in her fine book *The Eyes of The Few*, published by Macmillan.

During the hot summer days of 1940, the Battle of Britain as it came to be known raged over the Southern and Eastern counties, and the Luftwaffe, now confident that the R.D.F. Stations with their towers were part and parcel of the defences, attempted to knock them out. Several took a battering as the enemy tried to shut the eyes that were detecting their forces, but as fast as they were damaged, stalwart effort by the personnel had them operational again usually within hours.

About this time, Radio Location changed its name to Radar (Radio Detection and Ranging), an imaginative name, the same backwards or forwards, and completely descriptive. It played the great part that had been hoped for it. The outcome was that without the necessary air superiority needed to mount an invasion of the British Isles, the German High Command was forced to postpone and finally cancel plans for the operation.

When the Luftwaffe, having been unable to master the British skies by day, resorted to night bombing on a large scale they brought their radio aids into operation. The first was coded "Knickebein", a navigational radio beam, whilst the other two, "X-Gerat" and "Y-Gerat", were more sophisticated and gave greater aid in bomb aiming, as the ground controller could give release details. Knickebein had been detected by R.A.F. scientists and its beams located as they lay over the British Isles, and counter-measures were put into operation. The Luftwaffe then made the next move in this electronic game and counter-measured the counter-measures, enabling the bombers to wreak destruction on several British cities.

While the Battle of Britain was being fought above Southern England, Dr E. G. Barren and a team of dedicated scientists strove on at Bawdsey to develop a lightweight airborne location set suitable for installation in aircraft. This eventually became operational in time for the night battles of 1940-1941 and was then known as Air Interception (A.I.). These earlier sets had partial success in detecting the night bombers and were installed firstly in Bristol Blenheim Mk.1 twin-engined fighters, some of the first being those of No. 25 squadron based at Martlesham Heath, Suffolk. The range of these early sets was very limited, the aircraft being ground control guided to within three miles of the objective before the airborne set became effective. As development proceeded, so the range increased, resulting in Ground Control of Interception (G.C.I.).

During 1943, the equipment was developed so that it was possible to detect objects at up to 185 miles, whilst a year later the East Coast radar stations were able to detect all the V.1 flying bombs as they approached, and later still the V.2 rockets. The watch for the "V" weapons was code-named "Big Ben" and lasted from August, 1944 until March, 1945. As another example of the advance made in this electronic equipment from the low power of a few years previous the power output was now in the region of 3 million watts.

During 1944 a new Ground Control Interception Station came into operation at Trimley Heath alongside the Ipswich-Felixstowe road, and this in conjunction with the other stations in South East England was able to track any high-flying German reconnaissance aircraft which ventured towards the British Isles. Another station appeared on the cliff-top at Dunwich, Suffolk, this being a powerful jamming station whose function was to locate and identify the frequencies used by

German aircraft lying in wait for British bombers. When this had been identified an extremely strong jamming signal was radiated in order to confuse the enemy. It was learned after the war that the Dunwich station was capable of jamming enemy radar as far as the German capital.

Hand in hand with development went counter-measures. Many residents in the Eastern Counties woke up to find homes and gardens draped with long strips of metalized paper, known as "Window" which was dropped in order to confuse radar controllers, although the majority of the material found in the district was jettisoned from Royal Air Force aircraft.

In order to assist in protecting the aircraft of Bomber Command a new Group, No. 100, was formed to carry out radio-countermeasures work. Commanded by Air Vice Marshal E. B. Addison with headquarters at West Raynham, Norfolk, the Group initially comprised three squadrons, Nos. 141, 169 and 239. These were basically fighter units, being equipped with De Havilland Mosquito II night fighters fitted with devices to locate the radar in enemy night fighters. Operations were successful, it being recorded that Wing Commander R. Braham shot down six enemy night fighters in the first three months, whilst the Group claimed 31 enemy aircraft. At this time the Group Headquarters moved to Bylaugh Hall, near Dereham, Norfolk.

Heavy equipment was needed to carry out the jamming of enemy fighter direction transmissions, and it needed to be conveyed high and fast. The Royal Air Force heavies were unable to perform this function, so the American Boeing Fortress B.17.F was adapted for the task. Such aircraft, equipping No. 214 Squadron and painted black overall, operated from North Norfolk airfields such as Little Snoring, Foulsham, North Creake and Oulton, lifting their loads of electronic gear capable of at least three frequencies used by the enemy for long patrols high over the North Sea. They were later joined by another R.A.F. Squadron, No. 223, which also flew an American type, the Liberator B.24. A Unit of the U.S.A.A.F. also took part in the task, the 803rd Squadron, and this operated under the command of No. 100 Group.

"Window" dropping for special operations was also a major role of the Group, and engaged in this task were No. 199 Squadron with Stirlings and Nos. 171 and 642 with Halifax IIIs. These, fitted with a number of devices, including record players and carrying a German speaking crew member, were used to confuse the German fighter pilots. As the Luftwaffe night fighters direction control was based on a code of music, with women controllers, the No. 100 Group aircraft were able with the aid of powerful transmitters from high over the North Sea to give misleading directions both by music and word.

Although only coming into the conflict late, this Group carrying out its specialized tasks claimed 236 enemy aircraft destroyed.

When peace returned, the chain of radar stations had grown along the east coast, the pre-war ones being the major installations with smaller ones linking in the system. The rotating and nodding aerial arrays were a familiar sight in the district, but for the first time the public learned a little about the well-kept secret that had been such a valuable asset in the dark days. As the Services stood down, the radar defences, except for a thinning down of personnel, remained in their operational state with permanent stations responsible for Sectors. Those in the area were the Eastern Sector at Neatishead, Norfolk, and the Metropolitan Sector at Trimley Heath, Felixstowe, each with responsibility for its own Fighter Command airfields. The original "C.H." and "C.H.L." stations, which had done such yeoman service, were now phased out and their place taken by new equipment, known as British Type 80 radar, installed in the main in protected underground burrows. Such establishments were at Neatishead and Trimingham in Norfolk and at Bawdsey, Suffolk.

Bawdsey Manor was further developed after the war. During the early 1950s a top-secret installation was constructed 30 feet below the surface, its existence being known only to those who worked in it. Very few local people realised that it was in their midst. Known as "The Hole", it contained the control centre with the master controller and his staff who could gaze down on a huge map of the North Sea in the centre of the operations room. Before their eyes lay a complete picture of all air movements in the airspace controlled by Bawdsey radar, projected from below by a complicated automatic apparatus which photographed a high-definition radar screen, developed and dried the film and moved a new picture into the projection gate every 15 seconds.

Further development also took place at Trimley Heath when a large underground operations room, locally known as "The Big Hole" was constructed. As in so many cases before, it was outmoded before it became operational. Its service was limited but it was used as Station Headquarters for R.A.F. Felixstowe after the East Coast floods of 1953. The previous year, a serious fire which had started in a transformer in one of the consoles badly damaged the radar operations centre. During 1958, fire in similar circumstances damaged the operations room at R.A.F. Neatishead, Norfolk, two local firemen losing their lives in the underground inferno.

Sir Robert Watson-Watt, always a champion of women for radar work, furthered his association with the W.A.A.F. during 1966, when he married their former Director (1939-1943), Air Chief Commandant, Dame Katherine Trefusis Forbes, D.B.E., Ll.D.

During the early 70s much speculation was caused in the Orford district of Suffolk when a very large building began to rise on the eastern end of the Lantern Marshes, followed by scores of masts of varying heights and positioned in a gigantic circle not unlike a spider's web. Arranged to form an enormous sloping dish, the high side was at the inland edge with the lower edge towards the sea. At the end of 1973 it was announced that this giant radio installation, code-named "Cobra Mist", and largely financed by the United States, was to be dismantled, the reason for the action has never been given. Only the large building now remains, and there is much talk of it becoming the possible site of another nuclear power station.

Another U.S.A.F. installation hums away merrily at the bottom end of Bell Lane, Kesgrave, near Ipswich, with its tall barbed wire fence enclosing numerous masts which support large dish aerials as part of a microwave communications link. These too, caused considerable conjecture when first erected, but the local inhabitants well remember it by the shrill whine emitted from the installation and the 24-hour throb of the diesel generating sets.

The "Gee" chain radio navigation system which aided the R.A.F. bombing raids during the war closed down on the 26th March, 1970, after 28 years' service. Invented by a team of Bawdsey scientists led by Mr R. J. Dippy, it came into general use during 1942, the first aircraft to use the device being Wellington 1.Cs of No. 115 Squadron operating from Marham, Norfolk on 11th August, 1942.

The surveillance radar around the Eastern Counties carries on its ceaseless watch over the airways off the British Isles, and a not unusual situation arises when an unidentified "blip" appears on the radar map, distinct from that of Service aircraft and civil airliners known to be in that airspace. As it is watched across the "arena" the controller calls up R.A.F. Wattisham, near Ipswich, bringing a Lightning interceptor to first stand-by, followed by the order to take-off and intercept. Climbing swiftly high above the North Sea, the fighter is guided by the controller to the intruder, usually a large four-engined Russian reconnaissance patrol bomber. Flying alongside, the two crews survey each other and grins and waves are exchanged before the aircraft break away for their respective bases.

Radar has brought to the airways the safety long sought, and one of the most important installations in the region is the Military Control Zone Centre at R.A.F. Honington, Suffolk, practically the most complicated zone outside Heathrow, London. Keeping a twenty-four hour watch, seven days a week, it is the most up to date Royal Air Force controlled airfield. Over £250,000 worth of equipment is operated by 40 air traffic controllers whose job it is to keep apart British and American jet fighters, military and civil transports, crop-spraying machines, gliders and hedge-hopping helicopters. Another function is the ability to talk down a pilot for a landing in extreme weather conditions, using equipment whose initial development was carried out several years ago at Martlesham Heath and Sutton Heath. Squadron Leader Kenneth Cross, in charge of the centre has stated that they handled up to 15,000 aircraft movements a month and that their job was to abide by separation standards, keeping aircraft three miles apart laterally or 500 feet apart vertically aided by radar capable of "seeing" up to 70 miles, picking the aircraft up well over the North Sea.

Besides being one of the latter day operational radar stations, R.A.F. Bawdsey was the home of the School of Fighter Control, responsible for training fighter controllers and plotters for service all over the world. When in 1974 the Ministry of Defence decided that Bawdsey Manor and its radar installation, standing in 132 acres of woodland, should become non-operational the School of Fighter Control remained for a time in its classroom blocks and huts. However the School was largely dependent on the operational station and when the duties of the latter were taken over by R.A.F. Neatishead, in the heart of the Norfolk Broadland, it was clear the school would not remain in Suffolk for long. Consequently it moved to West Drayton in Middlesex on 1st April, 1975.

One of Bawdsey's longest serving civilian workers was Mr Percy White who had almost completed twenty-eight years and was allowed to stay on until May for his official retirement. A driver, he remembered Sir Robert Watson-Watt well and recalled that only a few years ago, equipment used by the scientist in his early work was discovered at Bawdsey and removed to the Science Museum at South Kensington.

Forty years of work, almost unknown and much still secret, is commemorated by a plaque at the entrance to the Officer's Mess;

IN THE YEAR 1936 AT BAWDSEY MANOR
ROBERT WATSON-WATT
AND HIS TEAM OF SCIENTISTS DEVELOPED
THE FIRST AIR DEFENCE RADAR WARNING STATION.
THE RESULTS ACHIEVED BY THESE PIONEERS PLAYED
A VITAL PART IN THE SUCCESSFUL OUTCOME OF
THE BATTLE OF BRITAIN IN 1940.

Sir Robert Watson-Watt returns to the scene of his labours, Bawdsey Manor to be presented with a commemorative plaque.   *E.A.D.T.*

CHAPTER NINE

They Also

DURING peacetime and the hectic days of war the Air Force's Fighter and Bomber Commands always tend to overshadow the many other essential formations and organisations necessary to ensure the efficiency of the strike force.

Whilst obviously one must pay tribute to the role played by the Army, and in particular that of Anti-Aircraft and Searchlight Units in air defence, this book is concerned with aviation. The scant references throughout the book does not mean that their role is forgotten, indeed it probably warrants a book on its own.

What we are concerned with are the back up services supplying information or service to the men who fly the planes.

The Observer Corps did not receive the Royal Warrant until 21st May 1947 to become The Royal Observer Corps (R.O.C.).

Its posts, positioned often in fields and on windy hilltops, were essential for the task of observing the skies. The men and women observers carried out a twenty-four hour watch in order to give the R.A.F. those few extra minutes to prepare for the enemy. They identified aircraft passing through their allotted airspace, and reported their progress to those needing the information. Before the advent of radio-location (later radar) this was the only indication of the presence of enemy aircraft, and even when the new electronic detection method was in action, visual information was still required to confirm the "magic eye" and give cover in the event of breakdown.

Inaugurated during the summer of 1924, the Observer Corps was at first equipped with posts in the South of England, attacks being expected to originate from the nearest point of the Continent over the English Channel. However, by 1926 the chain of observer posts had extended to the Eastern Counties, with No. 18 Group Headquarters at Colchester. In October, 1929, Coastguard stations along the South Coast were also on skywatching duties, the most northerly being the one at Orfordness. During October, 1933, a new Group, No. 16, was formed to cover Norfolk and Suffolk, and on 1st March, 1936, further growth was evidenced when No. 15 Group was formed at Cambridge, this centre controlling 21 posts. Air exercises during the summer of 1938 showed that further coverage of air tracking was needed, and so No. 14 Group with headquarters at Bury St Edmunds came into being.

An observer post at this time was manned by a crew of two observers, in a good visual position on top of a large building or on high ground. One member had an optical instrument mounted on a tripod with which he was able to estimate the speed, position and height of an aircraft, while the other member of the duty crew maintained a telephone link with the nearest sector operations room. In all some 1,500 observers were available to man the posts, day and night.

The Observer Corps was mobilised on 24th August 1939. By this time No. 18 Group, Colchester, which operated from a room in the Post Office Building in West Stockwell Street, consisted of the Control Centre and thirty-six posts. In the early days the personnel had been classified as Special Constables (unpaid), but on its earlier mobilisation, 3rd March, 1938, they were reclassified.

At the outbreak of hostilities, the Eastern area was reasonably covered by posts with Group headquarters at Colchester, No. 18, for Essex and South Suffolk, at Cambridge, No. 15, for that county, at Bury St Edmunds, No. 14 for West Suffolk, and at Norwich, No. 16, for Norfolk.

During the first months of the War, the Corps were able to train up to full war standard, and with both friendly and enemy aircraft in the region's airspace, they had adequate practice. The Battle of Britain brought additional pressures, and during this period the posts throughout the region worked non-stop, supplying the information essential to enable the R.A.F. fighters to contact the enemy.

When the Baedeker retaliatory raids began during the spring of 1942 Norwich was attacked on the nights of 27th/30th April and 8th/9th May with masses of incendiary, followed by high explosive bombs. The local posts tracked enemy aircraft and supplied information, as far as possible, on the altitudes of hostile aircraft and the friendly aircraft endeavouring to engage them.

Supplementing the vigilance of the Observer Corps were the civilian observers in their "crow's nests" on the roofs of many of the large works in the region. They did yeoman service, saving countless production hours when the workers would have needlessly been confined to air raid shelters.

Since the Munich Crisis days, local factories had been preparing for war. The air raid precaution scheme of Messrs Reckitt and Colman, Carrow Works, Norwich, was launched during September, 1938, under the chairmanship of Sir Basil Mayhew, and worked in full co-operation with the Works Council. The Chief A.R.P. Executive Officer was the Works Manager, and Section Leaders were appointed. Two types of warning were installed, one using the Works steam hooter or "Bull", whilst new klaxons were installed for the "crash" warning. Basically the steam hooter was sounded and internal bells rung when an air raid alert was given by the R.A.F. or Observer Corps. The civilian observers in their posts kept an intense watch on the skies, and when they observed enemy activity, sounded the "crash" warning on the klaxons, signaling all personnel still at work to take cover. This worked well, as raids had become frequent and the trek to the air raid shelters took so much time and led to valuable production time being lost. In factories where workers could "work on" concrete refuges were constructed close to their workplaces.

The Carrow Works aircraft-spotting tower was 82 feet high and 200 feet above sea level, situated in the grounds of a large house at No. 15 Bracondale. It was a joint venture by Boulton and Paul Limited, Laurence Scott and Electromotors Limited, and Colman's, and was manned day and night. The observers on duty, equipped with protective clothing, binoculars and identification charts, gave the "crash warning" during an alert if they spotted a non-British aircraft by day or an unidentified aircraft, gunfire, flares or aircraft illuminated by searchlights at night.

In passing it must be noted that this same firm looking ahead during 1939, bored five tunnels through the chalk substrata under the Carrow Abbey meadow with five entrances. The tunnels extended 100 feet and at the end joined up with a 12 foot transverse tunnel ventilated by 9 inch shafts from above. The tunnels were

Some of the men who stood at the top. Observers who manned the Norwich tower and who were able to save a great deal of badly needed production times in the factories by their vigilance. *Colman Foods*

The observers' tower or "crow's-nest" at Norwich which was manned for twenty-four hours a day and gave warning of imminent attacks. *Colman Foods*

between 5 feet 6 inches and 12 feet wide and lined with steel plates. Fourteen feet of undisturbed chalk lay over the top of the tunnels, which could accommodate 1,000 people.

There was a similar post on the office roof of Messrs Ransomes, Sims and Jefferies' Orwell Works at Ipswich. It took the form of an all "glass" post high up on a brick tower above the General Office, manned on a rota system all round the clock. This post stood in a most advantageous position with wide clear views over the Docks and down the River Orwell towards Harwich, the usual incoming direction of raiding aircraft. In another department of the same firm some distance from the "crow's nest" stands a large four storeyed warehouse with a flat roof, and during the early days of the conflict it was the author's duty, armed with a steel helmet and binoculars, to ascend to this roof when an alert was sounded. Being nearer the incoming enemy aircraft, it was the observer's duty to sound the emergency "crash warning".

The memory is still vivid of being on the roof one wet and windy afternoon, as the light was fading, low cloud scudding across the sky, and the "alert" sounded. Suddenly on the wind came the sound of throttled back aero motors, and out of the murk emerged a Heinkel 111K, bomb doors open, and a massive bomb dropping away towards the nearby gasworks. Breaking all records to the other end of the flat roof, almost 100 yards, the writer hit the "crash button" in passing, went down eight

A massive German bomb which fell in Holywells Park, Ipswich, and did not explode. The author had a personal interest in this bomb as he was underneath the Heinkel bomber which dropped it and was equally grateful that it fell into swampy ground. *Mr Ian Scrivener*

flights of steps in even better time and waited at the bottom for the bang. None came, as fortunately the bomb, one of the largest dropped up to the time, fell in swampy ground and did not detonate.

Another organisation formed during 1940 was the National Association of Spotters' Clubs, instituted to control and administer the many aircraft recognition clubs which were springing up. Clubs in the area were S.C. 430 Norwich Spotters Club, S.C. 97 Saffron Walden, S.C. 3 Chelmsford, and S.C. 540 Rayleigh. Meetings were held by interested spotters, aircraft recognition tests held, proficiency examinations conducted and aerodromes visited. The fortnightly journal "The Aeroplane Spotter", issued alternative Thursdays, priced 3d., carried reports of the association activities and incorporated the bulletin of the National Association of Spotter's Clubs. The editor was Mr Peter Masefield, M.A.(Eng.)Cantab., A.F.R.Ae.S., who after the war became the first British Civil Air Attaché Washington, U.S.A.

During the heavy night raids on Norwich, bombs damaged the communication system between the Norwich headquarters and the telephone exchange. Temporary repairs were quickly carried out and the work carried on. The Norwich group was sent a message of appreciation by the Air Officer Commanding in Chief, Fighter Command, congratulating them on the manner in which they carried out their duties in the face of the enemy.

When radar was established, members of the Observer Corps were trained in its use, and the coastal posts of local Groups were issued with G.L. sets to identify aircraft crossing the coast at altitude and as an aid to sorting out enemy intruders crossing over with the returning bomber streams.

On 12th March, 1943, the Observer Corps were reorganised with the appointments of Centre Controller and Observer Group Officer being combined and known as Group Commandant, with the rank of Observer Commander.

Although during 1943 the number of enemy aircraft over the Eastern Counties had decreased appreciably, a new menace appeared in the shape of the Messerschmitt 410 twin engined fighter bomber, used on intruder duties by the Luftwaffe. With these fast aircraft flying low, the Observer Corps had to be really on their toes to track them, but they did with a fair measure of success. The same applied to the fast low-flying Focke Wulf FW.190 which swept in from the sea, dropped its bombs and roared out to sea again.

During the summer of 1943 the overall command of the Corps moved to the responsibility of the respective R.A.F. Fighter Command Groups which covered the areas of the posts, and thus the local Groups came under No. 11 Group Fighter Command.

In June, 1944, the V.1 Flying Bomb, flying at an average airspeed of 340 m.p.h. and relatively small, called for quick detection and the varying height of approach also posed a problem.

Many Allied pilots returning home in adverse weather conditions owed their lives to the vigilance of Observer Corps members who were able to plot the courses of the often completely lost aircraft and pass the information to the R.A.F., who in turn were able to give the pilot a course to a suitable airfield. Another aspect of the work was the warning of homecoming bomber crews of the presence of enemy intruder aircraft in their midst.

Many U.S.A.A.F. aircraft returning from daylight raids over Europe arrived home later than anticipated, and in the gathering dusk circled awaiting directions for landing. It fell to the Observer Corps once again to identify these machines, their course and altitude in order that directions could be radioed to them to get them back to their bases.

Earlier during the conflict it is recorded that the information from a post was relayed direct to Spitfires from an Eastern Counties base and the observer guided the fighters to the enemy fighter which was successfully shot down. Another task, although not so frequent, was the capturing of German aircrews parachuting down or crawling from the wreckage of their aircraft. On 2nd October, 1940 two observers from the Brightlingsea, Essex, Post helped an Army Officer disarm four members of the crew of a Junkers Ju.88.

The post on the banks of the River Orwell at Woolverstone, near Ipswich, had the distinction of being one of the first to observe the flying bomb, on 16th June, 1944. Later in the year the men of the Aldeburgh, Suffolk, post had the more nerve-racking experience of looking down from their perch 20 feet up on a V.1 as it passed within yards of them, to crash a little further on when it struck the barrel of an anti-aircraft gun.

Many officers and men and women of the Observer Corps had narrow escapes from death or injury, whilst some paid the supreme prices for their duties which were carried out on a civilian basis against the might of the Luftwaffe.

The National Association of Spotters' Clubs was disbanded on 23rd March, 1946. On 30th November, 1946, Mr Herbert Morrison announced that the Observer Corps would be reorganised on a voluntary system based on the war-time methods of operation.

One year after re-enrolment and recruitment opened for the Royal Observer Corps, 13,509 persons — 11,715 men and 1,794 women had applied to join. Now regrouped and re-organised R.O.C. still carries on its duties, forming an integral part of the air defence and early warning system of the British Isles.

Felixstowe still operated in the marine aircraft role, no longer with its experimental craft but as a fighting station with units of Coastal Command and Air Sea Rescue Units with its high speed launches playing an extremely valuable role.

During 1940 the upper component of the Short Mayo composite aircraft which had been at the Marine Aircraft Experimental Establishment pre-war returned to the East Coast. Short S.20 G-ADHJ "Mercury" was flown to Felixstowe by Captain D. C. T. "Pathfinder" Bennett and served there with a Dutch flying boat unit, until returned to its makers during 1941 and later broken up. An unusual aircraft which moved with the M.A.E.E. to Helensburgh was the Short Scion Senior G-AETH, four engined light airliner. This was transferred to the R.A.F. as L9786 in order to continue experiments as a single float seaplane with a wide planing float under the fuselage.

At Martlesham Heath another unusual aeroplane, during the early months of the War, was the British Brunelli OA-1 G-AFMB, the only British-registered example of this American-designed aeroplane which employed a lifting fuselage and twin booms to carry the tailplane. It had been constructed by Cunliffe Owen Aircraft of Eastleigh, Hampshire. Another unusual feature was that it was a civil aircraft and was granted its Certificate of Airworthiness during November, 1940. Eventually transferred to the Free French Forces, it was flown out to West Africa by the famous pre-war pilot, Jimmy Mollison.

Unsung heroes of the airways were the members, men and women, pilots and flight crews of the A.T.A., the Air Transport Auxiliary, who in all weathers and conditions delivered the new or refurbished aircraft to the squadrons. Mainly composed of pre-war civilian pilots, who had flown as club members at week-ends, with a sprinkling of ex-R.A.F. pilots and also the helpful addition of many Commonwealth and American volunteers, this organisation contributed a great deal to the capability of the R.A.F. Theirs was the responsibility for delivery from either the manufacturer or a Maintenance Unit where modifications had been carried out on new aircraft of all types. Nothing seemed to daunt the pilots of the A.T.A. and even on a miserable day when all flying appeared to be cancelled a fighter or bomber would appear out of the scud, to make a landing and trundle up to the dispersal point. The uninitiated were even more surprised when out of the fuselage door of perhaps a huge Stirling, Lancaster or Halifax would step a petite blonde, accompanied by only one other crew member, a flight engineer. Flying often without the usual navigational aids, sometimes with only its rudimentary radio set, they shuttled to and fro, returning to their Ferry Pool, as the base was known, in an ancient D.H. Rapide or Avro Anson, and more often than not, in an "impressed"* Moth of some description. This work was not without its dangers, as the aircraft were unable to defend themselves if they met the enemy, but the weather conditions were the worst hazard. On 5th January 1941, Mrs Amy Mollison, better known before the War as Amy Johnson, was posted missing presumed killed when the Airspeed Oxford she was ferrying became lost and crashed into the icy waters of the Thames Estuary off Southend. Thirty four years later on 3rd April, 1975, bones found on the edge of the Thames at Canvey Island, Essex were thought to solve this wartime mystery. At the time of writing investigations are being carried out to identify them, to ascertain if they are in fact those of Amy Mollison, whose body was never found. It certainly wasn't the money that attracted the pilots of the A.T.A. as during 1940 the pay was £230 per annum, with an additional £8 per month flying pay!

The full story of these brave men and women is told in *The Forgotten Pilots* by

*Civil aircraft taken over by the R.A.F. for the war period.

Lettice Curtis. Before passing, it must be mentioned that the A.T.A. also performed a valuable spare parts service, flying urgently needed parts to the squadrons to enable grounded aircraft to become operational so much more quickly.

Many leaders have advised "get them young" and that is what the Air Defence Corps (A.D.C.), later the Air Training Corps (A.T.C.), did, enrolling young lads and giving them the basic training of various trades in the R.A.F. Squadrons. Corps sprang up in all the towns and larger villages in the region, one, No. 308 Squadron A.T.C., at Colchester, formed on 22nd February 1941 was commanded by Flight Lieutenant Enoch. The Squadron grew in strength, and during the War over 600 cadets from the unit joined the R.A.F. No. 356 Squadron A.T.C. Felixstowe was formed on 10th February, 1941 under the command of the late Flight Lieutenant Walter Dollan. The first Felixstowe cadet was Ronald Vernon Lee, who rose in the ranks to an N.C.O. and left to join the R.A.F. where he served as a pilot flying Hurricanes, Spitfires and Typhoons. Mr Lee, who still lives in Felixstowe, typifies many of the cadets, 610 of whom passed through the squadron between 1941 and 1966. Other squadrons like No. 759 at Beccles, No. 301 Bury St Edmunds, No. 432 Woodbridge, No. 469 Lowestoft, No. 1331 Stowmarket, No 1334 Manningtree, No. 1379 Leiston and No. 301 Sudbury catered for lads throughout the counties of Suffolk and Essex. The cadets learned the rudiments of arms drill and then took up courses in all manner of technical subjects at which the majority became very proficient. A highlight of the wartime A.T.C. was the weekend visits to R.A.F. Stations, where many were lucky in gaining air experience, eagerly queuing up to take their place in a bomber or transport for their first experience of "feet off the ground". Later in the war primary gliding schools for the A.T.C. came into being, such as the one formed during January 1944 at Berechurch, near Colchester and commanded by Flying Officer S. W. Haward.

Mr Morphew of Ipswich recalls an incident from his A.T.C. days. One Sunday morning at Ipswich Airport, then an A.T.C. Gliding School, the Unit's new Commanding Officer was sitting at the bar when in walked a very young cadet officer. Starting to tell the C.O. what a thrill it was gliding, he explained all about the procedures and then, as an afterthought, said "But perhaps you are not flying

Air Training Corp cadets prepare their Slingsby Grasshopper TX.1, WZ 791 for a "bungee" assisted hop. This type of machine was ideal for imparting the feel of the controls in a short hop.

types". The C.O. smiled. What the cadet officer did not know, was that the seemingly grounded C.O. had been shot down and rescued three times during his overseas service.

Operating in the region also were a number of Maintenance Units where damaged aircraft were either repaired or stripped. With the large population of aircraft in the Eastern Counties it was essential that a large repair and recovery organisation operated, as on a morning after a large raid the countryside would be littered with disabled aircraft and burned out wrecks. The large "Crash drome" at Sutton Heath catered for such emergencies, but many could not or did not make it.

At the time of Munich, it was more fully realised that the defences were nowhere near the state of preparation needed for a confrontation. Fighter squadrons were unable to operate at the altitudes that raiders were expected to fly, balloon barrages and anti-aircraft guns were well below establishment and new aerodromes were behind schedule.

The balloons of the R.A.F. Balloon Command were all under the operational command of the A.O.C., Fighter Command. During September, 1939, some 1,400 balloons could be mustered, rising to some 2,300 by the end of 1941. The barrage at Harwich and Felixstowe arrived during the early weeks of the War and claimed an unidentified victim on 9th September, 1940. After hitting a cable about midnight, the aircraft burst into flames and dived into Harwich Harbour. Similar occurrences happened several times during the hostilities, tragically often the victims being Allied aircraft.

Coastal guns were not able to give protection to inshore convoys all the way round the East Anglian coastline, so four squadrons of Blenheims were drafted into the region to provide this protection.

A task allotted to Anti-Aircraft Command was the provision and manning of smoke screens to obscure target areas during enemy attacks. Local factories were also permitted to produce more smoke than peace-time regulations allowed in order to create industrial haze.

Several unorthodox defence systems came into being during the early months of the war, one such being a scheme using semi-obsolete Handley Page Harrow bombers to tow aerial mines on calbes across the path of oncoming bombers. Another scheme utilized aerial mines, suspended from balloons, but thankfully both ideas were short lived. Another device installed at several airfields, including Martlesham Heath, was P.A.C. (Parachute and Cable)—rockets located around the perimeter of the defended zone were electrically fired and carried up with them a long length of thin piano-wire. At maximum altitude the rocket detached and a parachute deployed, allowing the dangling wire to descend slowly, it was hoped in the path of approaching dive bombers. The Martlesham Heath installation was only fired once, in error, and on this occasion the festooning wires "shorted out" electric transmission lines and telephone wires for miles around.

A night fighter version of the American built Douglas Boston, called the Havoc,

Dornier 215 seen from another aircraft of the same type. All the Dornier bombers followed the slim fuselage, high wing design and the layout ran through several series of aircraft.

Barrage balloons at low hoist. Their silver shapes rose over many regional towns and cities, and became familiar sights to friend and foe alike.

was fitted with a powerful searchlight in the nose known as the "Turbinlite" but by the time it became fully operational the night bomber menace had greatly diminished.

The public at this period must have noticed the difference in the positions of the regional searchlights, as at the beginning they were used singly, but early in 1941 they appeared in groups of three and then later in the year in a new formation. This was a box some 44 miles by 14 miles wide, with the lights 6 miles apart at the ends of the box and 3½ miles apart down the sides. One single fixed vertical light was used as a reference point for a night fighter which patrolled the area of the box.

Barrage balloons arrived at Ipswich on 14th September 1942. Located around the perimeter of the borough, they were flown for the first time, during the night of the 15th and for the first time during daylight on the 18th September. Whilst in Ipswich, one of the gasbags broke away and after a devious float over the western side of the town, finally descended on No. 14 Castle Road, off the Norwich Road. The Auxiliary Fire Service was quickly on the scene in case the hydrogen gas ignited, but it was removed without incident. Throughout the stay of the balloons in the Eastern Counties, a number of them broke adrift and floated over the region until they landed, or were destroyed, whilst a number fell in flames after being struck by lightning. One such incident occurred on Thursday, 28th March 1940, when a flaming balloon fell on a building at R.A.F. Felixstowe.

Another place protected by a balloon barrage was Norwich, where the winch lorries and balloons were sited on parks and recreation grounds and on bombed sites around the city. One was stationed in a corner of the King Edward VI Grammar School sports field close to Pull's Ferry and only a short distance from the Cathedral.

Local people always knew when an "alert" was imminent because of the whine of the winch motors as the balloons were sent up to their operational height. In normal conditions they were kept at medium height, and when bad weather was expected they were often hauled down and secured to ground anchors.

From 1942 until 1944, when the winds were favourable, balloons carrying incendiary devices and communication and power cable interference gadgets were launched from the region towards enemy occupied territory.

The autumn of 1943 saw the return of the night bomber attacks on the region and at this time the Luftwaffe dropped its first "Window", metallized paper strip similar to that used by the R.A.F., causing considerable difficulty to the defensive radar.

Another weapon employed by the A.A. Command in the region was the multiple rocket launcher gun, but these could not be used to their full capacity owing to a continued shortage of rocket missiles, the Navy taking priority for the defence of merchant shipping. From 24th April until 28th September, 1944, the coastal areas were declared Controlled Areas by law. Special military or police passes were required by persons in order to enter these areas. Other areas like

Multiple Rocket Projector sometimes referred to as the "Z Gun". Mainly used by the Royal Navy, several were also manned by the Home Guard units as defence against aircraft in the region.

Landguard Fort, Orfordness and the like were "Protected Zones" and had special passes for entry and exit. On 1st May, all roads to the coast in the region were closed to the public for military reasons and civilians with telephones were told by the police not to allow strangers to use their telephones.

With the advent of the V.1 Flying Bomb, night flying Mosquitos from the Eastern Counties airfields destroyed many of the V.1 launching Heinkel 111s over the North Sea, whilst working in close co-operation with R.A.F. Tempest fighters, a belt of searchlights stretching from Sudbury, Suffolk to Southend, Essex, enabled the fighters to destroy some 50 missiles.

At the end of June, 1944, the Harwich harbour balloon barrage was withdrawn after being in operation since the beginning of the war.

A small and almost unknown section of the Army operated its aircraft from Suffolk during the early months of 1940, this being No. 656 Air Observation Post Unit based at Westley, near Bury St Edmunds. The Auster A.O.P. aircraft were used for gun ranging and artillery spotting, and one of the ex-pilots, Captain N. J. King of Bramford, was with the unit in those days. After their spell in Suffolk they went to North Africa and Italy, and finally Europe, finishing up in Holland. These joint Army-R.A.F. units did valuable work in the front line with their small unarmed light planes, the descendents of which still fly from Ipswich Airport.

CHAPTER TEN

Flying Lifeboats

WITH the airfields of the Eastern Counties all located in close proximity to the North Sea, it fell to them to provide homes for various Air Sea Rescue units whose duties were to assist those of their fellow airmen in trouble in the sea as well as, in latter days, sailors and yachtsmen who, at times, needed their help.

The need for a speedy and efficient rescue service for dealing with aircraft casualties first became apparent when regular air services were instituted between London and Paris, and the Royal National Lifeboat Institution (R.N.L.I.) built a special high-speed lifeboat which was stationed at Dover. With the coming of the War it was realized that a much wider service, involving specially equipped aircraft as well as high-speed launches and the R.N.L.I.'s lifeboats, would be required, and the daily comings and goings of Allied bombers and fighters provided proof of the need for the service.

In order to save valuable aircrews, both the R.A.F. and the U.S.A.A.F. established airborne air-sea rescue units, the former from 1940 onwards and the Americans during 1943. One of the first units to operate was No. 278 Squadron (A.S.R.), coded MY and sharing the fighter aerodrome at Martlesham Heath, and equipped with ex-operational Supermarine Walrus amphibians and Westland Lysander monoplanes originally designed for army co-operation duties.

On receiving a "Mayday"* call, the faster Lysander would take off carrying dinghies and smoke floats on its undercarriage stub-wings and working from the latest information available to proceed to the area, where a search would commence. On sighting a dinghy or any wreckage, a smoke float would be dropped. This would give an indication of wind speed and direction and also guide the following Walrus, which could then alight on the sea and pick up any survivors. If, however, the men on the surface appeared to be in imminent danger the Lysander would drop one of its dinghies, and also a pack of provisions for their comfort. This procedure was also adopted if the sea was too choppy for the Walrus to alight, and then the aircraft would mount guard over the area until surface vessels arrived to pick up the men.

During the latter part of 1941 the A.S.R. units were provided with ex-operational Spitfire II's and Defiants, which could speed out to the search area and drop their smoke floats and dinghies, and also hold off any enemy interference, which was becoming more apparent at this time.

During the first two years of the War Martlesham Heath remained the only A.S.R. equipped aerodrome in the area, but after a while Coltishall and Horsham

*From the French 'M'aidez (Help me) International Distress Call replacing S.O.S.

St Faiths near Norwich and Bircham Newton, also in Norfolk, housed similar units.

Many deeds of valour were carried out by the not so glamorous men and machines.

During July, 1940, Warrant Officer Thomas Ormiston was sent out to pick up an R.A.F. bomber crew who were in their dinghy, 90 miles off Orfordness, Suffolk. Although very heavy seas were running, he skilfully brought the Walrus down on the heaving surface and took the bomber crew aboard. Owing to the heavy swell, he was unable to take-off again and radioed for assistance which was despatched to him in the shape of four gunboats. The local press takes up the story: —

"Escorted by four gunboats, an Air Sea Rescue pilot who had saved a bomber crew from the North Sea, taxied his Walrus flying boat through heavy seas for seven hours in an effort to reach the English coast. Then, in darkness, his fuel ran out and the flying boat was taken in tow by one of the escorting gunboats. An hour later the Walrus had to be abandoned for the night and the rescued crew and the pilot were brought to Lowestoft by the motor patrol boat." Ormiston, of Brighton, was awarded the D.F.C. for "great courage, fortitude and resource in very trying circumstances".

Many an aircrew in their dinghy, or even floating in the water in inflatable jackets, were relieved to see the obsolete Walrus rumbling along at low altitude, and then circling into the wind in order to make a rescue landing whilst, higher up, to maintain better radio contact with base, circled the Defiant or Spitfire.

Barely a day passed without a call being received for the services of the A.S.R. units, and as the tempo of the R.A.F. operations rose, both by night and day, the units rapidly became overworked, which necessitated fresh aircraft being drafted into the work.

Mr W. L. Cope of Niagara Falls, Canada, an ex-member of No. 277 Squadron, another A.S.R. unit based at Martlesham Heath kindly sent the author the Squadron's "A" Flight score-board and it makes very interesting reading.

When the Eighth Air Force took up residence in the Eastern Counties business became even more plentiful and during the summer of 1943 the U.S.A.A.F. set up its first A.S.R. unit at Hornchurch, Essex, though it soon moved to Saffron Walden. To boost the search radio system, new mobile radio fixing stations were set up in the region at Leiston, Suffolk, Palling, Norfolk, and Tolleshunt D'Arcy, Essex, so that more accurate radio fixes, by means of cross-bearings, could be obtained from the all-too-often weak dinghy signals. Working in very close liaison with the R.A.F., the U.S.A.A.F. organisation soon got into its stride, and on the 22nd June, 1943, the joint services rescued seven R.A.F. and eight U.S.A.A.F. aircrew members from the North Sea.

Useful though inflatable dinghies were, they had one disadvantage; they could do little more than drift with wind and tide, and the provision of sails on certain of them was no more than an aid to morale. What was needed was a boat in which

No. 277 SQUADRON
"A" FLIGHT. MARTLESHAM HEATH

Date	Pilot	Crew	Aircraft	Details of Rescue	Details of Rescued	Total
7.12.41.	F/Lt. Hawes F/S Boddy	F/S Leighton Sgt. Hazeltine	Lysander Lysander	Destroyer directed to raft	4 merchant seamen.　　Alive	4
1.6.42.	Sgt. Arundel	F/S Pickles Sgt. Markey	Walrus	Picked up	W/O Stillwell　,, 65 Sqdn.	5
3.6.42.	Sgt. Arundel	Sgt. Markey Sgt. Bunn	Walrus	Picked up	F/S Gibbs　　,, 85 Sqdn.	6
1.8.42.	P/O Hilton	F/S Pickles F/S Leighton	Walrus	Picked up	F/O Skinner　,, Sgt. Bernstein　,, Sgt. Quinn　Dead	9
6.10.42.	W/O Ormiston	P/O Nault F/S Pickles	Walrus	Picked up	Sgt. Air Gunner 418 Sqdn.　Alive	10
27.1.43.	F/Lt. Brown	F/O Sheppard	Walrus	Picked up	W/O Greenfield ,, F/S Harran　,, 277 Sqdn.	12
13.2.43.	W/O Ormiston	F/O Sheppard F/S Leighton	Walrus	H.S.L.s directed by Walrus	Lt. Powell　　,, 336 Sqdn. USAAC	13
20.2.43.	F/Lt. Brown	F/O Sheppard F/S Rance	Walrus	Picked up	F/O Brenner　,, F/S Rave　　,, Sgt. Glass　　,, Sgt. Vauher　,, 415 Sqdn.	17
15.4.43.	W/O Greenfield Sgt. Brodie		Spitfire Spitfire	Hawkinge Walrus directed to pick up	Col. Petersen　,, USAAC	18
20.4.43.	F/Lt. Brown	F/S Leighton F/S Errington	Walrus	Picked up by Air Sea Rescue Boat	German pilot　,, German airman ,,	19 20
31.5.43.	W/O Boddy Sgt. Grainer		Spitfire Spitfire	Directed H.S.L.'s	F/O Tarley　,, 402 Sqdn.	21
12.6.43.	W/O Greenfield	W/O Rance	Walrus	Picked up	P/O Abbot　　,, 198 Sqdn.	22
12.6.43.	W/O Greenfield	W/O Rance F/S Leighton	Walrus	Picked up	Lt. Beattie　　,, 335 Sqdn. USAAC	23
22.6.43.	W/O Boddy Sgt. Campbell		Spitfire Spitfire	Directed H.S.L.'s	8 Aircrew　　,,	31
22.6.43.	W/O Greenfield	W/O Thoran F/S Leighton	Walrus	Directed H.S.L. 2862 to dinghy	3 Aircrew　　,,	34
22.6.43.	W/O Ormiston	F/S Errington Sgt. Mann	Walrus	Picked up and taxied back. Relieved by M.G.B.	4 Aircrew　　,,	38
24.6.43.	W/O Ormiston		Spitfire	Directed H.S.L. 2668	6 Aircrew　　,,	44
4.10.43.	S/Ldr. Bawring F/Lt. Mackerlach		Spitfire Spitfire	Directed H.S.L.	10 Aircrew　　,,	54
20.10.43.	F/Lt. Mackerlach	F/O Sheppard Sgt. Lawrence	Walrus	Directed H.S.L.'s	10 Aircrew　　,,	66
	W/O Ormiston	S/Ldr. Ellis W/O Errington	Walrus			

By the 13th April, 1944, this unit with its Walrus and Spitfire aircraft had picked up 100 men from the sea, 98 alive, 2 dead.

aircrew survivors could make their escape from enemy waters and in which they would be safer and more comfortable until it was possible to pick them up. Thus was conceived the airborne lifeboat, designed by famous yachtsman Uffa Fox to be slung beneath the belly of an aircraft and lowered by a cluster of parachutes.

The debut of the airborne lifeboat coincided with the appearance in an A.S.R. role of the Vickers Warwick, an enlarged version of the Wellington which had not really been successful as an operational bomber machine. Endowed with great endurance and lifting capacity, it was the ideal carrier machine for the airborne lifeboats.

These boats were of two types, one weighing approximately 1,700lbs, 22 feet long and equipped with two engines giving it a range of 100 miles on one engine or 60 miles with both running. The other, larger type was 32 feet long, weighing in at 3,000lbs and had a range of almost 500 miles. Both were examples of ingenuity, as when they touched the water on their cluster parachutes lines were electrically fired from the boat so that the men in the water could grab them, the mast erected itself and stabilizers deployed in order to keep it upright.

No. 278 Squadron "B" Flight at Bradwell Bay, Essex, was engaged in development work on the lifeboats with Warwick aircraft. At first, they were dropped on five parachutes, two at one end and three at the other, but after several attempts it was found that if one of the cluster was caught up, or failed to open, the boat did not land in the water the right way up. On one attempt only the parachutes at one end opened and the boat went straight under, stern first. This tendency was corrected by having a group of five parachutes mounted in the centre of the boat.

One of the first Warwick A.S.R. units was that at Beccles, Suffolk, comprising two Squadrons, Nos. 279 (A.S.R.) and No. 280 (A.S.R.). The first boat was dropped on 5th May, 1943, when a Halifax bomber came down in the sea off Norfolk. The ditched crew boarded the lifeboat and began the westward journey of 50 miles, but when only a few miles off Wells-next-the-Sea the fuel ran out. They were sighted and towed the remainder of the way home.

Early in May, 1944, an American A.S.R. unit was formed at Boxted, near Colchester, its main function being to spot ditched aircrews and to drop the first dinghies or marker flares. Ex-operational P.47 Thunderbolts were used for this function and they collaborated with naval vessels from Great Yarmouth, Lowestoft and Harwich which maintained standing patrols under the flight paths of the bombers.

On 19th May, 1944, a large A.S.R. operation took place off the Norfolk coast when an Eastern Counties based B.17 came down in the sea some 250 miles off Great Yarmouth. Lockheed Hudsons of the R.A.F. from Langham, Norfolk, went to the scene with airborne lifeboats, escorted by Eighth Air Force Mustangs based at Debden, Essex. After searching for almost 24 hours they located the dinghy, and one of the Hudsons parachuted its lifeboat down as near as possible. The ditched crew boarded the lifeboat, started the engines and set course for home through the night but about midnight on the 21st May they encountered a Danish fishing vessel. When dawn broke the crew of a patrolling Warwick saw the dinghy crew taken aboard the Danish vessel, which then made towards its German-occupied home port. However, the tables were turned when the Warwick dropped down and fired several long bursts of machine gun fire across the vessel's bows, persuading the Danish fishermen to turn about again. It was eventually sighted by a motor launch which took on the much-travelled B.17 crew and landed them at Great Yarmouth. They could have said that they spent part of their service on the Dogger Bank!

Five weeks later, on 29th June, 1944, another B.17 from the 390th Bomb Group at Parham, Suffolk, ditched some 20 miles off the Dutch coast, and one of the patrolling high speed launches positioned 60 miles off Great Yarmouth dashed to the rescue. The crew of eight in their two dinghies were located and picked up, and the launch started its journey home. Running into bad weather, the escorting Warwick aircraft lost sight of the launch, which was attacked and set on fire by a marauding Junkers 88. The launch foundered and another rescue launch which dashed to the aid of the stricken vessel found four dead and seventeen survivors from the boat and the aircraft. Amongst the dead was the gallant coxswain of the patrolling launch, Flight Lieutenant Lindsay. The Walrus from Martlesham Heath now took part in the operation, flying two doctors out towards the homecoming launch to care for the badly injured survivors of the affray.

It is interesting to note that at the time of writing an airborne lifeboat of the smaller type still lies on the foreshore at Orford Quay, not so far from the area where many were used 30-odd years before.

Daily life on a war-time A.S.R. squadron is well presented by Mr Patient, of Chelmsford, who joined "D" Flight of No. 278 Squadron at Martlesham Heath.

"Our dispersal was what was known as the Main Gate Dispersal, near the Main Road end of 'B' Flight Road or later Portal Avenue and the large house used by the Commanding Officer of the American squadrons. There were two Nissen huts and two long wooden huts in the shape of a letter 'L' which contained the Aircrew Room, the C.O.'s office and a general room for the 'Bods', and connecting the huts was a large 'blister'* type hanger which could just accommodate a Walrus and a few drums of oil. Hanging from the roof of this hangar was a sign in the form of an illuminated box with the initials W. and S. When a hooter sounded as a scramble signal we rushed from the crew room, looked up at the sigh and if the 'W' was alight, rushed over to the Walrus and started her up. If it was the 'S' then it was the turn of the two Spitfire II's, whilst if both initials were lit, they both were started.

At this time we had 'on the strength' two or three Walruses (at least two of which carried the code letters AA and BB, an unusual scheme, after the squadron letters MY), several Spitfires all with square cut wing tips, a couple of Ansons, one Oxford and the C.O.'s Auster."

*So named because of their shape.

Crowds look over a war-weary Walrus as its captain explains to the gathered people what it was all about.

Towards the end of hostilities the U.S.A.A.F. had a large A.S.R. organisation in the Eastern Counties and the 5th Emergency Rescue Squadron moved from Boxted, near Colchester, to Halesworth in Suffolk. This was a specific unit with several aircraft designed for this work, including the amphibious version of the Consolidated Catalina, known as the PBY-5, sometimes called the "Canso". This long-range amphibian was ideal for the job, as it was able to alight on the water near the enemy coast, pick up ditched aircrews and land them back at base. This unit also investigated the possibilities of dropping medically-trained men by parachute to men in the water, a system which developed into the "para-medic" that we have at the present time. This unit carried on until the end of hostilities, when it was disbanded and flew home for a well-earned rest.

Before passing, it is interesting to note that during the war years the A.S.R.

units of both Air Forces rescued some 3,723 R.A.F. and 1,998 American aircrew members. Separate figures are not available for this particular part of the coast.

An exciting new type of aircraft developed during the late years of the war had tremendous possibilities in the A.S.R. role. This was, of course, the helicopter, capable of hovering flight and with the ability to take off and land in confined places. The R.A.F. took delivery of several American-designed and built helicopters, and although at first they operated with the Army in observation role, eventually some were drafted to the A.S.R. section of the R.A.F.

The fact that the rescue service was still needed, although the calls on its aircraft were not so frequent as before, was illustrated during January, 1951, when a Miles Hawk Trainer G-ALGK used for ground radar calibration work crashed into the sea off Burnham-on-Crouch, Essex.

During the night of 1st-2nd February, 1953, a giant tidal surge swept down the East Coast and into its estuaries causing widespread destruction and loss of life. The R.A.F. sprang into action with a fleet of rescue boats and supplies of bedding and food. The Duke of Edinburgh, who was at Sandringham at the time, flew from R.A.F. Bircham Newton with his instructor to see from the air the destruction caused by the water pouring through the broken sea walls. Three R.A.F. stations were evacuated, Felixstowe, North Coates and Theddlethorpe, the latter two in Lincolnshire, and the Research Station at Orfordness was wrecked, two Air Ministry policemen marooned on a hangar roof being rescued by a motor boat.

At Felixstowe the waters broke in behind the Air Station and rushed through a block of "prefabs", resulting in many deaths, whilst a railway signalman at Felixstowe Beach Station was never seen again after closing down his box. Canvey Island, Essex, was also badly affected. The total deaths were as follows: —

Norfolk	King's Lynn 15, Hunstanton 12, Sea Palling 7, Great Yarmouth 6, Snettisham 6, Heacham 4, Salthouse 1, Winterton 1, Dersingham 1.
Suffolk	Southwold 1, Felixstowe 26.
Essex	Jaywick 10, Great Wakering 4, Southend 7, Clacton 14, Canvey Island 100.

The distinctive R.A.F. high-speed air sea rescue launches still operated from R.A.F. Felixstowe and Gorleston and although still engaged basically in the rescue of ditched airmen they assisted the lifeboats of the R.N.L.I. in their lifesaving operations.

The region saw its first R.A.F. helicopters when the Whirlwinds of No. 22 Search and Rescue Squadron moved into Martlesham Heath during 1955 and soon the "alert-yellow choppers" were a familiar sight and sound to the residents of the region. Many will recall on fine sunny weekends when the beaches were covered with holidaymakers the Whirlwinds flew along the coast the crowds waving to them and the crews returning the salutations. Their aircraft were engaged in all manner of operations, from rescuing swans in ice-bound rivers to flying badly injured people to distant hospitals and even flying the Prime Minister, Sir Anthony Eden, round

A Westland Whirlwind helicopter carries out a practice rescue in co-operation with an R.A.F. High Speed Launch off Felixstowe. This operation was usually carried out whilst the launch was under way and often in bad weather as well.

Mr R. Malster

the area when he visited it. During 1956 the yellow helicopters took up residence at the Felixstowe Air Station, their nearness to the scene of impending action giving them that extra few minutes to reach the trouble.

On Monday, 19th May, 1958, a more sombre report appeared: — The winchman was killed when an R.A.F. Air Sea Rescue helicopter crashed into the sea off Felixstowe. He was named as Sergeant D. W. Frampton, of Manor Park, London, whilst the pilot, Flight Lieutenant K. Alderson, of Felixstowe, suffered a broken leg and spine injuries. The third member of the crew, the navigator, was uninjured.

Another casualty but with less tragic results was the Coltishall based Whirlwind helicopter of No. 288 Squadron, which plunged into the sea off Gorleston whilst carrying out a practice rescue. The engine failed and the aircraft dropped into the water, but the pilot, Flying Officer S. Smith from Coltishall, the signaller, Sergeant F. Ray from Colchester and the Master Navigator G. Perrell, who was down on the end of the winch rescue wire at the time, were all picked up. The aircraft which was lying in eight fathoms of water was pulled out of the sea a few days later.

On 23rd June, 1967, another Coltishall-based Whirlwind plunged into the sea 100 yards off the shore off Caister, Norfolk, and unfortunately the crew of three were all killed. The pilot, Flight Lieutenant Archie Gavan was very popular and greatly respected in the district for his work with the fishermen. Also killed with him were Flight Lieutenant Gil Pink and Master Navigator Harry Crossman, and at the funeral service held a few days later, the village church of All Saints, Scottow, was packed to overflowing by people from all walks of life who wished to pay their last respects to a crew who had given so much for others.

As a gesture of its long association with the town, Felixstowe Urban District Council granted the freedom of entry to R.A.F. Felixstowe, and during the celebrations Whirlwinds of No. 22 Squadron landed on the Pier carpark near the sea front and were inspected by the public.

Before the fixed wing aircraft departed from Felixstowe, a prototype amphibian intended for A.S.R. Duties, the Vickers-Armstrong Seagull was tested by the Marine Aircraft Experimental Establishment there. Mr W. Curtis, of Ipswich, who was engaged in these tests, remembers this aircraft with its unorthodox layout, variable incidence wings, contra-rotating airscrews and Rolls-Royce Griffon engine. While the aircraft was flying on a test one afternoon, the engine rapidly overheated and caught fire, so a hurried descent was made in order to extinguish the blaze.

Around this period several films were made in the Felixstowe area, one based wholly on the A.S.R. theme and titled "The Sea Shall Not Have Them". Others were "The Net", featuring a large nondescript flying boat involved in a spy story, and "Yangtse Incident", the story of H.M.S. *Amethyst* and her exploits in China. The latter was interesting in that one of the last Short Sunderland flying boats was used, landing and taking off from the River Orwell.

A Whirlwind lands on the Spa Car Park at Felixstowe on the occasion of the official reception for the Felixstowe A.S.R. Unit by the Urban District Council.

When Felixstowe closed down No. 22 Squadron's "B" Flight moved to the South of England, but search and rescue duties in East Anglia were carried on by a detachment of another helicopter squadron based at Horsham St Faiths. In 1963 this unit moved to nearby Coltishall.

The aircraft of "D" Flight, No. 202 Squadron (S.A.R.)* left Coltishall, Norfolk, during April, 1973, and were replaced by those of "B" Flight, No. 22 Squadron (S.A.R.) and Flight Lieutenant P. J. Thompson of the unit told the author that since then they had carried out 179 operational sorties and picked up 86 people. No. 22 Squadron has flown the Westland Whirlwind helicopter for over 20 years, having received its first HAR.2s during 1955. With four flights detached around the British Isles, its aircraft had been scrambled 6,451 times up to 1974 and

*Search and Rescue, a redesignation of the older A.S.R.

assisted 3,549 people during its life and collected 87 awards.

The value of the helicopter for sea rescue work was illustrated on the 15th November, 1968, when disaster hit a drilling platform and its supply ship off the coast of the Eastern Counties. The supply ship *Hector Garrett* capsized and sank in heavy seas, and the platform *Hewett* radioed "We ourselves are in trouble — we have a gas blowout and are preparing to abandon". Four helicopters sped out to the scene, accompanied by the Cromer R.N.L.I. lifeboat. Flying low over the huge waves, the helicopters located the survivors in the water and guided the trawler *Boston Hornet* to them. It picked up 15 men, 10 from the supply vessel and the others from the *Hewett* platform. Altogether 33 men were ferried from the disaster scene and the drilling platform to Great Yarmouth, while another helicopter flew out a team of engineers to seal off the fractured gas line and so prevent an explosion.

In just one year, 1973, the helicopter crews at Coltishall were "scrambled" no fewer than 63 times and in those missions they saved 39 lives. One of the men they saved was an R.A.F. wing commander who had ejected from his Lightning fighter, several others were holidaymakers who had got into difficulties while swimming or in small boats, and others were sick or injured seamen or fishermen lifted from vessels at sea and taken to hospital.

Those 39 lives included 10 men from a collier sinking off the North Norfolk coast on 2nd April, 1973; another six were rescued from the same vessel by a helicopter from another search and rescue flight at Leconfield. The collier, the *Amberley*, had developed a 20-degree list while en route from Goole to Shoreham with a crew of 16 men. Two Coltishall helicopters took part in the rescue, XP.354 piloted by Flight Lieutenant Jim Ross with Flight Lieutenant Tony Cass as the navigator and Master Signaller Ron Meager as winchman, and XP.350, flown by Flight Lieutenant Ian Christie-Miller, the flight commander, with Sergeant Dick Amor as the winchman and Flight Lieutenant Don Arnold as the navigator. A back-up helicopter with Flight Lieutenant MacGregor, Master Navigator Melton and Master Signaller Derili also flew out from Coltishall, and an HH-53 Jolly Green Giant came from the U.S.A.F. base at Woodbridge in Suffolk. Flying in winds up to 65 knots, the helicopters winched up the crew of the *Amberley* and landed them at Wells.

Master Signaller Meagher won the Air Force Cross and Sergeant Amor the Air Force Medal for their part in this rescue, while the two navigators from Coltishall both gained the Queen's Commendation for Valuable Service in the Air, awards which were undoubtedly well earned.

On that occasion, as on many others, Avro Shackleton aircraft provided an escort for the helicopters, directing them to the scene and overseeing their rescue work. Shackleton maritime reconnaissance aircraft were operated by No. 204 Squadron which was stationed for a time at Honington, Suffolk. In its year at Honington No. 204 Squadron launched 97 aircraft on distress calls, the planes flying up to 16 hours at a time and taking part in missions all round Britain's coastline and half-way across the Atlantic. Air Marshal Nigel Maynard, Chief of Staff to R.A.F. Strike Command, took the final salute at the disbandment parade at Honington on 1st April, 1972, when the squadron ceased flying the maritime reconnaissance Shackletons.

Much of the work done by the search and rescue helicopters is carried out over the sea, which presents particular difficulties for the pilots and navigators. On Wednesday, 23rd January, 1974, one of the helicopters from Coltishall flown by Flight Lieutenant Ian Christie-Miller went out 60 miles over the wind-swept North Sea to find the Lowestoft trawler *Boston Tristar* with one of her crewmen with a badly broken arm. Whilst the Whirlwind hovered over the pitching vessel, Sergeant Dick Amor lashed the injured fisherman to a stretcher and then supervised the winching up to the "chopper", the pilot holding the pitching and drifting aircraft just above the vessel's swaying mast. During this operation a second helicopter from Coltishall provided an escort for the flight commander's aircraft, a very necessary precaution when carrying out lengthy flights over the sea.

The range and capability of the R.A.F. Search and Rescue flight at Coltishall was greatly increased when the ageing Whirlwinds were replaced by the more powerful twin-engined Sea King HAR Mk3. The Falklands war brought about a further change, however, when "C" Flight of No. 202 Squadron became No. 1564 Flight and was sent to R.A.F. Port Stanley in the Falklands to provide search and rescue facilities for British forces garrisoning the islands.

Their place at Coltishall was taken by "F" Flight of No. 22 Squadron operating Westland Wessex helicopters, the other flights of this squadron being based at Chivenor in Devon, Leuchars in Fife, Leconfield in Yorkshire and Manston in Kent.

The introduction of the Sea Kings greatly enhanced the chances of the helicopter crews in carrying out their rescue work, but nothing can entirely eradicate risk from such an enterprise, as was tragically underlined in November, 1980. Two of the U.S.A.F.'s A-10 tank-buster aircraft from Bentwaters were en route to the Wainfleet range in Lincolnshire on 18th November when they were in collision over North Norfolk, one of the pilots, Major Stephen Kaatz, ejecting successfully before his aircraft crashed in flames at Itteringham, near Aylsham and not many miles from the helicopter base at R.A.F. Coltishall. The other, flown by Lieutenant Colonel Bill Olson, remained airborne for some time but went out of control when the pilot attempted to lower the undercarriage.

Bill Olson baled out as the jet plummeted into the sea off Winterton, but for some reason he failed to operate the quick-release mechanism on his parachute harness when he hit the water. In high winds the still-inflated parachute dragged him through the rough seas at 12 to 15 knots.

When a Sea King from Coltishall came on the scene the winchman, Master Air Loadmaster David Bullock, went down to try to lift Colonel Olson from the sea. With the parachute still attached he found he could not lift the American airman, but he refused to be winched up and continued his efforts until the strain imposed by the waterlogged parachute snapped the cable by which he was suspended from the helicopter. Both David Bullock and the man he attempted to rescue were drowned.

Master Air Loadmaster Bullock was awarded the George Medal, the citation stating that "he had every opportunity over a period of three or four minutes to disconnect himself from the pilot and save his own life. However, consciously and with conspicuous courage, he chose to remain with the pilot in the hope of saving him."

In spite of such tragedies the work goes on, the helicopter crews not only carrying out their primary task of picking up ditched aircrew, be they British, American or of any other nationality, but also taking part in any kind of rescue work for which they are called upon. Much of their day-to-day work consists of airlifting seriously ill patients from East Anglian hospitals to specialist hospitals elsewhere; on 6th May, 1984, a Wessex of No. 22 Squadron landed on a school playing field at Ipswich adjacent to the expanding Heath Road Wing of the Ipswich Hospital to investigate the possibility of using the field as a landing ground whenever it becomes necessary to carry out a "medevac" operation from that hospital. The crews frequently collaborate both in exercises and in rescue work with the volunteer lifeboatmen of the Royal National Lifeboat Institution based around the East Anglian coast, men with whom they maintain most cordial relations.

Before concluding, mention must be made of some of the more notable rescues carried out by the helicopters of Nos. 22, 202 and 228 Squadrons whilst operating from their bases over the years at Martlesham Heath, Horsham St Faiths and Coltishall.

12th November, 1956.   Two Whirlwinds from Felixstowe picked up two Norwegian seamen from the s.s. *San Miguel* 35 miles off Orfordness after an engine room fire on the vessel. The two men were flown to Ipswich hospital for urgent treatment, one being critical and the other in a "moderate condition".

27th April, 1963.   A No. 74 Squadron B.A.C. Lightning flown by Flight Lieutenant Burns caught fire at 10,000 feet off Cromer and the pilot ejected and landed in a field. A Coltishall Whirlwind was soon on the spot, and within 20 minutes of landing, the pilot was back at his home base. The rescue unit, No. 228 Squadron had only moved a few days previously to Coltishall from Horsham St Faiths.

6th May, 1964.   A Whirlwind from Coltishall sped out to a spot 24 miles east of Southwold, where is searched for a seaman who had fallen overboard from the French trawler *Viergermarie*. It was escorted by an aircraft from R.A.F. Stradishall, and eventually the body was spotted, recovered by the Whirlwind and landed at Southwold Common.

11th August, 1963.   A new venture for the R.A.F. Air Sea Rescue helicopters was when a Coltishall Whirlwind picked up an ill Spanish seaman. Antonio Liopez, from the *Conoco I* oil drilling rig, 50 miles off Cromer.

Royal Humane Society Testimonials in vellum by the Air Officer Commanding No. 18 Group, Air Vice Marshal Desmond Hughes.

2nd April, 1973.   The m.v. *Amberley,* a collier en route from Goole to Shoreham with a crew of 16 men, ran into difficulties near the East Dudgeon Buoy, 15 miles off Wells, Norfolk. Two Coltishall helicopters took part in the rescue, XP 354 piloted by Flight Lieutenant Jim Ross with Flight Lieutenant Tony Cass as the navigator and Master Signaller Ron Meagher as winchman, and XP 350, flown by Flight Lieutenant Arnald with Sergeant Dick Amor as the winchman. The back-up aircraft was also from Coltishall with Flight Lieutenant MacGregor, Master Navigator Melton and Master Signaller Derili. Flying in winds up to 65 knots, the helicopters winched up the crew and landed them at Wells. They were assisted also by another Whirlwind from Leaconfield, Yorks, and a U.S.A.F. machine from the Woodbridge base.

January, 1974.   A badly injured seaman was lifted off the Lowestoft trawler *Boston Tristar* 60 miles off Great Yarmouth by a Coltishall's No. 22 Squadron Whirlwind flown by Flight Lieutenant Christie-Miller.

22nd November, 1975.   A Coltishall Whirlwind picked up the two-man crew of a U.S.A.F. F.4D Phantom which had encountered trouble whilst on a training flight over the North Sea. Twenty-eight miles from Great Yarmouth, Captain James C. Evans and First Lieutenant George Kurprian, flying from Lakenheath. ejected and parachuting down landed in a rough sea with eight foot waves running. Climbing into their dinghies, they were rescued by the helicopter within 20 to 30 minutes and returned to Lakenheath.

CHAPTER ELEVEN

Cousins in Peace

A FTER the United States Army Air Force had returned home to the United States of America at the end of the War the American presence in the United Kingdom was very thin, but the Berlin crisis caused some units to return to the British Isles during July, 1948. Soviet forces making loud noises in Eastern Europe caused concern in the R.A.F. and the U.S.A.F. camps, and once again preparations went ahead for co-operation between the two forces if the need arose. This took the form initially of preparing four bomber stations in the Eastern Counties to receive the American Boeing B.29 Superfortress four-engined bomber. These stations were at Lakenheath, Suffolk, Marham, Norfolk and Scampton and Waddington in Lincolnshire and the bombers arrived during July and August 1948. Co-operating with the R.A.F. in training flights, the duration of their stay was on a 90-day rotation, under command of the Third Air Division. Need for further accommodation became apparent and so the ex-R.A.F. bomber station at Sculthorpe in Norfolk became a further U.S.A.F. base.

These were not the first B.29s in the United Kingdom, for on the 9th June, 1947, nine Superfortresses had arrived at Marham, Norfolk, on a goodwill and training mission. Before they returned to the U.S.A. on the 16th June, the formation made flights over London and Southern England. The B.29s belonged to the 340th, 341st and 342nd Squadrons and carried the unit marking B.E. on their otherwise all-metal finish.

Marham, Norfolk, was also the landing place on 18th November, 1949, for a U.S.A.F. C74 Globemaster transport aircraft which had flown the Atlantic non-stop from Malade, Alabama, carrying 103 persons, which to that date was the largest number to cross in one aircraft.

The big noise arrived in Suffolk during the summer of 1950 when six U.S.A.F. B.36 bombers landed at R.A.F. Lakenheath, as part of a global training flight which had brought them to England on a 5,000 mile non-stop flight. Weighing 150 tons and powered by ten engines, six piston and four jet, the 162 foot long monsters with their 230 foot wingspan and tail fin reaching up 55 feet flew at an altitude of eight miles and a speed of 435 m.p.h. Carrying a crew of sixteen, and with a capacity of 10,000 lbs. of bombs, the aircraft was said to have a range of 10,000 miles, the tanks carrying enough fuel to drive a car sixteen times round the world. The bomber contained twenty-seven miles of electrical wiring. It was also stated that the B.36 cost £800 an hour to fly! First Lieutenant C. F. Horton, one of the captains, said that they had experienced "bits of everything" weather and the trip

The United States Air Force returns to the region when giant Boeing B.29s arrive at R.A.F. Lakenheath during the spring of 1951. These were U.S.A.F. aircraft and not to be confused with the B.29 Washingtons which operated with the R.A.F. *Mr and Mrs Hall*

had been uneventful. "But," he added, "I think it's the longest night I have ever spent. Of those 24 hours, 16 were in darkness, and we got in a good bit of instrument flying."

When the Korean War broke out in June, 1950, it was felt that further strengthening of the force in the United Kingdom was necessary and as the result of agreement between the two Governments, a "Special Construction Programme" was instigated with provision for 26 new bases plus the original four, under the command, as from 1st May, 1951, of the Third Air Force. The programme grew and by June, 1952, the Third Air Force had over 27,500 personnel in the United Kingdom, whilst further amendments to the plan brought about a signing during September, 1953, of an agreement under which the British Government would spend $63 million on airfields and the United States Government would cover all costs above that figure, estimated to rise to $300 million.

Peak activity was reached during 1954, after which many units were de-activated and during 1955 the involvement had dropped to 26 sites in the United Kingdom. During 1958, agreement of a new kind was reached when the U.S.A.F. supplied 60 Douglas Thor inter-continental ballistic missiles and assisted in their installation, whilst the R.A.F. took over the operation of missiles, which became operational during 1960. Familiar sights in the more northerly districts of the Eastern Counties, these missiles stood sentinel until April, 1963, when they were gradually dismantled and the equipment returned to the U.S.A.

Whilst flying low over the River Orwell at Ipswich during March, 1958, a U.S.A.F. P.80 Shooting Star from R.A.F. Woodbridge struck the high tension electric cables crossing the river from the Cliff Quay generating station. The damaged aircraft, leaving part of its structure with the fallen cables, managed to remain airborne and returned safely to its base. That mishap luckily did not result in any loss of life, but the U.S.A.F. had one of their fortunately infrequent tragic events during the last week of December, 1958, when two F.100 Super Sabres took off from R.A.F. Woodbridge in a climb towards Ipswich. When passing over the River Deben one of the F.100s suffered an engine fire, and the pilot ejected and landed safely. The fighter continued to climb, and then dropped its nose and eventually crashed into the house and office of Falcon Caravans on the A.12 road at

A North American F100 Super Sabre comes in over the hedge at Wethersfield. For several years this interceptor was the backbone of the U.S.A.F., being one of the first supersonic aircraft in service.

Myron Burak

Kesgrave, near Ipswich, exploding on impact. The blast killed the lady in the office, whilst an electricity meter-reader who was just entering the building was blasted on fire across the lawn and into a fish-pond, which no doubt saved his life. The jet engine careered towards the home of a Mr Ward, who was in his garden where he was enveloped by the blazing kerosene; he died later in hospital. Mrs Riches, the site owner's wife, was at the back of the building when the aircraft hit, and in her flight from the oncoming plane went through a thick hawthorn hedge almost without getting a scratch. At the time of writing, Mr Charles Riches is still recovering pieces of the F.100 as they come to the surface in his lawn.

With a shattering roar a Phantom F.4 takes off from Lakenheath with an assortment of long-range tanks and stores mounted beneath the mainplanes. Aircraft of this type also operate from R.A.F. Bentwaters and R.A.F. Woodbridge and the small national markings are unusual on this example.

U.S.A.F.

Open Day at R.A.F. Bentwaters with all eyes on the Spitfire, a Mk.XVI TE.471, whilst in the background are a Fairchild Packet, Douglas Destroyer, North American Super Sabre F.100 and a Lockheed Shooting Star.

As a result of the late President de Gaulle's decision to withdraw from N.A.T.O.* some U.S.A.F. units based in France returned to the United Kingdom during 1966, making a sizeable increase in numbers in the Eastern Counties as many of the displaced units took up residence in the region.

The 48th T.F.W.† arrived at R.A.F. Lakenheath on 15th January, 1966, from Chaumont, France. It was then equipped with the North American Super Sabre F.100 single seat interceptor, but these were exchanged during 1972 for the McDonnell F.4 Phantom two-seat interceptor, capable of becoming airborne in less than 3,000 feet and climbing to intercept at over 1,500 m.p.h. In the ground attack role they are capable of carrying 18 750 lb. bombs, 4 Sidewinder missiles, 15 680 lb. mines, 3 20 m.m. Vulcan gun pads which fire 6,000 rounds per minute, or combinations up to 15,000 lbs.

The largest U.S.A.F. facility in the United Kingdom, this airfield near Brandon covers nearly 2,000 acres, and has a base population of 10,600 persons. It also houses the main U.S.A.F. Hospital and the U.S.A.F.E.** Purchasing Region United Kingdom, covering airfields from Oslo, Norway, to Dublin, Eire.

Co-operation between the two Air Forces increased as time went by and many operations were now carried out on a joint basis, such as R.A.F. tanker aircraft refuelling U.S.A.F. fighters, and joint participation in radar and defence systems.

It is interesting to note that all the U.S.A.F. bases still carry their R.A.F. site names, i.e. R.A.F. Bentwaters, R.A.F. Sutton Heath, R.A.F. Sculthorpe etc., and all have a senior R.A.F. officer in a liaison role.

Whilst all the hustle and bustle of a big air display was going on at Bentwaters on Saturday 6th May, 1967, an American surgeon and his team operated for two hours on a nine-year-old Ipswich boy, Richard Crabtree. Whilst running underneath a parked jet, he cut open his head on the fin of a missile. Later he was transferred to an Ipswich Hospital where he recovered. The attendance at the open day was 35,000 some 10,000 more than the previous year.

During July, 1968, residents at Kesgrave and surrounding district speculated at the high pitched whine which emanated from the U.S.A.F. installation at the

*North Atlantic Treaty Organization.
†Tactical Fighter Wing.
**United States Air Forces Europe.

bottom of Bell Lane, Kesgrave. The answer was supplied by a U.S.A.F. spokesman who stated that temporary diesel-electric generators had been installed to supply power for communications equipment. A sound barrier of quilts was erected to surround the motors. The spokesman stated that the communications unit was a vital link in the N.A.T.O. system and must be in operation every minute of the night and day.

Four members of the Ipswich Peace Action Group were arrested at R.A.F. Bentwaters during the open day display on Saturday, 25th May, 1968, when they attempted to deliver a letter of protest to the commander, Colonel R. R. Melton.

Five years later, on Saturday, 24th May, 1973, no such commotion occurred when Armed Forces Day was held at Bentwaters, with a mixed batch of United States, R.A.F. and European aircraft present. The United States Naval aerobatic team "The Blue Angels" flying their six F.4.J. Phantoms performed the "breathtaker" in which four aircraft flew in a tight box with only some three feet from an aircraft's wingtip to its partner's cockpit canopy. The R.A.F. was represented by the Gnats of the "Red Arrows", the Chipmunks of the "Blue Chips" and the Jet Provosts of "The Red Pelicans". The Belgiums gave a noisy and spirited display with the "Shivers" flying Lockheed Starfighters.

During September, 1974, the U.S.A.F.'s newest jet fighter aircraft, the McDonnell Douglas F.15 Eagle, serial 10291, visited Bentwaters after flying almost 3,000 miles from the United States of America without refuelling. This was the first visit of this type to Europe, and the aircraft spent a short time at the Suffolk base prior to its visit to the Farnborough Air Show. Whilst at Bentwaters the Eagle was flown by General John W. Vogt, Junior, Commander of the U.S.A.F. in Europe and of Allied Forces in Central Europe, who was the first U.S.A.F. (Europe) pilot to fly the F.15.

At the same time, the Sikorsky S.67 Blackhawk prototype helicopter M.671SA was visiting the disused airfield at Ellough, near Beccles, Suffolk. The helicopter tragically crashed at Farnborough a few days later whilst performing a low level barrel-roll, with the loss of both the crew members.

Suffolk did well as a result of the Society of British Aerospace Constructors Show, as a gem visited Mildenhall in the shape of the Lockheed SR-71A No. 17972 on 9th September, 1974. The all-black Blackbird had recently broken the Atlantic crossing record with a timed run from New York to London of 1 hour 55¾ minutes. It was also attempting a record run home to California from Mildenhall, but owing to mechanical trouble it took 3 hours 47 minutes to cover the 5,645 miles.

Mildenhall saw another unusual visitor during January, 1975, when a Lockheed U-2, strategic reconnaissance aircraft, serial No. 68-10345, devoid of all national markings, and with an unusually long nose section, arrived there. Later in the year, during May, five more Lockheed U-2C's from the 344th Strategic Reconnaissance Squadron 100th Wing of the Strategic Air Command under command of the 3rd U.S.A.F. arrived at Mildenhall.

A modern maid of all work, the Lockheed C130 Hercules, powered by four Allison turbo-props, operates with U.S.A.F. units in the region, as well as several from other Air Forces when they make exchange visits
Myron Burak

Purported to be carrying out precision navigational exercises, the aircraft were said by the Press to be taking part in a project to detect the operation of electronic transmissions on the ground. One of the U.2Cs, No. 66700, crashed on 29th May near Winterburg in Germany, but the pilot ejected.

A nostalgic return was made during June, 1975, when a large party of ex-U.S.A.A.F. personnel visited the Eastern Counties to see the old bases. Visiting Duxford they saw the B24J Liberator 258522 and the Mustang P51D 472258 currently based at the East Anglian Aviation Society and Imperial War Museum collections. Among the party was the well-known film star and ex-U.S.A.A.F. pilot, Mr James Stewart, who had served at Tibenham, Norfolk during the War.

R.A.F. Mildenhall has a background unparalleled by other United Kingdom bases as it was the first "modern" aerodrome to be built in the early 1930s. The first "Yanks" didn't arrive at Mildenhall until August, 1950, when a detachment of the 28th Weather Squadron was posted there and is still stationed there.

It was not until 1966 and the arrival of the 513th Tactical Airlift Wing from France that Mildenhall became a fully operational U.S.A.F. base. Since that time the base has been one of the busiest in England.

Boeing Flying Command Post 10282 of the U.S.A.F. at Mildenhall. These aircraft can be used as flying tankers.
U.S.A.F.

A giant Lockheed C.141 Starlifter of the 438th Military Air Wing, Military Airlift Command rests at Mildenhall. A turbo-prop C.133 can be seen behind it and both these aircraft types are regular visitors to this base, flying non-stop from airfields in the U.S.A. *U.S.A.F.*

Formed on the 6th April, 1966, at Evreux Air Base, France, the unit was equipped with the Lockheed C-130 Hercules four-turbo-prop-engined heavy transport. Weeks after the wing's formation, an announcement from the Secretary of Defence stated that the 513th would move to Mildenhall on 1st July, the first U.S.A.F. unit to leave France as part of the American withdrawal.

On 1st July, 1967, the unit was re-designated 513th Tactical Airlift Wing and shortly afterwards received the Air Force Outstanding Unit Award for its movement performance and its participation in Exercise Pathfinder Express, the largest joint Spanish/United States exercise ever held.

The 513th usually has two squadrons of C-130s which rotate from the U.S.A., and is supported by the 5th Aerial Port Squadron, the only one of its kind in Europe. The 10th Airborne Command Control Squadron rounds off the operational side of the base, flying Boeing EC-135 aircraft which provide an aerial communication platform for the European Command. One-half to two-thirds of the U.S.A.F.'s tactical airlift force in Europe is provided by the 513th T.A.W. and its area of operation covers all Europe and parts of the Middle East and Africa.

Mildenhall is also the main entry airport for U.S.A.F. aircraft from the United States, and massive facilities are provided to cover all aspects of the military airline role. Its runways are used by many giant aircraft such as the Lockheed C-5 Galaxy, the Lockheed C-141 Starlifter, Boeing EC-135 Stratotanker, C-135 Stratolifter and the C-133 Cargomaster.

The 81st Tactical Fighter Wing came to the United Kingdom on 28th July, 1951, the first aircraft, North American Sabrejets, touching down at R.A.F. Bentwaters, near Woodbridge, and Shepherd's Grove, near Bury St Edmunds. Six months later it converted to the Republic F.84F Thunderstreak and was redesignated the 81st Fighter-Bomber Wing. Early in 1955 the Wing was scattered round three bases, the 91st Squadron at Bentwaters the 78th at Shepherd's Grove and the 92nd at Manston, Kent. During 1957, another move was made when the 78th transferred

Resembling a manned missile, the stub winged Lockheed F104 Starfighter of the U.S.A.F. draws the crowds when it appears at Open Days such as this one at Wethersfield during 1967. *Myron Burak*

to Woodbridge (Sutton Heath) and the 92nd to Bentwaters. Re-designated again on 8th July, 1958, the Wing became the 81st Tactical Fighter Wing and on 4th December received its new aircraft, the McDonnell F.101 Voodoo, which lasted until 1965, when it re-equipped with the McDonnell F4C Phantom. At the present time the 81st T.F.W. maintains three tactical fighter squadrons at R.A.F. Bentwaters and Woodbridge, the 91st T.F.S.* (Bluestreaks) and the 92nd T.F.S. (Avengers) at Bentwaters, and the 78th T.F.S. (Bushmasters) at Woodbridge, all prepared to conduct all-weather tactical air operations as directed by higher command.

The 81st Tactical Fighter Wing when equipped with the McDonnell Voodoo F.101 aircraft at Bentwaters helped to build up 100,000 hours on this type of machine. When Colonel William C. Clark, the Commander of the 81st T.F.W., landed his F.101A, at Bentwaters on 8th August, 1963, it had registered that number of hours. This time had been recorded since the aircraft arrived in England during January, 1959.

Sixty Voodoo aircraft flew at 1,300 feet and 2,000 men lined the edge of the runway when the new Wing Commander of the 81st T.F.W. was installed. Colonel Robin Olds, who graduated from West Point during 1943, was a well-known

*Tactical Fighter Squadron.

footballer in the U.S.A. and this was not his first visit to the United Kingdom as he served in England during the Second World War.

In May the following year, the 81st T.F.W., still at Bentwaters, was awarded the U.S.A.F. Flying Safety Award, Major-General R. W. Puryear presenting the award plaque to Colonel Robin Olds.

A McDonnell F4C Phantom jet fighter crashed whilst landing at Woodbridge on 13th September, 1967, but the two-man crew ejected safely using the aircraft's English-made ejector seats. They were Captain Joseph T. Kirling and First Lieutenant James B. Pierce, whose £600,000 aircraft belonged to the 78th Tactical Fighter Squadron. Mr J. A. Bloomfield of Sutton who witnessed the crash said, "There were two of them flying together and they started to turn and then one broke away from the other. It went over on its back, then made a screaming noise and went straight into the ground where it dug a large crater."

Current Press records state that Bentwaters will be the first European unit to receive the new McDonnell Eagle air-superiority fighter. Woodbridge houses the 67th Aerospace Rescue and Recovery Squadron (A.R.R.S.) which moved to its present home from Moron, Spain, in early 1970 to provide greater rescue coverage in the North Atlantic. As the world's largest rescue squadron it is charged with responsibility for an area which stretches from the North to the South Poles and from mid-Atlantic to the border of Burma, an area of approximately 68,000,000 square miles. To carry out these tasks the 67th A.R.R.S. uses the Lockheed Hc-130 Hercules which has a range of 4,000 miles, and the Sikorsky Super Jolly Green Giant HH.53C helicopters, the largest and fastest rotary wing aircraft available.

In addition to these duties the 67th A.R.R.S. had the primary recovery responsibility for Atlantic Ocean splashdowns of N.A.S.A. space endeavours. It covered all the Apollo missions and also the Skylab projects.

The work of the unit is summed up in its creed and motto: —

It is my duty as a member of the AEROSPACE RESCUE AND RECOVERY SERVICE to save life and aid the injured. I will prepare at all times to perform my assigned duties quickly and efficiently, placing these duties above personal desires and comforts.

Known worldwide for over three decades, the Douglas C.47 or Dakota has served as a universal workhorse, and can still be seen over the region now on civil freighting work.   *Myron Burak*

Other U.S.A.F. bases in the region were at Wethersfield in Essex which operated the F.100 Super Sabre and laterly the Lockheed U.2s and at Sculthorpe in Norfolk, which housed a variety of U.S.A.F. aircraft, and in 1976 it was planned that it will be the home of aircraft which have finished their service with N.A.T.O. Air Forces and have been returned to the U.S.A.F. In addition to the airfields proper, many U.S.A.F. installations of one type or another exist in the region, such as the large U.S.A.F. Transportation Centre at Felixstowe Dock, and many jointly operated with the R.A.F. on sites covering radar and communications.

The first U.S.A.F. aircraft to land at Ipswich Airport since the Second World War touched down on 10th July, 1975, when a Jolly Green Giant HH.53C helicopter from the 67th A.R.R.S. based at Woodbridge arrived. It dropped off Lieutenant Loren C. Stendahl, Sergeant Russell J. Tanner and Airman First Class Gordon F. Randolph, plus several items of equipment. The reason for the visit was to give a lecture on air sea rescue to Air Cadets learning to fly at the Airport. The HH.53C was about to go on "Standby" for the last Apollo space flight to link up with the Russians.

Although now operating from fewer bases than during the War, the U.S.A.F. is part and parcel of the life of the Eastern Counties. The members of the U.S.A.F. live not only on the bases but in the towns and villages of the region, and in many ways join in the activities of the community. Many of the larger types of cars seem to have disappeared, giving way to the smaller British types, the shortage of fuel appearing to be a common leveller! Nevertheless the U.S.A.F. and its members are no longer regarded as the "gum-chewing Yanks" but partners in the air defence system of N.A.T.O.

T.29, 017892 piston engined short haul transport based at Mildenhall and used for flights to other European U.S.A.F. airfields. *U.S.A.F.*

CHAPTER TWELVE

Commercials

E AST Anglia's first international airline, based at Southend and later at Stansted in Essex, was inaugurated during 1946 by Squadron Leader R. J. Jones, an ex-R.A.F. Transport Command pilot who had also served in the Royal Navy as well as doing a spell as a farmer.

His first aircraft, an early 1930 De Havilland Puss Moth registered G-ABKZ was the forerunner of what was later to be a large fleet of modern aircraft. The name on the three-seat monoplane was East Anglian Flying Services. Operating in the southern sector of the region, it spent its first season flying from a field close by a holiday camp at Herne Bay, Kent, where holiday makers were taken aloft for a short joy flight at ten shillings a time. Formed as a company on 16th August, 1946, East Anglian Flying Services gave many people their first glimpses of Canterbury from the air during that first summer.

Southend Corporation's new municipal airport opened on 1st January, 1947 at Rochford, the ex-R.A.F. fighter airfield on the outskirts of the town, and so for the 1947 season Squadron Leader Jones moved back to his home town and became the first resident operator. The need for more staff now arose, and so Captain Hugo Parsons and Captain Angus Pascoe joined the company. The advent of a regular service came during early 1947 when a service was run from Southend Airport to Rochester Airport in Kent, and this continued into the following year. The firm was now able to boast a fleet of nine aircraft, five De Havilland Dragon Rapides, a Miles Aerovan G-AJKM, an Auster, an Airspeed Courier and the original Puss Moth. The Aerovan made its mark in aviation history during 1947 when this low powered transport flew a charter flight to Cyprus and back with a party of Servicemen's children.

Business was brisk, and the young company opened its wings and pioneered inclusive holiday tours to Ostend in conjunction with two tour operators, the first British independent airline to do so. So promising was the first year's results that Squadron Leader Jones decided that the next step would be to go for more of this business and a licence was obtained for a scheduled service to Ostend from Southend. Another licence obtained was that for the Channel Isles route to Jersey and coupled with the holiday side, this arrangement offered good traffic.

Restrictions in foreign travel and currency difficulties brought about by the severe economic conditions during 1951 almost killed off the promising little airline. Only the joy flights now kept E.A.F.S. alive with "Jack" Jones doing the flying, the other two members of the staff temporarily taking up again their previous trades as a tailor and garage owner.

Appearing almost motionless a Channel Airways Dakota wheels into Ipswich Airport.

Nicknamed "The Whispering Giant", the Bristol Britannia turbo-prop airliner is no stranger to the Eastern Counties in the house colours of British United Airways. *Myron Burak*

However, keeping its head above water E.A.F.S. soldiered on and kept solvent and so during 1953 a long lease was taken out on Ipswich Airport, it being anticipated that this site would become a secondary charter base. Further routes were opened, including the one to Paris, Guernsey and Rotterdam and soon things were looking very promising again. Three De Havilland Dove twin-engined feeder airliners were purchased from West African Airways Corporation, followed by two Bristol 170 Wayfarers. During 1957 these aircraft carried the remarkable number of 30,000 passengers on the various routes.

The little airline had its ups and downs and the various members of the staff carried on all manner of duties other than their allotted ones in order to see the job well done. Mr Leslie Firman of Ipswich recalls flying back from Paris one autumn in the early days in one of the Rapides. Having cruised for some time towards England, the pilot appeared to be having some difficulty in locating his bearings, and sought advice from his passengers. As both pilot and passengers scanned the shrouded surface of the sea hoping to sight the coast, the Cork lightvessel off Felixstowe hove into sight, whereupon they were able to make for the coast, locate the River Orwell and fly up it until Ipswich Airport came into sight on its banks.

On 29th October, 1962 the company changed its title to Channel Airways and bought up another Southend based company which had fallen on bad times, Tradair, and which counted among its fleet Vickers Vikings, Douglas DC.3s (Dakotas) and a four-engined Douglas DC.4 ex-Skymaster. The incorporation of Tradair marked another advance as Channel Airways now possessed their first turbine powered aircraft, a Vickers Viscount Series 700. This spurred the company to go ahead with re-equipment and it purchased another seven Viscount 700s from British European Airways, two from Bahamas Airways and one from Starways, eleven Viscount 812s from the American Continental Air Lines, which had run into trouble, and then also placed an order for four Hawker Siddeley 748 twin-engined medium range airliners. The largest order the company placed was that of £5.5m. for B.A.C. One-Elevens.

Another step forward was taken when a subsidiary named Mediterranean Holidays Limited was formed to deal with the holiday side of the business, with sales offices throughout the Eastern Counties. A new service came into operation named the "Scottish Flyer", the firm's first venture into the bus-stop type of air travel, linking Southend with Aberdeen, intermediate stops being made at Ipswich, Norwich, Leeds, Teesside, Newcastle and Edinburgh. This service was operated by the new turbo-prop Hawker Siddeley 748s, the four of which had been delivered at a cost of £1.5 million. For the first time, they brought big airline comfort to the grass surfaced airfields of the region, and the outward bound departure from Ipswich at around 10.00 hours each day was always an impressive sight. The

Undergoing maintenance in the front of the hangar a Channel Airways De Havilland Dove G-ANVU is prepared for the next day's work. Used on the internal routes these were regular visitors to Ipswich and Norwich as well as Southend their home base.

quietness of the Rolls-Royce built turbo-props was in marked contrast to the roar of the Dakota's Wright Cyclones as they climbed out in a far shallower circuit.

Channel Airways' next move to Stansted was necessary in order to operate its newly acquired Hawker Siddeley Tridents and Comets. All Channel's new jet aircraft were adorned with golden fins and became known as the "Golden Fleet". With these machines the company was able to operate further afield, the Tridents going as far as Istanbul, Turkey, when they operated on a Berlin based contract. Working for the large operators such as Cosmos, Clarkson's, Lyons, Wallace Arnold and Martin Rooks, Channel airlines aircraft could now be seen at the majority of the Continental airports. With the new concept of holidays in the sun, the aircraft were kept busy for most of the year, but all major maintenance was carried out during the winter months, and any surplus aircraft were chartered out so that they were never laid up.

Thus in 1971, the streamlined and modernized fleet comprised two Trident IE.140s, two B.A.C. One-Eleven Series 400s, five Comet 4Bs and one Comet 4, nine Viscount 812s and six Heron feeder liners. All looked well, until that fateful day during 1973 when the axe fell and the money tragically ran out. Overnight Channel was no more, its aircraft grounded, offices closed, and crews looking for other jobs. What had been one of the big independents, with 27 years service to the Eastern Counties and a staff of over 430, just disappeared. Aircraft were picketted out awaiting buyers, and when sold eventually appeared again in the house colours of other airlines.

Southend Airport still has a scheduled service to the Continent, operated by British Air Ferries Limited (B.A.F.) and British Midland. B.A.F. are unique in that they operate the bulbous nosed Douglas DC6 conversion known as the Carvair A.T.L.98, designed and converted by Aviation Traders (Engineering) Limited at their Southend works. With a capacity of between 17 and 65 passengers and three to five cars or equivalent cargo, these aircraft carry a steady stream of cars to the Continent. The first flight of the Carvair took place on 21st June 1961 with Mr D. B. Cantledge at the controls.

Aviation Traders (Engineering) Limited or A.T.E.L. was formed during 1940, starting in the aircraft maintenance field but later launching out and designing a twin engined medium range turbo-prop airliner similar to the Hawker Siddeley 748 and named the Accountant; unfortunately it did not go into production. The first flight of the A.T.L.90 Accountant I took place during July, 1957, the aircraft being registered G-41-1, and later appropriately enough G-ATEL. It successfully passed through all its tests, but was abandoned and scrapped during February 1960.

During 1956 A.T.E.L. bought 149 surplus R.A.F. Percival Prentice single engined trainers with a view to converting them for civil use. Many of these aircraft had served with No. 3 Flying Training School at Feltwell, Norfolk, and later with the Air Signalling School at Swanton Morley in the same county. Between April and July 92 of these aircraft went to Southend, the remainder going to Stansted. The high cost of conversion killed off this enterprise, and eventually when only a few aircraft had been sold the residue were scrapped. The last unconverted example G-AOPY which had spent its life in a children's playground at Basildon, Essex, finally disappeared during March 1975, and was carried away to a scrapyard. One of the last flying examples is G-AOW, which operates from Aberdeen but returns to East Anglia occasionally for overhaul by Air Anglia at Norwich. Still mainly engaged in the component design and manufacture field, A.T.E.L. carries out work for the major contractors and can count among its achievements the design of the air intake dump doors for Concorde.

During 1950, several Handley-Page Halton HP.70s (ex Halifax bombers) were operated from Southend Airport by Bard Air Services Limited and Aviation Traders Limited, but all were scrapped there by the end of the year. The Haltons included ex-B.O.A.C. G-AHON "Flamborough", G-AHDO "Forfar", G-AHDS "Fremantle", G-AHDU "Falkirk" and G-AHDN "Falaise".

Later in the year, several HP.71 Halifax Mk.9s were flown to Southend for conversion by A.T.E.L. but although nine were refurbished for the Egyptian Air Force, the balance of eighteen at Southend were scrapped for spares.

Southend as an airport had one of its very few accidents on 9th October, 1960, when a Handley-Page Hermes 4 G-ALDC "James Robertson Justice" owned by Falcon Airways Limited made a crash landing, finishing up on the railway line alongside the airfield, resulting in its scrapping.

North from Southend in mid-Essex lies Stansted, the possible third airport for London, with its long runway which can accommodate the largest modern jet aircraft. Used mainly in the freight role, its visitors include the large CL44 freighters of Transmeridian which carry out large amounts of freight annually.

During May, 1967, opposition to the Government's decision to build London's third airport at Stansted grew stronger. The South Essex Economic Planning Committee, annoyed because it had not been consulted (though it did not exist when the enquiry was held, and the rules apparently precluded consultations after the enquiry and before a decision was made), came out against Stansted on regional planning grounds and thought a Thames Estuary site would be more favourable. Foulness was suggested as an alternative, before the further proposal of a site on the Maplin Sands was put forward. Ipswich was concerned at the Stansted proposal, as it would mean a high level stacking area over the town and surrounding district, some 20 miles long at top level and 15 miles wide over Sudbury, Needham Market, Wickham Market, Felixstowe and Harwich. In this area, airliners would be in waiting stacks at 1,000 feet levels from 10,000 feet to 14,000 feet. This area also includes the military flight patterns of R.A.F. Wattisham, Bentwaters and Woodbridge, and although these stacking arrangements would only be used when certain conditions prevailed it was thought that a certain amount of risk existed.

During 1975 controversy began to rage again about the siting of the new proposed four runway London Airport, after the cancelling of the Maplin Sands project. Essex County Council recommended Cublington, Buckinghamshire and Thurleigh, Bedfordshire, in order to take the limelight off Stansted, a favourite because of its existing facilities. Although with a passenger handling capacity of 3,000,000 passengers per year, Stansted only handles some 200,000 at the moment, due to the demise of some of the operating companies. Equipped with modern terminal buildings, a large apron and a road link with London via the M.11 Motorway, it also boasts a 3,048 metre runway, one of the longest in the U.K. It is anticipated that the British Airports Authority will, however, make further moves to enlarge this airport, and it has already taken steps to enlarge the airspace by making a Special Rules Zone operating from 24th April, 1975.

Also at Stansted, occupying buildings originally constructed for the U.S.A.F., is the Civil Aviation Authorities Fire Service Training School. Moving to Essex from Cardiff during 1959, the school trains the fire prevention personnel from Britain's airports, as well as students from overseas.

Equipped with a modern fire station, watch-tower, drill tower and smoke chamber, it also has its resident aircraft for training purposes. These fall into two categories, those used for rescue operations, which are fully fitted out with life-like articulated dummy passengers and crew, and others which are used for firework. This takes place on a realistic area, with a variety of ground surfaces, and the aircraft are "fired" for the students to extinguish. If the crews are fast enough, the same aircraft can be used several times. The types range from service fighters and bombers to large commercial jet-liners. Research work is also carried out in connection with the guidance and movements of fire and rescue vehicles.

Another interesting unit at Stansted is the Civil Aviation Flying Unit, which operates two Hawker Siddeley 748s, G-AVXI and G-AVXJ, for radio calibrating work and radar research. By the very nature of their work, much of the flying is carried out in peak conditions.

Turning north-east we come to the university city of Cambridge, another centre of East Anglian flying and the site of the region's only other aircraft industry, Marshalls of Cambridge (Engineering) Limited, under the chairmanship of Sir Arthur Marshall.

Cambridge Airport was opened on 8th October, 1938, by the then Secretary of State for Air, Sir Kingsley Wood, who arrived in the Air Councils D.H. 86. The Spitfire Is of No. 19 Squadron from nearby Duxford made their public debut during the afternoon, rather stealing the thunder from nine Avro Tutors of the resident Cambridge University Air Squadron. Both civil and service reserve flying carried on until the outbreak of hostilities, when all civil aviation ceased, the majority of the light aeroplanes being impressed, many serving with No. 22 Elementary Flying Training School based at the airfield.

Service aircraft resided for a while after Dunkirk when Lysanders of No. 16 Squadron flew coastal patrols around the north Norfolk coast, until replaced by machines of No. 2 Squadron.

With the increase of the aeroplane population in the region, Marshalls rapidly expanded and carried out a large amount of repair and modification work at Cambridge, as well as sending civilian working parties to many R.A.F. Stations. Many service aircraft including Whitleys, Albemarles, Oxfords, Gladiators and the powerful Typhoon came direct from the factories for modification and overhaul. During 1943 the first of many Mosquitoes arrived for modification, and Marshalls worked on this type right through until the 1950s. During the war years, Marshalls' labour force grew until at one time it reached over 3,200, but with the workload dropping off after the war it was down to approximately 1,200 during 1946.

Another wartime achievement of Marshalls was the Elementary Flying Training School No. 29, which they operated for the R.A.F. at Clyffe Pypard in Wiltshire, using the ever faithful D.H. Tiger Moth.

With the return of peace, civil flying came into being again, the majority of the types available being ex-service aircraft. Charter flying also sprang into being, one of the first aircraft to be used for this purpose being a De Havilland Dragon Rapide G-AHED, which after many years hard work is now preserved in the Royal Air Force Museum at Hendon as RL-962.

When the aircraft work fell off, Marshalls looked around for fresh outlets for their efforts, and ventured into the commercial vehicle body building field. From small beginnings, it has now grown into a part of the firm which is internationally renowned for the excellence of its design and workmanship.

Cambridge was the starting point during August, 1948, for a local housewife, Mrs Richanda Morrow-Tait, who was attempting a round the world flight in a light aircraft. Named "Thursday's Child", the Chrislea Super Ace, G-AKUV, chosen for the flight unfortunately met with a landing accident and was ruled out for the flight. Replacing the damaged aeroplane by a Percival Proctor IV G-AJMU bearing the same name, the intrepid lady pilot and her navigator, Mr Michael Townsend, set out on 18th August. After many adventures the aircraft arrived in Alaska during November, after covering half its journey, but in attempting a landing on the Alaska Highway it was damaged beyond immediate repair, and the navigator decided that he had had enough and returned to the United Kingdom.

Mrs Morrow-Tait shopped around for another aircraft and eventually purchased an American built Vultee BT13A low wing monoplane, which became "Next Thursday's Child", and after another series of adventures the flying housewife made Croydon on 19th August, 1949, 366 days later. The plane was ferried to Cambridge where it spent a considerable time picketted out, until suddenly it disappeared, no one quite knowing where it went.

With more aircraft business available, Marshalls were now in the modification and conversion field more and more, work on Vampires, Venoms and Canberras being on the increase. When the Lockheed Hercules C-130 four-engined heavy transport was introduced into Europe, Marshalls were appointed the European centre and carried out all painting and modifications for the manufacturers. Thus it is that when one passes their works, aircraft of this type are to be seen in the colours of many different Air Forces. Another sight is numbers of Viscounts, Vanguards and Britannias awaiting their turn for refurbishing or overhaul, to emerge some time later in the colours of a different airline bound for some far corner of the globe.

Marshalls were responsible for another Eastern Counties design when during the 1960's they redesigned the Auster VII, VF.665, with a new wing and powered by a Harwich-manufactured Budworth gas turbine. Known as the MA-4, the aircraft met with disaster when it dived into the ground on 8th March, 1966, both crew members being killed instantly.

Further east, at Norwich Airport, Horsham St Faiths, Air Anglia operates its scheduled services to the Continent with increasing frequency, using at the present time the Dutch-built Rolls Royce turbo-prop powered Fokker F.27 Friendship. Like the other operators in the area, Air Anglia started in a small way, being formed from three former air charter companies. Norfolk Airways was founded during 1950 by Mr James Crampton, an experienced aviator with many hours flying taxi work and charters combined with pleasure flights from Clacton during the summer. The original equipment was an American built Fairchild Argus four seat high wing monoplane with a Warner Scarab radial motor. During 1950 Anglia Air Charter was founded by Mr Gordon Wright, who, flying from Caister near Great Yarmouth, carried out local charter flights and taxi work. With the advent of the North Sea gas and oil industry more work became available and the two companies formed a joint venture called Rig-Air in order to offer a better service, operating a Dakota G-AMPZ, Islander G-AXUP and a Cessna 172.

During 1970 the three firms merged to become Air Anglia, and began daily flights to Amsterdam. Making a cautious approach, they also started a service from Norwich to Edinburgh and Aberdeen, operating a Britten-Norman Islander, which proved so successful that a further aircraft of the same type was brought into service. New routes were inaugurated with journeys to Manchester and Liverpool and later in the year, to Cambridge and Jersey.

At this time another new company known as Progressive Airways joined in the operations from Norwich, but apart from applying for licences, this company did little and it had faded out by August, 1971. One aircraft did appear in Progressive Airways colours, a De Havilland DH114 Heron II four engined feeder airliner named "City of Norwich".

Still engaged in the oil rig industry, Air Anglia now also has a base at Dyce near Aberdeen and runs an East Anglia service for the movement of oil company personnel. With a potential market of two million East Anglians, Air Anglia provides links between Norwich and the Continent and also with the north east of England and Scotland. Anglia Holidays is a wholly owned subsidiary of the parent company and operates taxis in the United Kingdom and Europe. During 1975 the fleet comprised the 44-seat Fokker Friendships, 36-seat Dakotas, 8-seater Navajo and 5-seater Aztec. Another facet of the company's operations is the executive charter service provided for such local companies as the Norwich Union, Rowntree-Mackintosh and Erie Electronics. Air Anglia have also during the present year been granted a licence to carry Her Majesty's mails between Norwich and Aberdeen, and before leaving the company, it is interesting to record that until recently the company operated a real veteran machine, Douglas DC-3, G-AOBN, a delight to see still in the skies of the region.

Also operating from Norwich is another charter firm, Peters Aviation, also in the oil business and using on the Norwich-Aberdeen route three De Havilland Heron IB's, G-ANSZ, G-ANXB and G-APKW. Charters are flown to anywhere in the United Kingdom and frequent trips are also made to the Continent. This lively concern, under the managership of Mr Ridley Thomas, demonstrates that it is not necessary to use ultra-modern equipment to keep abreast of the times.

Fortunately civil aircraft crashes in the region are rare. A lucky escape came to a Fanjet Falcon of Norwegian ownership LN-FOE which crashed during take-off at Norwich on 18th December, 1973. The twin-engined jet flew into a flock of birds when it was only just airborne and managed to make a fast wheels-up landing on the edge of the airfield, luckily without fire resulting. The aircraft was dismantled at Norwich and flown back to the manufacturers in France later in the year in a massive French-owned Super Guppie Freight aircraft. Earlier in the year, members of a party of farmers returning from an agricultural show were killed at Shipdham, Norfolk, as their Piper Twin Comanche G-AXPW crashed as it approached the airfield in the dusk. The following year Harwich business man and engineer Mr David Budworth was killed when an aircraft of the same type crashed as he was approaching Norwich Airport.

As a result of trials carried out during 1947 by the G.P.O. and B.E.A. with helicopters operating a mail service in the West of England, it was decided that rural areas of Norfolk and Suffolk could benefit from such a service. The basis of the scheme was that mail would be collected from a main distribution centre on a main railway line, in this case Peterborough, and then flown round several rural distributing and collecting points, the collected mails being despatched via the rail centre again.

Using a Westland Sikorsky S.51 helicopter powered by a 450 h.p. Pratt and Whitney air-cooled radial motor giving it a top speed of 103 m.p.h. and a cruising speed of 85 m.p.h., a primary service was flown on 12th May, 1948. The route was from Peterborough, with the Norfolk stops at King's Lynn, Wells, Sheringham and Dereham. Having proved the route, dummy mail was conveyed from 24th to 29th May, in preparation for the real thing.

The experimental service began on 1st June with outward calls at King's Lynn, Wells, Sheringham, Cromer, Norwich, Thetford, Diss, Harleston and Great Yarmouth. The homeward journey brought in Lowestoft, Beccles, Norwich and Dereham, with the collected mail put on the mailtrain at Peterborough. A time of 2 hours 54 minutes was taken for the outward run, and 1 hour 55 minutes for the return, these times allowing five minutes at Norwich for refuelling. Some 13,000 letters were posted in the area for the initial flight for which no airmail fee was charged, but B.E.A. did commemmorate the occasion with special envelopes. The service operated Monday to Friday, whilst on Saturday a morning service only was flown from Peterborough to Norwich and return, the last flight being made on 25th September. The average amount of mail carried per flight was about 680 lbs.

Reporting on the operation, the Post Office showed that it was reliable with 95 per cent success. On two days the service was cancelled due to fog and on another occasion the aircraft was delayed ten minutes, again because of fog.

After the successful daylight flights of the previous year, B.E.A. and the G.P.O. embarked on a series of night mail carrying flights, starting with some proving flights between Peterborough and Downham Market. The full service, inaugurated on 17th October, 1949, between Peterborough and Norwich, also proved successful and operated two-way at night until 15th April, 1950, with only a few services cancelled due to weather conditions. The take-offs were timed for 01.50 hours with arrival at Norwich at 02.46 hours, the aircraft being a Westland Sikorsky S.51 registered G-AJOV.

The airspace above the relatively sparsely populated countryside of Norfolk was sometimes used for test-flying new aircraft. The Hawker Siddeley, ex-De Havilland, Trident IC G-ARPY was on its maiden flight from the builder's airfield at Hatfield early in June, 1966, and was carrying out stalling tests in the area north of Norwich when disaster struck.

It went into a deep stall and a resultant flat spin from which the crew could not extricate it. All four of the crew died as the aircraft crashed at Felthorpe.

Sikorsky Dragonfly G-AJDV belonging to British European Airways and on hire to the Post Office for Helicopter Mail Trials takes on its cargo at Beccles, Suffolk. The area of cut grass illustrates the small space needed for these type of operations. *Mrs G. Wilton*

At the inquest on the pilot, Mr Peter Barlow, 2nd pilot Mr Geoffrey Errington, flight engineer Mr Edgar Blackstone-Brown and radio operator Mr Charles Patterson, the coroner said that the four men had performed a great service to British aviation. They were, he said, all at the zenith of their careers and had done great service to Britain in their lives, whatever the circumstances of their deaths.

As a result of the investigation into this crash the tail unit of the Trident was modified to prevent a similar accident occurring again.

In a large country house not far from Norwich is a rural aircraft manufacturing centre, producing unorthodox aircraft at that, Reymerston Hall is the place, and the man behind it all Wing Commander K. H. Wallis, C.Eng., A.F.R.Ae.S., R.A.F. Retired. Followers of James Bond films will be familiar with Mr Wallis's aircraft, firing rockets, dropping bombs and roaring all over the sky.

Wing Commander Wallis is a member of a family which has been linked with flying since 1909, when his forebears constructed one of the first aeroplanes to be made in the Eastern Counties, the "Wallbro Monoplane". The Wallis family are at present engaged in constructing a replica of this early aircraft, Wing Commander Wallis being fortunate in having photographs of the original machine. After the aeroplane, Mr Wallis Senior turned to airscrew-driven hydroplanes, all of which were named "Per Ardua" and during 1957 Wing Commander Wallis won the Missouri Marathon in "Per Ardua VIII".

Learning to fly during 1937 at Marshalls, Cambridge, young Wallis made it after twelve hours, and £14, and eventually joined the Civil Air Guard and then at the outbreak of war the R.A.F.V.R.

Always interested in rotary-winged aircraft, Wing Commander Wallis studied the German aircraft captured by the Allies and mulled over the technical problems until during 1957, when on an exchange visit to the U.S.A.F. Strategic Air Command, he was able to glean more information. On his return to the U.K. he made a start on the construction of an ultra-light autogyro.

The first Wallis "rotary", "The Argyle" G-ARRT, which took to the air during May, 1959, was used mainly in the capacity of a "test hack". Next followed WA.116 which made its debut during August, 1961, at the A. & A.E.E.* Boscombe Down, and this raised military interest. As a result several WA.116's were constructed by Beagle Aircraft Limited for Army Trials, but the service was already interested in helicopters and thus the autogyro venture was short-lived.

Leaving the Royal Air Force during 1964, Wing Commander Wallis formed Wallis Autogyros Limited with his cousin Mr G. V. Wallis and his wife as co-directors, and proceeded with small scale production of WA.116s at Cambridge.

During 1966, much time was spent in flying the Wallis "gyros" for film work in Brazil, Japan, Italy and Spain, and during 1968 the WA.116 prototype gained the autogyro altitude record, 15,220 feet. The speed record fell to Wing Commander Wallis in 1969 and the closed circuit range record during 1974.

Further development resulted in a series of new designs, the WA.117, the

*Aircraft and Armament Experimental Establishment.

Wing Commander Kenneth Wallis in his record breaking Wallis autogyro G-ATHM in which he set up a new distance flight record for this type of aircraft. The long-range petrol tank which made this possible can be seen beneath the fuselage and also worthy of note is the simplicity of this small aircraft.

W/C. K. Wallis

WA.118 "Meteorite", the WA.120, and the WA.121, G-BAHN. At the present time, eleven machines operate from Reymerston Hall. An unusual assignment during 1970 was when the WA.117, G-AVJU, specially silenced, was used in the Loch Ness investigations.

For his outstanding work in this field, Wing Commander Wallis was awarded the Alan Marsh Medal in 1963, the Seagrave Trophy in 1969 and the Breguet Trophy five years later.

From this picturesque Norfolk base has sprung technology of a high standard in an interesting field, and another approach to man's search for safety in the air. It has resulted in the breaking of several records and on 28th September, 1975, Wallis WA.116/F, G-ATHM was flown by the designer from Lydd in Kent to Wick in the north of Scotland to set a new world record for autogyros. Average speed was 92 m.p.h., time in the air 6 hours 25 minutes, and the fuel consumption was 24 miles per gallon, with a 60 h.p. Franklin engine.

From Reymerston one flies east to reach Great Yarmouth and the North Denes airfield, used as a base for rig servicing helicopters and pleasure flight light aircraft during the holiday season. A grass surfaced airfield, it is ideally suited for helicopter operations, but with the rapidly encroaching housing estates plans have been submitted for the site to become a holiday leisure area, or as an alternative, an industrial commercial area. Mr L. F. Whight, who opened the airfield, is the joint managing director of Air Anglia, and he has submitted that the field is not used to capacity and that operations would be better suited at Norwich. During the holiday season of 1970, Anglian Air Charter Limited operated an Islander BN2A G-AXVP light feeder airliner, one of the original Air Anglia machines, from the North Denes.

Few inventors can have had so great an impact on established technology as Mr Christopher Cockerell, now Sir Christopher, who having retired from a senior position with Marconi's in the electronic field was running a small boat building establishment in Norfolk and investigating the problem of cutting down the friction of a boat's passage through water. One Saturday evening in 1954, he decided to put his latest idea to the test, and using a vacuum cleaner and some empty coffee tins, he proved for the first time the hover principle.

After further experiments involving the building of a series of successful models, the time seemed ripe for the building of a full-size machine. This was built by Saunders-Roe on the Isle of Wight and completed on 28th May, 1958. On 25th July, 1959, it made the first successful crossing of the English Channel by this new kind of craft and from this machine have stemmed the large fast craft which now cross the Channel several times each day.

When British Overseas Corporation disbanded its flying boat operations several of the aircraft came to Felixstowe for storage and stood at the back of the hangars until 1953 when Aquila Airways purchased a few, which returned to Hamble. The remainder presented a sorrowful sight as they gradually succumbed to the elements, and grass could be seen growing in the control surface gaps and out of the engine cowlings. The boats were eventually sold to a scrap merchant, broken up and carried away from the place where the prototypes had been tested some years earlier.

Ipswich Airport had originally been opened in 1932 by the Prince of Wales, who had remarked at the time on the excellence of the site and its nearness to the town of Ipswich. Extended and reopened by the Whitney Straight Corporation during July, 1938, it became the home of R.A.F. light bomber squadrons at the outbreak of hostilities.

After the war flying gradually gathered momentum but the greatest step forward was made during 1955 when Channel Airways took over the lease and started rebuilding the airport buildings, operated scheduled services and ran the flying school which was part of the leasing agreement. Development of the services continued apace, with coaches running a regular service to pick up passengers from surrounding districts for onward flights to the Channel Isles.

When Channel Airways went out of business during 1973, the lease was taken over by Lonmet Aviation, who set about modernizing the site and improving facilities. It is reported that between 1972 and 1975 Lonmet spent over £100,000 on Ipswich Airport, and aircraft movements are also reported to have grown from 10,000 in 1972 to over 46,000 during 1974.

The British School of Flying based at Ipswich ran Ministry of Defence Scholarship courses and Civil Aviation Authority Traffic Control cadet courses. The Ministry of Defence cadets were able to do 30 hours' flying each, and with an extra five hours' flying they were able to qualify for their Private Pilot's Licence.

Two noisy small aircraft which operated from Ipswich were the N.H.1 H.3 Kilibrie 2 seat helicopters owned by European Helicopters Limited for crop spraying. Powered by ram-jets at the blade-tips, these small "rotaries" operated until G-APRZ was sold to Equador and its partner crashed whilst working in Scotland.

Ipswich Airport has now come under the control of the Ipswich Co-operative Society and the light aircraft and air taxi business continues, although there have been threats that the land will be used for massive building development and flying will have to be curtailed or stopped altogether. As early as 1975 the chief executive of Ipswich Borough Council, owners of the airfield land, said that expiry of the lease in the late 1980s would give the council opportunity to "balance the advantages of continuing the aerodrome on its present location for a further period against other needs existing at that time, e.g. land for housing or industry."

A large and growing parachute club based on the airport helps to increase the number of aircraft movements, though the so-called Martlesham Heath Parachute Club now operates from the former U.S.A.A.F. airfield at Flixton, near Bungay, some forty miles from the airfield that provided its name.

Since the first edition of this book appeared in 1977 Norwich Airport, home of Air-U.K., formerly Air Anglia, has increased its business, especially to the Continent, with turbo-prop aircraft operating what amounts almost to a ferry service. Southend Airport continues in the ferry role but is somewhat limited in its aircraft acceptance owing to the restricted runway length.

In the west of Essex controversy has continued to rumble on over the possible future of Stanstead as a third London airport, with no sign that a firm conclusion on its future is any nearer. A most unusual and noteworthy visitor to Stanstead in the summer of 1983 was the Boeing 747 Jumbo and Space Shuttle combination, which drew very large crowds to the airport during its short stay.

Despite the recession the light aircraft population of the Eastern Counties has continued to grow. Particularly notable has been the increasing number of "home-builds," many of them operating from private farm strips and using barns for hangars.

The advent of the hang-glider and the microlight has brought flying more truly within the reach of the man-in-the-street than was the case with the ill-fated Flying Flea of the 1930s. There was good news for the region in 1984 when David Cook, of Aldringham, Suffolk, designed a breed of light aircraft called "The Shadow" and established a number of outstanding records with the machine. There were plans to produce the machine at Leiston, while Wing Commander Wallis's diminutive autogiros, having passed through many stages of development, also reached production status, plans being made for a Bury St Edmunds company to manufacture them.

CHAPTER THIRTEEN

Peace Till Now

WITH the War over, the British Isles had many more military aircraft than it could possibly use. At the same time there were not enough civil aircraft for the country's immediate needs, and there was little money available for the design and production of new types of aeroplane for the airlines that would soon be reorganizing.

The Auxiliary Air Force was reformed on 2nd June, 1946, and those who had learned the art of flying were able to carry on their duties at week-ends and at the annual summer camps.

On the 16th December, 1947, King George VI gave permission for the prefix "Royal" to be used by the Auxiliary Air Force Squadrons, which now became "Royal Auxiliary Air Force Units" (R.A.A.F.).

It was a dark day for the air-minded during January, 1957, however, when those same units were disbanded, and this was regarded by many as a retrograde step.

In the Eastern Counties, where almost every other field was an airfield, the quiet of peace was most noticeable as only a few aerodromes were operating, military flying being on a very restricted basis. In the main the pre-war expansion 'dromes were the ones that were still used, as the wartime "fields" had more primitive amenities. Another great factor, of course, was the departure of the U.S.A.F., and all the airfields which they had occupied were now rapidly becoming vacant.

The Aeroplane and Armament Experimental Establishment did not return to Martlesham Heath, its pre-war home, but remained at Boscombe Down, though the Marine Aircraft Experimental Establishment did return to Felixstowe. First to be tested on the M.A.E.E.'s, return was the Short Sunderland V, TX. 293 which was used for hydrodynamic experimental work, whilst the modified Sunderlands MZ.269 and MZ.271 were also in residence.

A setback to British aviation occurred in the early hours of the 28th January, 1946, when the largest flying boat constructed in the British Isles caught fire and sank at its moorings at Felixstowe. The giant Short S.40 Shetland DX.166, one of only two of its type, was moored off the slipway where an electrical fire involving the auxiliary generator started in the galley. The ventilator had been accidentally left closed, and a flash fire fed by the generator's fuel supply soon destroyed the aircraft. Another unique marine aircraft was the Saro A.37 Shrimp, G-AFZS, TK.580 two-seat flying scale research flying boat, used for testing scaled down components, which remained at Felixstowe until it was scrapped during 1949.

The Saro A.37 Shrimp, G-AFZS was used at the M.A.E.E. Felixstowe post-war in an experimental role including flight testing scaled-down components for larger prototypes.   *Westland*

A feature of interest to the observer at Felixstowe in the early post-war days was a number of ex-Luftwaffe marine aircraft to be seen at their moorings. Used for research and evaluation, they included the Arado 196 and the Blohm und Voss BV.138, a three-engined (diesel), twin-boomed flying boat, the Dornier Do.18 twin and the Dornier Do.24 three-engined boats. The giant Blohm und Voss BV.222 C-012 "Wiking" paid a visit, whilst at the other end of the scale was the one and only FGP-227 flying scale model of the 197 foot Blohm und Voss BV.238 six-engined flying boat. The "baby" had six two-stroke petrol engines of only 21 h.p. each, and was similar in every detail but size to its giant sister, which had six 1,750 h.p. Daimler Benz DB.603V engines. Coming into Harwich Harbour, a keen observer on a "leave boat" recorded three Junkers Ju.52/3m, three-engined floatplanes, two Blohm und Voss BV.138 and a Dornier DO.24 three-engined flying boat, all painted black overall.

Mr Parke of Felixstowe, who was with the M.A.E.E. at the time, remembers the "visitors". One afternoon a severe gale blew up suddenly and he was despatched to move one of the Dornier Do.24s from the Felixstowe to the Harwich side of the harbour. With the aircraft's hull obeying the pull of the ebb tide and the tailplane serving as a "weathercock" to turn the boat into wind, a wing dropped and the aircraft eventually turned turtle just as the crew scrambled into an accompanying launch. It was not possible to start the engines to get out of trouble as the water in the bilges had flooded the auxiliary generators needed to start the main engines. Many years later parts of this Do.24 were dredged up, the light alloy engines components in a very bad state owing to the salt water corrosion but the airscrews still in good shape.

The captured "boats" were ferried from ex-Luftwaffe bases in North Germany, and when Mr Parkes went over to assist in bringing the "prizes" back he was surprised to be given operating instructions in perfect English by a Luftwaffe technician. Asking the speaker where he had obtained his knowledge of the language, he replied that he had worked for a number of years at the British Small Arms factory in Birmingham.

The testing of flying boats and seaplanes went on apace at the M.A.E.E. Felixstowe, but another valuable prototype was lost during 1949 when the Saro SRA/1 jet flying boat fighter, TG.271, crashed on a Saturday morning whilst preparing for a Battle of Britain flying display. Plunging into the sea near the Cork Lightship, the aircraft was lost and the pilot, Squadron Leader Major, killed.

Another serious setback to British aviation on Friday, 27th September, 1946, was the death of Flying Officer Geoffrey de Havilland, O.B.E., R.A.F.O., a distinguished son of a famous father who was killed when the second DH.108 Swallow tail-less research jet monoplane broke up over the Thames Estuary. The aircraft had been at Sutton Heath using the large runway for its early flights.

The marine aircraft chapter ended in the region when on 21st June, 1962, the Marine Aircraft Experimental Establishment at Felixstowe closed. Among the guests at the closure ceremony was the late Air Chief Marshal, Sir Arthur Longmore, who had served at the Station. Sir Arthur was the holder of the Royal Aero Club Pilot's Certificate No. 72 dated April, 1911, the oldest held by any serving R.A.F. Officer.

At the other end of the region, Duxford returned to the R.A.F. from the Americans but lacked aerial activity, the occupants of the buildings being officers accommodated from Cambridge where they were on a Russian language course.

Duxford did hear the sound of Merlins again early in 1946 when No. 165 Squadron returned with its Spitfires, but during July this squadron reformed as No. 66 Squadron flying the later marques of Spitfires and early Gloster Meteors. A new aircraft appeared in the region when No. 74 Squadron re-equipped at Coltishall with the Gloster Meteor F.3 twin-jet single-seat fighter. Later No. 56 and No. 245, together with No. 74, were stationed at R.A.F. Bentwaters with these aircraft and became the first R.A.F. jet fighter wing.

Bentwaters was used as the Fighter Command base for the Battle of Britain fly-past on the 11th September, 1946, the aircraft taking part in the massed formation fly-past over London taking off and landing at the Suffolk airfield. Later in the day fly-pasts were made by the same aircraft over Ipswich, Great Yarmouth and Norwich districts.

R.A.F. Horsham St Faiths, Norfolk, was the only Flight Command station open that year, and a crowd of over 10,000 flocked to the excellent flying display. Many aircraft of the Command performed, including a Meteor IV, Mosquito 30, Hornet I, Auster V, Lincoln I, Harvard II, Mustang III, Vengence IV and a Spitfire XVI. Seven Meteors of No. 74 Squadron and nine Mosquito 30's of No. 307 (Polish) Squadron gave an immaculate formation flypast, whilst the twin-engined Hornet fighters of No. 64 Squadron performed single-engine demonstrations. Squadron Leader Peter M. Gardner outdid them by making a pass with both airscrews feathered, whilst Flight Lieutenant R. Large and Wing Commander Bird Wilson thrilled the crowds with aerobatics in a Meteor III and Vampire respectively. Two days later the Empire Radio School at Debden, Essex, was open, also attracting large crowds who were entertained with flying and static displays.

Early in 1948 the Horsham St Faiths Meteor Wing was re-equipped with the Gloster Meteor F.4 jet fighter. Their main assignment in the years ahead was the interception of Russian TU.4 reconnaissance aircraft off the East Coast, and in order to practise those procedures the fighters carried out constant exercises with the B.29 Washington bombers based at R.A.F. Marham.

The Aeronautical Press during 1949 acclaimed the aerobatic displays performed by Flight Lieutenant Lyres of No. 74 Squadron based at Horsham St Faiths. Carrying out complicated manoeuvres in his Meteor F.4, he was in great demand for displays all over the country.

The first fighter squadron to convert to the new Meteor F.8 jet fighter in 1950 was No. 245 at Horsham St Faiths. Several of the fighter airfields in the Eastern Counties were now equipped with various marques of Meteor fighters. Fighter personnel was also well represented as R.A.F. Wattisham had a well-known fighter pilot as commanding officer, Group Captain Peter G. Wykeham-Barnes, D.S.O., O.B.E., D.F.C. and bar, A.F.C., victor during the War over 15 enemy aircraft.

During the annual air exercises held during the summer of 1948, a de Havilland Vampire jet fighter engaged a de Havilland Hornet twin piston engined fighter over Ipswich in mock combat. The defending Odiham-based jet flown by Squadron Leader Beddow had refuelled at Martlesham Heath and taken off to intercept the attacking Hornets. Whilst involved in a series of tight turns, the Vampire whip-stalled, turned on its back and crashed onto the road in front of houses in Myrtle Road, Ipswich. Exploding as it impacted the blazing paraffin scattered and enveloped a small girl playing in the road, who died the next day. The pilot was killed instantly, the remains of the jet crashing through a high brick wall and into Holywells Park.

Further exercises, coded "Operation Dagger" were carried out by Fighter and Bomber Commands from 3rd to 5th September. Bombers from bases in Germany attempted to raid regional airfields and the fighters intercepted them.

Ipswich has an unhappy record of crashes, for during June, 1952, a Meteor encountered trouble whilst flying over Ipswich and dived vertically into houses on the Castle Hill Estate, Whitton, Ipswich, the pilot being killed instantly although fortunately no other casualties resulted. Seven years later a Hunter based at Wattisham experienced trouble also over Ipswich and dived into houses in Tuddenham Avenue, Ipswich, causing considerable damage but fortunately no loss of life. The pilot baled out to safety.

During October, 1949, it was decided that the Duxford runways needed major repair works, and so new runways and perimeter tracks were constructed. The work, which continued until 1951, gave the airfield a 6,000 feet runway and all facilities for fighter operations. When these works were completed jet aircraft were the order of the day at Duxford, where for the third time, a Duxford Wing was in residence, Nos. 64 and 65 Squadrons operating their Meteors and later Javelins, which remained until the airfield shut down during 1961.

Hawker Hunter.

The Duxford squadrons led the R.A.F. Flypast on Coronation Day, 2nd June, 1953, flying over London as the newly-crowned Queen Elizabeth II stood on the balcony of Buckingham Palace.

During the Battle of Britain open days for 1955, it was estimated that over 23,000 people visited R.A.F. Duxford for the flying and static displays.

On 26th July, 1961, two Hunters of No. 1 Squadron, Duxford, broke the London-Valetta speed record. Flown by Wing Commander Bennett and Flight Lieutenant Davidson, they made an average speed of 633 m.p.h., aided by a tail-wind, and broke the existing record held by the Royal Navy by nine minutes.

The famous Duxford airfield began to run down during January, 1961, and No. 65 Squadron disbanded during the following April, the Duxford Station Flight the next month, and No. 64. Squadron moved to Waterbeach in July. The last flight was made by Air Vice Marshal R. N. Bateson on 31st July, when he took off and landed in a Meteor IV. The Station transferred from Fighter Command to Training Command on 1st October, 1961.

The music of Merlin motors came back to Duxford in the late 60's when the United Artists film "Battle of Britain" was made largely on the Station. In the course of the action one of the original hangars was blown up, causing far more damage than was ever inflicted by the real enemy.

During April, 1949, the R.A.F. formed its B.29 Washington heavy bomber squadrons at Marham, Norfolk, and Nos. 35, 90, 115 and 207 Squadrons were all equipped with the large American-built four-engined bomber. Also in residence on the airfield was the Washington Conversion Unit, to train pilots and aircrews up to operational standards on these aircraft. It was a coincidence that No. 90 Squadron was equipped during the war with the Boeing Fortress I, and now it should receive the big brother of its original equipment.

On 22nd March, 1950, the first Boeing B.29 Superfortress, 44-61787 and now named Washington by the R.A.F. touched down at Marham. The purchase of 89 of these ex-U.S.A.F. bombers, enough to equip eight squadrons, cost some £14 million and was hotly opposed by the aircraft industry as it was reputed that approximately 38,000 jobs would be lost to the British industry. It was also stated that the Superfortress was only marginally superior to the Avro Lincoln, which it replaced.

Taken out of plastic cocoons in the U.S.A., the B.29s were brought up to operational standards and then allocated to No. 3 Group. In spite of the criticism the Washington, the first American aircraft to enter R.A.F. service since the War, proved to be a useful component of Bomber Command. The crews passed through the Conversion Unit and then No. 115 Squadron was formed at Marham. Eventually the Washington equipped Nos. 15, 35, 44, 57, 90, 115, 149, 192 and 207 Squadrons, several of which were based at Marham.

Starting during January, 1954, and finishing during May, the Washington bombers were returned to the United States, flying westwards across the Atlantic in an operation coded "Homerun". They were replaced during May by the new

English Electric Canberra twin jet medium bomber, the first of its kind which remained until 1956, when the first of the "V-Bombers", the Vickers Valiant, arrived to equip No. 207 Squadron. The new age dawned on 11th October, 1956, when Valiant WZ.366 commanded by Squadron Leader E. J. G. Flavell, A.F.C. from Marham dropped the first British atomic bomb at Maralinga, South Australia. With the flash action in Egypt over the Suez Canal, Nos. 138, 148, 207 and 214 Squadrons left the region for Malta, to carry out operations over Suez using conventional bombs.

During March, 1957, No. 90 Squadron which seemed to live permanently in the Eastern Counties received its Valiant B.I's at Honington, Suffolk, with the aircraft being finished in all-white anti-radiation style with pale national insignia. On 15th May, another Valiant XD.818 of No. 49 Squadron, Marham, and commanded by Wing Commander K. C. Hubbard, O.B.E., D.F.C. and A.F.C. dropped Britain's first "H-Bomb" off Christmas Island in the Pacific in "Operation Grapple". This aircraft is still preserved at Marham at the time of writing (1975), sole survivor of a graceful first of the "V" bombers.

Distinguished visitors at Marham arrived in the shape of Mr N. Kruschev, Mr I. V. Kurchabor, a nuclear scientist and the famous Russian aircraft designer, Mr A. N. Tupolev. Guided by the Secretary of State for Air, Sir Nigel Birch, and the British Ambassador to Russia, Sir William Hayter, the party was shown round the station and its aircraft. July saw Nos. 35 and 90 Squadrons leave Marham, followed by No. 115 Squadron, as the Valiant force grew, whilst Nos. 214 and 148 arrived to take their place, followed later by No. 49 Squadron.

First of the V-Bombers, a Vicker Valiant, WZ 403 comes in to land at Marham, Norfolk in all-white anti-radiation finish. The long probe protruding from the nose is for in-flight refuelling. *Vickers*

The seven man crew of two R.A.F. bombers were killed when they collided at night over Norfolk, five being the crew of a Victor "V" bomber from Marham and the remaining two being in a Canberra from R.A.F. Bruggen, Germany. The market town of Holt was showered with wreckage but fortunately no one was hurt by the falling debris.

No. 214 Squadron at Marham developed the technique of in-flight refuelling pioneered before the Second World War by Sir Alan Cobham, using some of their Valiants as tankers. They employed in-flight refuelling during the spring of 1960 when Valiant B.I. XD.858 of No. 214 Squadron flew 8,500 miles around the British Isles in a time of 18 hours, 5 minutes, the longest flight so far achieved by an R.A.F. aircraft. The valiant refuelled twice whilst airborne. On 25th/26th May another Valiant B.I. WZ-390, again from No. 214 Squadron, flew nonstop from England to Singapore, a distance of 8,110 miles in 15 hours, 33 minutes at an average speed of 523 m.p.h. Piloted by Squadron Leader Gousten, the Valiant was refuelled twice on route, once over Cyprus and again off Western Pakistan. The return flight was also made in record time.

The tanker force gradually increased with the arrival of Nos. 55 and 57 Squadrons. When the Valiants went out of service, somewhat prematurely, their place was taken by Handley-Page Victors which at the time of writing, 1975, are still very much in operation.

Whilst refuelling two Buccaneers in 1975, a Victor tanker from Marham, broke up in the air and crashed into the North Sea about 70 miles off Scarborough. The two strike aircraft returned to their base at Honington, Suffolk, but only the Victor's captain, Flight Lieutenant Keith Handscomb, of Ipswich, escaped by ejector seat and parachute and was picked up from the water.

In May, 1954, No. 5 Flying Training School at Oakington, Cambridgeshire, was re-equipped with the De Havilland Vampire T.11 jet trainer. This was the first school to put into use the joint training programme, carrying out initial training on Provosts at Ternhill, Salop, and finishing on the T.11 at Oakington. Pupils received 110 hours on this aircraft, the training including all facets of Service flying.

During March, 1954, No. 23 Squadron at Stradishall became the first unit to receive De Havilland Venom NF.2 night fighters, these eventually being replaced by the improved NF.3. The two Wattisham based units, Nos. 257 and 263, were re-equipped with Hawker Hunter F.6s, a variant of the type powered by an Armstrong-Siddeley Sapphire turbo-jet engine instead of the more usual Rolls-Royce Avon.

During March and April, 1955, the Day Fighter Reduction Board visited fighter stations in the Eastern Counties to assess the need and disposition of the combat forces. As a result of June, No. 74 Squadron was the only day fighter unit left in this sector. During the previous month the first exchange of North Atlantic Treaty Organization squadrons had been made when No. 74 Squadron went to Holland and a Dutch Air Force squadron visited Horsham St Faiths. Further exchange visits with N.A.T.O. squadrons occurred during March, 1956, when No. 74 went to Leewarden in Holland while No. 324 Squadron of the Netherlands Air Force came over to Horsham St Faiths. During June, No. 25 Squadron of the Belgium Air Force visited Horsham, and the joint activities of No. 74 Squadron, R.A.F. and No. 25 Squadron, B.A.F. were directed by controllers on both sides of the North Sea.

No. 74 Squadron was honoured on 27th July, 1956, when Princess Margaret inspected the unit and spent a considerable time looking at the aircraft and talking to the personnel.

The same squadron suffered a casualty on 21st August, 1958 when Flight

Belgian pilot and his Hawker Hunter are welcomed at R.A.F. Wattisham by an R.A.F. officer where they have arrived on an exchange visit.

Lieutenant Tester crashed into the sea off Winterton, Norfolk whilst flying a Hunter. At a memorial service held later in the year at Horsham St Faiths, Flight Lieutenant Tester's parents, Air Commodore J. A. Tester, C.B., C.B.E., and Mrs Tester, presented the Squadron with their son's 1922 Rolls-Royce car.

After many petitions by the people of Norwich regarding jet noise, the fighter aircraft at Horsham St Faiths moved to nearby Coltishall and it was at this station during 1959 that the first English Electric Lightning F.I interceptors entered R.A.F. service at the Central Fighter Establishment. These were followed by those of No. 74 Squadron at the same station during July, 1960, under the command of Squadron Leader J. E. G. Hare. This unusual large swept-wing machine with its unorthodox lines attracted a lot of attention, especially when one saw a Lightning take-off for the first time. The aircraft of No. 74 Squadron were resplendent in black fins and fuselage spines and the unit's bright tiger badge displayed on the fin. No. 56 and 111 Squadrons at Wattisham later received Lightning F.2s and these became a familiar sight in the skies of the Eastern Counties.

Big noises were heard at Sutton Heath too, on 20th January, 1961, when the 79th Squadron, U.S.A.F. were hosts to No. 74 Squadron R.A.F., the reason for the get-together being that both units were officially known as "Tigers", the 79th with its North American Super Sabre F.100s and No. 74 with its Lightning F.1s. A further "Tiger Meet" was held during July, three squadrons participating, one each

H.R.H. The Duke of Edinburgh walks through a hangar at R.A.F. Wattisham and looks at a Hawker Hunter of No. 111 Squadron. This is one of the famous "Black Arrows" aircraft with its distinctive raked tail fin flash. 29th March, 1960.

from the R.A.F., the U.S.A.F. and the French Armée de l'Air. In 1963 the Luftwaffe flew in East Anglian skies again when a fighter unit operated from Coltishall for ten days as part of a N.A.T.O. interchange programme.

On 31st July, 1968, a detachment of the Italian Air Force arrived at R.A.F. Wattisham and consisted of Lockheed Starfighters F.104s with 10 officers and 17 senior N.C.O.s led by Captain Fabio Colossi; the detachment was visiting No. 29 Squadron from their base at Grossetto, 90 miles north of Rome and stayed for ten days carrying out joint exercises.

On 7th May, 1963, No. 74 Squadron was again honoured when Princess Margaret visited R.A.F. Coltishall to present the unit with a Squadron Standard. The previous year Princess Marina had presented squadron standards to Nos. 55 and 57 Squadrons at R.A.F Honington.

During February, 1964, No. 74 Squadron left Coltishall for Leuchars in Scotland, thus ending a long stay in the region, but the roar of Lightnings was heard again when No. 226 Operational Conversion Unit moved into the same airfield.

An ex-bomber station came under Fighter Command on 1st July, 1958, when No. 263 Squadron commanded by Squadron Leader L. de Garis, A.F.C. and equipped with Hunter F.6s arrived at R.A.F. Stradishall. This unit consisted mainly of personnel of No. 1 Squadron, which had been disbanded under the "Sandys Axe", the Defence White Paper of 1957, which had drastically reduced the R.A.F. strength. It later became No. 1 Squadron again and as such led a mass fly-past of 45 Hunters over the Society of British Aero Constructors Show at Farnborough held during September.

No. 54 Squadron at Stradishall formed a Hunter Wing with No. 1 Squadron and was then known as No. 54 Wing with Wing Commander Boyle as Commanding Officer.

On 17th February, 1959, a pilot from Stradishall had a lucky escape in his Hunter F.6. Flying Officer Brook was approaching the airfield in very poor visibility, under radar assistance, when he hit a tree on the aerodrome perimeter. Although the Hunter was considerably damaged, the pilot managed to gain height and was then directed to R.A.F. Honington, where it was thought the weather would be better. With his fuel now extremely low he found the weather at Honington to be no better, but made a remarkable landing in the down-wind direction at high speed without causing further damage. About this time another Hunter dived at supersonic speed into the sea off Felixstowe, and it is thought that the pilot made one of the first supersonic ejections. Although injured he was picked up from the sea.

No. 54 Hunter Wing moved from Stradishall to Waterbeach to become part of No. 38 Group, employed on ground attack duties. Whilst at this station they were visited by Mr Julian Amery, M.P., the Secretary of State, who flew in a Hunter T.7 over the Stanford battle area on a rocket strafing mission. Some time later the Wing

The Vickers Varsity was well known in the region as a crew trainer and served for some time at R.A.F. Stradishall. Developed from the Viking airliner, the last Varsities left the Service during 1975.

Vickers

moved from Waterbeach to West Raynham, Norfolk, and it was here that the squadrons developed the technique of small bomb skip bombing.

In 1965, No. 1 Air Navigators School was at Stradishall and as it turned out was the last unit to reside at this famous airfield. It was equipped with the Hawker Siddeley Dominie twin jet navigational trainer, which had gradually replaced the long-serving Vickers Varsity piston-engined trainers. The two types worked together, the 472 m.p.h. jets being used for high, fast instruction whilst the slower Varsities were employed on the low and slow exercises.

On 1st April, 1968, the Jubilee of the Royal Air Force was celebrated by a large gathering at R.A.F. Stradishall, at the invitation of the Station Commander, Group Captain A. G. Davies.

A new era in R.A.F. training aircraft appeared when the first Scottish Aviation Jetstream navigational trainer was handed over to No. 5 Flying Training School at Oakington, Cambridgeshire in 1973. The twin turbo-prop monoplane, designed by the now defunct Handley-Page firm, and then taken over by the present manufacturer, was a step forward in R.A.F. training aircraft.

After the announcement by the Air Ministry regarding the closure of R.A.F. Stradishall, the Clare Rural District Council were very concerned as the station, which was rated at £55,000 during 1967, represented about 25 per cent of the rating income. Still close it did, and after much speculation it has now become one of H.M. Prisons.

General Franco started his first rumblings regarding Gibraltar during February, 1965, and consequently No. 1 Squadron was hastily despatched from the region to back up the British forces there. The movement appeared to have had the desired effect as the noises died down and No. 1 came home to the Eastern Counties again.

Further stirrings from the same gentleman two years later saw No. 1 Squadron rushing out to Gibraltar again, and the operation then lasted for a considerable time with aircraft rotating for spells of duty on the Rock.

The Commanding Officer of No. 1 Squadron, Wing Commander J. A. Mansell was killed on 31st May, 1969, whilst carrying out combat manoeuvres off the Norfolk coast in hazy conditions. Witnesses on the sea front at Wells-next-the-Sea saw a Hunter aircraft dive into the sea and explode, but only small fragments of wreckage were recovered.

On 15th October, 1964, a unique squadron was formed at West Raynham, this being the three-nation evaluation squadron to test the Hawker Siddeley Kestrel vertical take-off fighter for the R.A.F., the U.S.A.F., the U.S. Navy, U.S. Army and the Luftwaffe. A special symbol was carried by the aircraft comprising the roundels of the three nations. The German representative was Colonel Gerhard Barkham, who was credited with shooting down 301 Allied aircraft during the War.

After a period of operation the squadron proved the aircraft and the crews became familiar with their charges, and as a result of experience, the makers

Two Hawker Siddeley Kestrels GFA.I Vertical Take-off single seat fighters of the Tripartite Squadron which was formed at West Raynham, Norfolk to evaluate this aircraft. Note the multi-national Markings.   *Hawker-Siddeley*

incorporated various modifications and the new aircraft emerged as the Harrier. First to receive this new revolutionary machine was No. 1 Squadron based at Wittering, but the conversion flying for the new type was carried out at West Raynham.

The first Intercontinental Ballistic Missile Squadron, No. 77, was formed at Feltwell, Norfolk during August, 1958, under the control of Bomber Command and equipped with the Douglas Thor missile. Each squadron consisted of three missiles on their own launching pads, the rockets having a range of 1,750 miles and carrying a two-megaton nuclear warhead. Mounted at a state of readiness, they remained as such until they ceased to be operational five years later. Other squadrons were stationed on the former bomber airfields at Shepherd's Grove, and Tuddenham, Suffolk and North Pickenham in Norfolk. During the Cuban Crisis of April, 1961, the missiles were brought up to a very high state of readiness, armed and fuelled and almost ready for off, but the only live firings were those carried out by R.A.F. crews while under training in the U.S.A. Several important modifications were carried out to the missiles by the R.A.F. whilst they were in residence to improve the motor performance and the heat shield.

At nearby Banham, the little mounds spread over a large site and all connected

A big white bird sits and waits. Douglas Thor Inter Continental Ballistic Missile on its launching gantry at a North Suffolk base.

by roads were the shelters where the armaments were housed for the neighbour-
hood, and at the time much speculation ensued regarding their true purpose — some
now grow mushrooms.

Fifty years of flying at Martlesham Heath was celebrated on 16th January,
1967, by an informal get-together, but low cloud and rain prevented all but one of
the visiting aircraft from arriving. Dozens of distinguished flyers, war dignitaries
and representatives of the R.A.F. and U.S.A.F. came by road to Martlesham at the
invitation of Mr Freddie Fausing, who ran an engineering distribution business in
one of the old hangars. Later in the day a wreath was laid on the Martlesham
Memorial by the Commander of the U.S.A.F., Bentwaters, Colonel de Witt R.
Seales.

With the high cost of aircraft design and production, constructors co-operated
internationally to produce their machines and one to emerge in this manner was the
joint Anglo-French Jaguar strike aircraft. The first Jaguar squadron in the R.A.F.
was No. 54 Squadron, which had been formed at R.A.F. Lossiemouth in Scotland,
where it had flown as an operational conversion unit. The unit moved to its new
home at Coltishall during 1972.

The Hawker Hunter came back into R.A.F. operational service that same year
when No. 45 Squadron was reformed at West Raynham as part of Strike

B.A.C. Jaguar.

Command. Pilots grew to operational capacity in the Hunters and then were able to undergo training in Jaguar procedures.

During May, 1950, R.A.F. Wattisham became a fighter base when No. 263 (F) Squadron was based there with their Meteor F.4s. Named "The Fellowship of the Bellows" Squadron it was presented by the British Community in the Argentine, and derived its curious name from the act of "raising the wind" to pay for it.

Air Commodore Hughie Idwal Edwards, V.C., C.B., D.S.O., O.B.E., D.F.C., returned again to R.A.F. Wattisham as station commander during 1953.

During April, 1957, the Black Arrows of No. 111 Squadron with their Hunter F.6s from Wattisham made the first of their spectacular displays in their gleaming all-black jet fighters. Later they became world-famous as a mass aerobatic team, being the only such formation to loop 22 aircraft at once. Under the leadership of Squadron Leader, later Group Captain, Roger Topp, and Squadron Leader, also later Group Captain, Peter Latham, the formation was the perfection of mass aerobatic flying and "Treble One" received the Britannia Trophy from H.R.H. The Duke of Edinburgh.

Wattisham had its own Battle of Britain survivor in the form of a Messerschmitt Me.109, a wartime capture which was painstakingly restored by Flight Lieutenant Jeff Hawke and a band of volunteers in their free time. It was full turn of the circle when some years later, the epic film "Battle of Britain" was made in the region and the Mitchell camera plane used to film the aerial sequences was flown by Jeff Hawke, who had by then retired from the R.A.F.

Two Lightning F.2s from No. 56 Squadron at Wattisham touched whilst carrying out aerobatics and XM.179 crashed near the aerodrome at Great Bricett, whilst its partner managed to make a landing although damaged.

A Messrschmitt Me.109 coming up Garrison Lane, Felixstowe — pushed by the local cadets for use as the main exhibit at their exhibition in the local Drill Hall. *F/O John Fuller*

Ready for the call an English Electric later B.A.C. Lightning stands on the tarmac. This is an early type machine depicted by the rounded tip to the fin, and the large finned tank under the fuselage is for extra fuel.   *R.A.F.*

Lightnings were based at Wattisham in the 1960s as a Target Facilities Flight, their function being to act as targets for the resident squadrons, and in this connection they operated off the East Coast, where over the years the occasional aircraft was lost, fortunately the majority of the pilots being saved.

On 20th April, 1968, Bomber Command and Fighter Command ceased to exist as individual formations, both being amalgamated to form Strike Command. A large formation of aircraft based in the region took part in a fly-past over the Battle of Britain control centre at Bentley Priory, Middlesex, on Thursday, 25th April, 1968, to mark the disbandment of Fighter Command. Taking off from Wattisham, the formation comprised 24 Lightnings, four Hunters, three Meteors and four Canberras.

The last piston-engined aircraft of Bomber Command had been phased out five years before, these were five Avro Lincolns of No. 51 Squadron stationed at R.A.F. Watton and on loan to Signals Command.

During 1974 two famous squadrons were disbanded at R.A.F. Wattisham, No. 111 always known as "Treble One" during September, and No. 29 during December. Both units flew Lightnings for some thirteen years but were fortunately reformed later to fly Phantoms from airfields in Lincolnshire.

Annual gloom descended when the 1975 Government White Paper was published, bringing massive defence cuts and it was announced that 12 R.A.F. stations would close, one of these being West Raynham, Norfolk. On 10th March,

Arriving in the region in increasing numbers, The Rolls-Royce Spey engined version of the Phantom, which has replaced the Lightning in many of the local squadrons.   *R.A.F.*

R.A.F. Oakington closed and the flag lowered for the last time after 25 years of service in Bomber and Training Commands. During its time it saw changes like the introduction of the Short Stirling, the first four-engined heavy bomber, the forming of the "Pathfinders", and in later years the introduction of the jet for training purposes.

Another famous station closed down during June 1975, when R.A.F. Debden had a day of ceremonies. As the R.A.F. Ensign was lowered, a Hurricane and Spitfire flew low over the parade.

As the years rolled by so the older squadrons reached seniority like No. 12 Squadron at Honington, which celebrated its 60th anniversary on 21st February,

1975. The unit was flying the Hawker Siddeley Buccaneer S.2A low level strike aircraft at this period of its life.

No. 56 Squadron also reached its 60th anniversary on 21st December, 1975, and to honour this unit a special series of postage stamps were issued depicting aircraft that were used by the squadron. Special envelopes were flown by Lightning aircraft, franked, and signed by the pilots, the proceeds from the sale of the same going to the R.A.F. Museum.

An operation of a warlike nature was undertaken by the Buccaneers stationed at R.A.F. Honington when they were called out to set fire to the 60,000 ton load of crude oil which was seeping from the ruptured tanks of the super-tanker *Torrey Canyon,* fast aground on the Seven Stones Reef off the Scilly Isles. Hunters dropped 100 gallon tanks of kerosene to burn the surface floating oil after the tanks had been bombed by the Buccaneers, but this attempt to deal with the pollution was unsuccessful. No. 1 Squadron Hunters were then called in to drop napalm bombs into the wreck, whilst other Hunters fired 3-inch rockets to further rupture the tanks and release more oil for burning.

Being a mainly agricultural area, and in the main of flattish contour, the region was well to the fore in the newly developing art of aerial crop-spraying. Small firms were formed and often using ex-R.A.F aircraft and ex-R.A.F. pilots they carried out a steadily growing operation for the farmer. Needing all the pilots' full

The 60th anniversary celebrations of No. 56 Squadron at Wattisham. Four Lightnings fly over the circle of famous aircraft which this unit has flown, including the Hunter, Spitfire, Lightning, Hurricane, Metoer and the S.E.5A in the centre.   *E.A.D.T.*

attention in order to fly the aircraft at the correct height, and at the same time look out for high-tension wire and other hazards, this work was not without its risks. Wing Commander Hatfield who had formed Airspray Limited and operated from the old airfield at Boxted, near Colchester, was killed when his Champion Challenger aircraft, G-ASSW, the only British registered example of this type crashed at Boreham, Essex. Wing Commander Hatfield was one of the pioneers of this work, and had previously had several narrow escapes whilst spraying. An unusual aircraft for this work was used by A.D.S. (Aerial) Limited of Southend, this being a LET.2-37 Omelak (Bumble-Bee) a Czechoslovakian design and construction with a Russian designed radial engine.

The two man crew of an R.A.F. Phantom jet strike fighter, and the pilot of a crop sprayer were killed in a mid-air collision near the Fenland village of Fordham during September, 1974. The Piper Pawnee sprayer, flown by a New Zealand pilot was struck by the fighter which was making a high speed low run in a low flying area. Exploding when it hit the ground, the Phantom was flown by the station commander of R.A.F. Coningsby, Group Captain David Blucke with Flight Lieutenant Terence Kinkland as his navigator.

Crop sprayers were not the only casualties as on 16th March, 1958, a Miles Messenger G-AKKI was in a fatal collision with an Auster Alpha G-APAH over Danbury, Essex, all the occupants of the two aircraft being killed. Luckier was an R.A.F. Auster which force-landed in Gippeswyck Park, Ipswich, owing to lack of fuel, but when replenished it took-off and continued its flight.

Another "oldie" crashed on 31st August 1955, when Tiger Moth G-ANCV, ex-R.A.F. T.6709, crashed at South Fambridge, Essex, but the pilot was not seriously injured, whilst four months earlier a rare Chrislea Ace 111 G-AKVB owned by Mr E. F. Thurston crashed at Rettenden, Essex.

Taylorcraft Auster V RT.560 with its ground crew. This machine is similar to those used for Air Observation Post duties and stationed at Westley near Bury St. Edmunds, and it was from these that the very successful civil Austers were developed. *John Langford*

Mr Stanley Ward in glasses formates G-AJUE over the River Orwell with Cliff Quay Power Station and the spread of Ipswich in the background.   *Mr Jim Empson*

Crowds at the Waveney Flying Group Display at Seething airfield near Bungay were thrilled by the daring aerobatics of sixty-two-year old Essex farmer, Mr Neville Browning of Stanford Rivers. Flying his special Czechoslovakian built Zlin Trener Master G-ASIM he showed the plane's capabilities to fly upwards, at speed and long spells of inverted flight. Mr Browning was killed on 22nd August, 1971, at the same airfield in the same plane giving a similar display, when he suffered sudden illness and the aircraft crashed in front of the watching crowds.

On 23rd August, 1975, a Druine Condor G-AYFC lost its propeller whilst flying to Ipswich and made a hurried landing at the airport, whilst on the 30th, a Bellance ECA, G-BOSR belonging to Hendon Air Services crashed at Martlesham Heath. Flying from Biggin Hill, the aircraft, flown by Mr Nigel Brendish, banked near the ground and impacted in poor visibility, the aircraft being "written-off".

During December, 1968, the East Anglian Flying Club's veteran Auster Autocrat J-1, G-AJAH which had been with the Club since March 1947 and had given stalwart service was withdrawn. Nacton aerodrome had one of its rare crashes on 17th March, 1971, when a French-built Jodel D11Z twin seat cabin monoplane G-AYBR took off without a pilot and crashed near the perimeter. Another local aircraft, Auster V G-AKJU, crashed at the strip at Whatfield, near Hadleigh, whilst glider towing and was badly damaged.

An unusual visitor to the region on 6th November, 1971, was the Tiger Club's Sea Tiger, G-AIVW, which was making a tour of the Eastern Counties. One of its refuelling stops was on the River Deben at Waldringfield, where it was serviced from the shore. Earlier in the year, whilst on a similar flight it had landed and refuelled at Fritton Decoy near Lowestoft.

Auster Autocrat G-AGXP of the East Anglian Flying Club, Ipswich. These machines carried out yeoman service for a number of years and safely trained a great number of pupil pilots.

Mr Stan Ward

The final development of the pre-war Pou de Ciel (Flying Flea) was the HM.293, one of which was home-built by Mr W. H. Gale near Chelmsford and flown from Purleigh airstrip. This was a more reliable version of the "aeroplane for the masses", and was registered G-AXPG. This example carried out a good deal of flying before being preserved.

Whilst engaged on filming work along the Essex coast during the early 70s, a Brantley B.2A helicopter G-ASHD crashed into the River Colne and was wrecked. Shortly afterwards the amateur designer and constructor, Mr John Taylor, of Leigh-on-Sea was killed when his Taylor Tich JT.2., G-ATYO crashed near Southend. The previous design by Mr Taylor, the JT.1 Monoplane, resulted in several being built by "home-builders", one such being G-AZSK built at Eye, Suffolk, by Mr R. R. Lockwood.

The old American airfield at Lavenham rejoiced to the roar of four Merlins on a wet 30th March, 1969, as veteran Lancaster NX.611 landed on a flight from Biggin Hill. Intended to be used as a museum exhibit she stood out in the elements, and gradually deteriorated until 7th February, 1970, when she took off

An ex-U.S.A.A.F. airfield hears the roar of Merlins again as the veteran preserved Avro Lancaster named at that time "Guy Gibson" trundles around the perimeter at Lavenham. It later flew to Blackpool, and is now preserved at R.A.F. Scampton.   *E.A.D.T.*

again, with the actor Richard Todd on board recording a commentary for television. The flight was to R.A.F. Hulborough, Wiltshire, where she was to be serviced and refurbished by a private firm. NX.611 stands now, beautiful as ever, as the "gate guardian" at R.A.F. Scampton, Lincolnshire, a tribute to all Lancasters and all the men who flew and maintained them.

The much weathered wooden hull of a 1925 Supermarine Southampton flying boat which had been moored at Felixstowe Ferry for over 30 years was moved during 1972 for preservation. The hull, believed to be the only one still in existence, was used as a houseboat for many years. The R.A.F. team of six men from R.A.F. Leconfield, after inspecting the hull, concurred that the structure was in remarkable condition for its age. After restoration at R.A.F. Henlow, the hull will be fitted out in its original condition, and then taken to rest in the hallowed hangars at Hendon, where the R.A.F. Museum houses the treasures of our Air Force.

In the south of the region we are blessed with an air museum which has catered for several of the more unusual aircraft, this being the Southend Historic Aircraft Museum. Of the static variety, nevertheless they are the genuine article and include

Spanish built Casa/Heinkel He.111H used in the film "Battle of Britain" and now resident at the Southend air Air Museum. It differed from the original mainly in being fitted with Rolls-Royce Merlin motors instead of those of German manufacture.   *Myron Burak*

a Spanish-built C.A.S.A. 2-111 (German Heinkel He 111H) G-ANHB which took part in the film epic "Battle of Britain". Also on exhibition are the Migret HM.14 Pou de Ceil G-ADXS, built during 1935 by Mr C. L. Storey but not flown, whilst the later version, the HM.293 mentioned previously is also resident. Other interesting items are the Miles Gemini G-AKGD, Percival Proctor 3, G-AOBW, D. H. Dragon Rapide G-AIUL and remains of Short Scion G-AEZE.

Many of the ex-operational airfields still operate as flying club centres, the Norfolk and Norwich Aero Club flying from Swanton Morley which it shares with the Air Training Corps Gliding School commanded by Flight Lieutenant Ron Page of Ipswich. The ex-U.S.A.F. airstrip at Shipdham serves as a centre for light aircraft servicing and charter flights. Engines still roar at another ex-U.S.A.F. airfield, Hethel, the home of the Lotus racing car firm who also run a fleet of three aircraft, a Cessna 414 N46833, a Seneca G-BABK and a Navajo G-AZME as well as Chipmunk G-BBMY of the Lotus "King" Colin Chapman. Little Snoring, Norfolk, is the base for the McAully Flying Group, who collectively own and fly a Piper Cub G-AKAA. The North Denes strip at Great Yarmouth is busy during the summer with many visiting aircraft movements due to the holiday season and the horse racing as well as the several large helicopters on oil-rig work. Even Martlesham

Heath has seen a revival with several aircraft being housed and serviced in the hangar on the "American" side of the airfield, the showpiece being the De Havilland Leopard Moth belonging to Mr John Parkes of Charsfield. Many of the regions ex-airfields are still the home of small groups of enthusiasts who own and fly an aircraft and these include Andrewsfield, High Easter, Earls Colne and Hanningfield in Essex, and Metfield, Beccles, Parham and the heath at Newmarket in Suffolk, the latter being well used during race weeks.

The local Air Training Corps Squadrons continue their good work and grow in numbers and their members in knowledge as the years pass. Several of the cadets were fortunate in gaining flights to the more distant R.A.F. stations in the world, and this is always a prize worth having.

The village policeman at Sibton, Suffolk, Police Constable Geoff Payne, is a local aviator, having constructed his own hot air balloon with 56,000 cubic foot capacity. The work took him two years assisted by a Saxmundham ambulance

Air Vice Marshal S. F. Vincent, the only pilot to fly fighters operationally in both wars, inspects the Felixstowe Squadron of the Air Training Corps. Flight Lieutenant Cowan, the Commanding Officer, is in attendance. *F/O John Fuller*

driver, Mr Jack Tomlinson. P.C. Payne became interested in balloons and joined the British Balloon and Airship Club in 1967 and summed it up by saying "It is one of the simplest forms of flying and you can land in almost any size field and move off again easily".

On 24th and 25th August, 1968, Heveningham Hall, Suffolk, was the venue for a large gathering of hydrogen and hot-air balloons. These graceful and picturesque machines of a former age made a wonderful sight as they filled and lifted off for their silent flight over the region, bringing to life the fine mural of an earlier balloon race painted in the converted stable tearoom at the Hall.

The sea around the Essex coast is a museum of aircraft wrecks, as during an exceptionally low tide on 8th August, 1975, a number of aircraft were observed, including a Dakota, Lancaster and a Spitfire lying on an exposed mudbank. The fishermen were not so enamoured with these relics, like Mr Lungley of West Mersea whose nets fouled them whilst fishing in the River Blackwater. Calling on the services of the Colchester Sub-Aqua Club and Mr Brian Jay of West Mersea, the divers discovered a buckled airscrew, a badly damaged engine and assorted wings and fuselages at a depth of 30 feet. One large portion lifted was that of a Hawker Typhoon, R.8895 which flew from Bradwell Bay, Essex, piloted by Flight Sergeant Pottinger of No. 3 Squadron and crashed during the night of 22nd March, 1944 and had laid on the river bed for over 30 years.

Not in the usual run of events, and further out than the usual "Blips" on the radar screen are the Unidentified Flying Objects reported by people in the region. One such incident occurred on 24th February, 1975, when Mr Mayer of Aldringham, Suffolk was walking along the beach with his dog during the early evening. He spotted what he thought was a shooting star, but as it approached, appeared like a green and yellow pumpkin with an illuminated glow. Remaining stationary in front of Mr Mayer for 30 seconds, it then swiftly made off in the direction from which it had come.

Earlier during 1956, the radar at Bentwaters picked up a mysterious object on its screen at about 21.30 hours on 13th August and recorded it as travelling at some 4,000 m.p.h. whilst at R.A.F. Lakenheath the radar operators watched their screens as a U.F.O. played cat and mouse with a high flying jet fighter.

A local gentleman who has carried out a great deal of research into U.F.O.s is Mr Martindale of Needham Market, headmaster of the Highlands School, who holds a degree in physics. With the aid of an ex-ship's radar set on the roof of his house, this ardent watcher has logged many sightings. Many people, mostly at night, have observed extraordinary objects over fields and woods, glowing and then making off at great speed. Almost weekly reports are made of unearthly objects which turn out to be everyday things, but nevertheless there still remains the unexplainable ones. During the last decade, a local businessman and his son, people sailing on the River Orwell, and a group of Ipswich schoolmasters have all sighted U.F.O.s, so the answer although we cannot say "yes" or "no" must be left as an open verdict.

Many changes have occurred in the East Anglian flying scene since the appearance of the first edition of this book in 1977. While many new shapes and sounds have become familiar to East Anglians, others to which people had become accustomed over the years have finally disappeared.

R.A.F. Wattisham is now home to the McDonnell F.4 Phantom, and its squadrons have changed. One of them, No. 23, has taken up residence at R.A.F. Port Stanley, in the Falklands, a location which was until the Falklands War little known. Other F.4s have vacated the Suffolk airspace, their place at R.A.F. Bentwaters and R.A.F. Woodbridge being taken by the quieter Fairchild A.10 Thunderbolt II tank-buster, a ground attack aircraft with formidable armament in the shape of a 30mm. multi-barrelled Gatling gun capable of firing at either 2,100 or 4,200 rounds a minute. Operating by rotation between the two Suffolk bases and forward bases in Germany, these somewhat unorthodox aircraft represent a major part of the N.A.T.O. answer to the threat posed by the Warsaw Pact's armoured columns.

Another new aircraft, the Tornado, has taken up residence at R.A.F. Honington. Successor to some of the R.A.F.'s larger bombers such as the Vulcan, the Tornado flies fast and low to its target, endeavouring to remain out of sight of enemy radar by hugging the contours. Flying with its mainplanes either swept back for high-speed flight or extended for slower speeds, the Tornado with its two-man crew often practices in mock combat with its near neighbour from R.A.F. Coltishall, the B.A.C. Jaguar.

Larger and faster transports now whine their way into and out of the extensive U.S.A.F. installations at R.A.F. Mildenhall and R.A.F. Lakenheath. At the latter the General Dynamics F.111s thunder in and out, their long front fuselages appearing to gain even greater length as the seemingly inadequate mainplane sweeps back into the high-speed configuration.

As the older aircraft are replaced by newer and, it is said, more efficient ones, their numbers decrease and the need for airfields also diminshes. As a consequence more of the well-known aerodromes have been reduced to a care and maintenance basis or have been closed down. Stradishall is now the site of H.M. Prison Highpoint, Bircham Newton is the home of the Construction Industry Training Centre, and Martlesham Heath is the home of the British Telecom Research Station, while much of the old airfield from which flew so many experimental aircraft is now covered with the houses of a new village whose road names recall the names of manufacturers whose aircraft were tested at the A. & A.E.E.

One of the strangest changes of role for an R.A.F. station must be that accomplished by R.A.F. Bawdsey*, the birthplace of radio location and radar, which has dropped its role as one of the country's main radar stations to become a base for Bloodhound guided missiles.

---

*The story of R.A.F. Bawdsey is told in *Bawdsey — Birth of the Beam*, by Gordon Kinsey, published by Terence Dalton, 1983.

Airfields in the Region 1938-1975

The following list of airfields used by the Royal Air Force, the United States Army Air Force, the United States Air Force and several Allied Air Forces is as complete as information received allows. The squadrons listed are, as far as can be ascertained, correct, but others could have visited or been deployed and their visits not recorded. Many additional units are listed in this Appendix over and above those in the first edition. For key to squadron designation abbreviations see Page 274.

ANDREWS FIELD (Great Saling), Essex

R.A.F.	No. 19 (F) Squadron	Mustang III
	No. 65 (F) Squadron	Mustang III, Spitfire LF. XVI E
	No. 74 (F) Squadron	Meteor III, Battle of Britain Flypast Base
	No. 122 (F) Squadron	Mustang III
	No. 129 (F) Squadron	Mustang III
	No. 276 (ASR) Squadron	Spitfire ASR II, Sea Otter ASR.II
	No. 303 (F) Squadron	Mustang IV
	No. 306 (F) Squadron	Mustang III
	No. 309 (F) Squadron	Mustang I, Mustang III
	No. 315 (F) Squadron	Mustang III
	No. 316 (F) Squadron	Mustang III
	No. 504 (F) Squadron	Spitfire IX
	No. 616 (F) Squadron	Meteor III
U.S.A.A.F.	96th Bomb Group, 8th A.F.	B.17F
	322nd Bomb Group, 9th A.F.	B.26B

ATTLEBRIDGE, Norfolk

R.A.F.	No. 88 (B) Squadron	Blenheim IV, Boston III
	No. 105 (B) Squadron	Blenheim IV
	No. 247 (F) Squadron	Typhoon
	No. 320 (B) Squadron	Mitchell B.II, Mitchell B.III
	No. 1508 B.A.T. Flight	Oxford
U.S.A.A.F.	319th Bomb Group, 9th A.F.	B.26B
	466th Bomb Group, 8th A.F.	B.26H J.L.M.

BENTWATERS, Suffolk

R.A.F.	No. 56 (F) Squadron	Meteor F.III
	No. 64 (F) Squadron	Mustang III
	No. 65 (F) Squadron	Spitfire LF.XVIE
	No. 74 (F) Squadron	Meteor F.III, Meteor F.IV
	No. 118 (F) Squadron	Mustang III
	No. 124 (F) Squadron	Meteor F.III
	No. 126 (F) Squadron	Mustang III
	No. 129 (F) Squadron	Mustang III
	No. 165 (F) Squadron	Mustang III

	No. 226 O.C.U.	Meteor F.III
	No. 234 (F) Squadron	Mustang III, Spitfire IX
	No. 245 (F) Squadron	Meteor F.III
U.S.A.F.	81st Fighter Interceptor Group	F.86A
	81st Fighter Bomber Wing	F.84A
	81st Tactical Fighter Wing	F.4 C.D., A.10
	87th Fighter Interceptor Squadron	F.86D
	91st Squadron	F.101
	92nd Squadron	F.101

BIRCHAM NEWTON, Norfolk

R.A.F.	No. 1 Anti-Aircraft Co-op Unit	Wallace, Henley
	No. 2 Armament Practice Camp	
	No. 2 General Recc. Unit	Wellington DW.I
	No. 15 Air Beam Training Flt.	Anson
	No. 18 (B) Squadron	Hind
	No. 18 Aircrew Holding Unit (R.C.A.F.)	
	No. 25 (B) Squadron	Blenheim IF, Blenheim IV
	No. 42 (GR) Squadron	Vildebeest, Beaufort GR.II
	No. 119 (GR) Squadron (R.N.)	Swordfish I, Albacore
	No. 206 (GR) Squadron	Anson GR.I, Hudson GR.I, II & III
	No. 220 (GR) Squadron	Anson GR.I,
	No. 221 (GR) Squadron	Wellington IC
	No. 229 (F) Squadron	Hurricane I
	No. 233 (GR) Squadron	Blenheim IV, Hudson I
	No. 235 (GR) Squadron	Blenheim IV, Hudson I
	No. 248 (B) Squadron	Blenheim IVF
	No. 252 (CC) Squadron	Beaufighter I, Beaufighter IV
	No. 254 (B) Squadron	Blenheim IVF
	No. 269 (GR) Squadron	Anson I
	No. 279 (ASR) Squadron	Hudson III, IIIA, V, VI; Anson ASR, Warwick ASRI, Hurricane IIc
	No. 320 (GR) Squadron	Hudson I
	No. 403 (MET) Flight	Blenheim IV, Hudson
	No. 407 (GR) Squadron	Hudson
	No. 409 (CC) Squadron	Beaufighter VI
	No. 415 (CC) Squadron	Wellington XIII, Albacore
	No. 500 (B) Squadron	Blenheim IV, Hudson III
	No. 502 (GR) Squadron	Whitley III
	No. 521 (MET) Squadron	Spitfire V, Hudson, Gladiator, Mosquito IV, Blenheim IV
	No. 598 (AC) Squadron	Martinet
	No. 601 (F) Squadron	Blenheim IF
	No. 608 (GR) Squadron	Blenheim IVF, Hudson
	No. 610 (F) Squadron	Spitfire I
	No. 612 (GR) Squadron	Anson I
	No. 695 (AAC) Squadron	Henley III, Hurricane IC
	No. 819 (R.N.) Squadron	Swordfish
	No. 826 (R.N.) Squadron	Albacore
	No. 855 (R.N.) Squadron	Avenger

AVIATION

	No. 1401 (MET) Flight	Gladiator
	No. 1403 (MET) Flight	Blenheim IV, Hudson
	No. 1409 (MET) Flight	Mosquito IV
	No. 1510 (BAT) Flight	Anson
	No. 1611 Flight	Henley
	No. 1612 Flight	Henley
	Coastal Command Elementary and Base Training School	
	Coastal Command Preparation Pool	Mosquito IV, Mosquito VI, Beaufighter, Wellington, Albacore
	Kestrel Trials Unit	Kestrel
	Officers' Advanced Training School	
	Transport Initial Conversion Unit	
	Warwick Training Unit	Warwick
Today	Construction Industry Training Centre	

BODNEY, Norfolk

R.A.F.	No. 21 (B) Squadron	Blenheim IV, Ventura II
	No. 61 (B) Squadron, "B" Flt.	Hampden
	No. 82 (B) Squadron, "B" Flt.	Blenheim IV
	No. 98 (B) Squadron, "B" Flt.	Mitchell II
	No. 105 (B) Squadron	Blenheim IV
U.S.A.A.F.	352nd Fighter Group, 8th A.F.	P.47D, P.51D, P.51K

BOREHAM, Essex

U.S.A.A.F.	394th Bomb Group, 9th A.F.	B.26B

BOTTISHAM, Cambridgeshire

R.A.F.	No. 22, E.F.T.S.	Tiger Moth
	No. 168 (AC) Squadron	Mustang I, Tomahawk
	No. 241 (AC) Squadron	Lysander, Tomahawk, Mustang I
	No. 652 (AOP) Squadron	Tiger Moth
U.S.A.A.F.	361st Fighter Group, 8th A.F.	P.47D, P.51B

BOURN, Cambridgeshire

R.A.F.	No. 15 (B) Squadron	Stirling I, Stirling III
	No. 97 (B) Squadron	Lancaster I, Lancaster III
	No. 101 (B) Squadron	Wellington IC
	No. 105 (B) Squadron	Mosquito B.IX
	No. 162 (B) Squadron	Mosquito B.XXV

BOXTED, Essex

R.A.F.	No. 25 (F) Squadron	Mosquito NF.XXX
	No. 56 (F) Squadron	Meteor F.III
	No. 222 (F) Squadron	Meteor F.III
	No. 234 (F) Squadron	Mustang IV, Meteor F.III
	No. 263 (F) Squadron	Meteor F.III
	No. 266 (F) Squadron	Meteor F.III
U.S.A.A.F.	5th E.R.S., 8th A.F.	P.47D, OA-10A, B.17G
	56th Fighter Group, 8th A.F.	P.47D

	354th Fighter Group, 9th A.F.	P.51B
	355th Fighter Group, 9th A.F.	P.51B
	386th Bomb Group, 9th A.F.	B.26

BRADWELL BAY, Essex

R.A.F.	No. 3 (F) Squadron	Tempest V
	No. 19 (F) Squadron	Mustang IV
	No. 23 (F) Squadron	Boston III, Mosquito II
	No. 25 (F) Squadron	Mosquito NF.XXX
	No. 29 (F) Squadron	Beaufighter IF
	No. 56 (F) Squadron	Typhoon IB
	No. 64 (F) Squadron	Spitfire LF. Vb
	No. 68 (F) Squadron	Mosquito XVII
	No. 124 (F) Squadron	Spitfire F.VII, Spitfire F.IX
	No. 126 (F) Squadron	Spitfire IXB
	No. 151 (F) Squadron	Mosquito NF.XXX
	No. 157 (F) Squadron	Mosquito II
	No. 198 (F) Squadron	Typhoon IB
	No. 219 (F) Squadron	Mosquito XVII
	No. 247 (F) Squadron	Typhoon IB
	No. 264 (F) Squadron	Defiant I
	No. 278 (ASR) Squadron	Walrus, Warwick, Anson
	No. 310 (F) Squadron	Spitfire LF.IX
	No. 312 (F) Squadron	Spitfire LF.IX
	No. 313 (F) Squadron	Spitfire IX
	No. 418 (F) Squadron	Boston III
	No. 456 (F) Squadron	Mosquito NF.XXX
	No. 488 (F) Squadron	Beaufighter VI, Mosquito XII
	No. 501 (F) Squadron	Tempest V
	No. 605 (F) Squadron	Mosquito FB.VI
	No. 611 (F) Squadron	Spitfire IX

BROME, Suffolk

U.S.A.A.F.	490th Bomb Group, 8th A.F.	B.24, B.17

BUNGAY, Suffolk

U.S.A.A.F.	93rd Bomb Group, 8th A.F.	B. 24D
	310th Bomb Group, 12th A.F.	B.25
	329th Bomb Group, 8th A.F.	B.24 H & J
	446th Bomb Group, 8th A.F.	B.24 H, J, L & M

BURY ST EDMUNDS (Westley), Suffolk

R.A.F.	No. 241 (AC) Squadron	Lysander
	No. 268 (AC) Squadron	Lysander, Tomahawk
	No. 652 (AOP) Squadron	Tiger Moth
	No. 656 (AOP) Squadron	Auster AOP 1, 3, 4, 5 & 6

CAMBRIDGE, Cambridgeshire

R.A.F.	No. 2 (AC) Squadron	Lysander I
	No. 4 Flying Instructors' School	Master I, Magister, Tiger Moth

	No. 5 Air Experience Flight	Chipmunk TX
	No. 7 (B) Squadron	Whitley
	No. 16 (AC) Squadron	Lysander I
	No. 22 E.F.T.S.	Tiger Moth, Auster AOP
	No. 22 Reserve Flying School	Hart, Hind, Battle, Tiger Moth, Prentice, Chipmunk
	No. 26 (AC) Squadron	Lysander
	No. 239 (AC) Squadron	Lysander
	No. 268 (AC) Squadron	Lysander
	No. 15 R.A.F. Guard Dog Unit	
	Cambridge Aero Club	Tiger Moth, Moth Minor, assorted light aircraft
	Civilian Repair Unit	Oxford
	Marshalls Limited	Whitley, Albemarle, Mosquito XXXV, I, XII, XVII, PR.XVI, XXV, Typhoon, Dakota, Dragon Rapide, Sea Hornet, Venom NF.II, Brigand T.IV, T.V., Valetta T.IV, Canberra, Britannia, Hercules, Viscount, VC.10, Belfast
	University Air Squadron	Bulldog, Tiger Moth, Chipmunk, Prentice

CASTLE CAMPS, Cambridgeshire

R.A.F.	No. 25 (F) Squadron	Mosquito NF.XXX
	No. 68 (F) Squadron	Beaufighter VIF
	No. 73 (F) Squadron	Hurricane I
	No. 85 (F) Squadron	Hurricane I
	No. 91 (F) Squadron	Spitfire XII
	No. 111 (F) Squadron	Hurricane
	No. 151 (F) Squadron	Mosquito VI, Mosquito NF.XXX
	No. 157 (F) Squadron	Mosquito II
	No. 257 (F) Squadron	Hurricane
	No. 307 (F) Squadron (Polish)	Mosquito NF.XXX
	No. 410 (F) Squadron	Mosquito XIII
	No. 486 (F) Squadron	Typhoon, Tempest V
	No. 517 Radar Calibration Squadron	Blenheim IV, Hurricane, Hornet Moth
	No. 526 (SD) Squadron	Blenheim IV, Hurricane,
	No. 605 (F) Squadron	Mosquito II

CHEDBURGH, Suffolk

R.A.F.	No. 214 (B) Squadron	Stirling I
	No. 218 (B) Squadron	Lancaster III, Stirling I, Stirling III
	No. 301 (B) Squadron (Polish)	Halifax VIII, B.V. Liberator B.VI, Warwick
	No. 304 (B) Squadron (Polish)	Halifax C.VIII, Warwick III, Wellington GR.XIV
	No. 620 (B) Squadron	Wellington XIII, Stirling I
	No. 1653 H.C.U.	Stirling

CHIPPING ONGAR, (Willingale), Essex

U.S.A.A.F.	387th Bomb Group, 9th A.F.	B.26
	Storage Unit	C.47, CG.4A
R.A.F.	Technical Training Unit	

COLTISHALL, Norfolk

R.A.F.	No. 1 (F) Squadron	Spitfire LF.IXb, Spitfire F.XXI
	No. 5 (ASR) Flight	Walrus
	No. 6 (F) Squadron	Jaguar
	No. 19 (F) Squadron	Spitfire Vb
	No. 22 (CC) Squadron	Beaufort
	No. 23 (F) Squadron	Mosquito NF.XXXVI, Vampire NF.X, Javelin FAW.VII
	No. 25 (F) Squadron	Mosquito NF.XVII
	No. 26 (F) Squadron	Mustang III
	No. 41 (F) Squadron	Javelin FAW.VIII, Jaguar
	No. 42 (CC) Squadron	Beaufort
	No. 54 (F) Squadron	Jaguar
	No. 64 (F) Squadron	Spitfire I, Spitfire LF.Vb, Mustang I, F.III, F.V.
	No. 65 (F) Squadron	Spitfire I, Lightning F.I.A.
	No. 66 (F) Squadron	Spitfire I
	No. 68 (F) Squadron	Beaufighter IF, Mosquito XVII, Mosquito XIX
	No. 72 (F) Squadron	Spitfire I
	No. 74 (F) Squadron	Spitfire IIA, Hunter F.VI, Lightning F.I, Lightning F.V.
	No. 80 (F) Squadron	Spitfire IX
	No. 86 (CC) Squadron	Beaufort
	No. 93 (F) Squadron	Havoc
	No. 118 (F) Squadron	Spitfire Vb
	No. 124 (F) Squadron	Spitfire IX
	No. 125 (F) Squadron	Mosquito NF. XVII
	No. 133 (F) Squadron	Hurricane IIB
	No. 137 (F) Squadron	Whirlwind I
	No. 141 (F) Squadron	Mosquito NF.XXXVI, Meteor NF.XI, Venom NF III, Javelin FAW IV
	No. 151 (F) Squadron	Spitfire IIA, Defiant I
	No. 152 (F) Squadron	Spitfire Vb
	No. 154 (F) Squadron	Spitfire IIA
	No. 167 (F) Squadron	Spitfire Vb
	No. 195 (F) Squadron	Typhoon IB
	No. 202 (ASR) Squadron, "D" Flt.	Whirlwind HAR
	No. 222 (F) Squadron	Spitfire I
	No. 226 O.C.U.	Lightning F.I
	No. 229 (F) Squadron	Spitfire IX, Spitfire LF.XVIE
	No. 234 (F) Squadron	Spitfire Vb
	No. 242 (F) Squadron	Hurricane I
	No. 255 (F) Squadron	Beaufighter IIF
	No. 257 (F) Squadron	Hurricane I
	No. 264 (F) Squadron	Mosquito NF.XXXVI
	No. 266 (F) Squadron	Spitfire
	No. 274 (F) Squadron	Tempest V
	No. 278 (ASR) Squadron	Defiant ASR
	No. 303 (F) Squadron	Spitfire LF.Vb, Mustang IV

	No. 306 (F) Squadron	Mustang III
	No. 307 (F) Squadron	Mosquito NF.XXX
	No. 309 (F) Squadron	Mustang IV
	No. 312 (F) Squadron	Spitfire HF.IX
	No. 315 (F) Squadron	Mustang III
	No. 316 (F) Squadron	Mustang III
	No. 346 (F) Squadron	Spitfire
	No. 402 (F) Squadron	Spitfire
	No. 409 (F) Squadron	Beaufighter VIF
	No. 416 (F) Squadron	Spitfire
	No. 453 (F) Squadron	Spitfire IXE
	No. 488 (F) Squadron	Beaufighter IIF
	No. 504 (F) Squadron	Spitfire
	No. 515 (SD) Squadron	Defiant
	No. 602 (F) Squadron	Spitfire IXE, Spitfire XVI
	No. 603 (F) Squadron	Spitfire LF.XVIE
	No. 604 (F) Squadron	Beaufighter I
	No. 610 (F) Squadron	Spitfire
	No. 611 (F) Squadron	Spitfire
	No. 616 (F) Squadron	Spitfire I
	No. 841 (FAA) Squadron	Swordfish, Albacore
	Air Defence Development Squadron	Lightning I

DAGENHAM, Essex

R.A.F.	No.910 Squadron (Balloon)	45 Balloons

DEBACH, Suffolk

U.S.A.A.F.	493rd Bomb Group, 8th A.F.	B.24H & J, B.17G
	German P.O.W. Camp	
	Displaced persons camp	

DEBDEN, Essex

R.A.F.	No. 17 (F) Squadron	Hurricane I
	No. 25 (F) Squadron	Blenheim IF, Beaufighter IF
	No. 29 (F) Squadron	Demon, Blenheim I
	No. 52 O.T.U.	Hurricane, Master, Battle
	No. 71 (F) Squadron (Eagle)	Spitfire V
	No. 73 (F) Squadron	Gladiator
	No. 80 (F) Squadron	Gladiator
	No. 85 (F) Squadron	Hurricane I, Defiant I
	No. 87 (F) Squadron	Gladiator, Hurricane
	No. 111 (F) Squadron	Hurricane
	No. 124 (F) Squadron	Spitfire VI
	No. 157 (F) Squadron	Mosquito
	No. 264 (F) Squadron	Defiant I
	No. 418 (F) Squadron	Boston III
	No. 504 (F) Squadron	Hurricane
	No. 601 (F) Squadron	Hurricane
	No. 616 (F) Squadron	Meteor I
	Air Cadet Gliding School	

	R.A.F. Technical College, Debden Divn.	Chipmunk, Varsity
	Dog Handler's School	
	Empire Radio School	
U.S.A.A.F.	4th Fighter Group, 8th A.F.	Spitfire V, P.47D, P.51B, Spitfire IX

DEOPHAM GREEN, Norfolk

U.S.A.A.F.	452nd Bomb Group, 8th A.F.	B.17G

DOCKING, Norfolk

R.A.F.	No. 2 Armament Practice Camp	
	No. 53 (B) Squadron	Blenheim IV
	No. 53 (GR) Squadron	Whitley VII
	No. 206 (GR) Squadron	Hudson
	No. 221 (B) Squadron	Wellington VIII
	No. 235 (B) Squadron	Blenheim IVF, Beaufighter IC
	No. 304 (B) Squadron	Wellington VIII, Wellington X
	No. 415 (B) Squadron	Albacore, Hampden, Wellington XIII
	No. 521 (MET) Squadron	Hampden, Hudson, Ventura
	No. 524 (B) Squadron	Wellington XIV
	No. 855 (FAA) Squadron	Avenger
	No. 1401 (MET) Flt.	Gladiator, Hampden, Hudson Spitfire V
	No. 1525 (BAT) Flt.	Oxford
	Warwick Training School	

DOWNHAM MARKET, Norfolk

R.A.F.	No. 214 (B) Squadron	Stirling III
	No. 218 (B) Squadron	Stirling III
	No. 571 (B) Squadron	Mosquito B.XVI
	No. 608 (B) Squadron	Mosquito B.XX
	No. 623 (B) Squadron	Stirling III
	No. 627 (B) Squadron	Mosquito IV, Mosquito XX
	No. 633 (B) Squadron	Stirling III
	No. 635 (B) Squadron	Lancaster I, III & VI
	Horsa Glider Storage Unit	

DUNMOW (Little Easter), Essex

R.A.F.	No. 190 (B) Squadron	Stirling IV, Halifax VII, Horsa
	No. 620 (B) Squadron	Stirling IV, Halifax VII, Horsa
U.S.A.A.F.	386th Bomb Group, 9th A.F.	B.26
	387th Bomb Group, 9th A.F.	B.26

DUXFORD, Cambridgeshire

R.A.F.	No. 13 (AC) Squadron	Lysander I
	No. 19 (F) Squadron	Gauntlet, Spitfire I
	No. 56 (F) Squadron	Hurricane IIB, Typhoon IA & IB, Meteor III

AVIATION

	No. 64 (F) Squadron	Blenheim IF, Meteor F.VIII, Meteor NF. XIV, Javelin FAW.VII
	No. 65 (F) Squadron	Meteor F.VIII, Hunter F.VI
	No. 66 (F) Squadron	Gauntlet, Spitfire I, Meteor F.III & F.IV
	No. 75 Signals Wing	Blenheim IVF, Cierva C.30A
	No. 91 (F) Squadron	Spitfire F.XXI
	No. 92 (F) Squadron	Spitfire, Meteor F.III
	No. 133 (F) Squadron (Eagle)	Hurricane IIB
	No. 165 (F) Squadron	Spitfire IX, Mustang III
	No. 181 (F) Squadron	Hurricane I, Typhoon IB
	No. 195 (F) Squadron	Typhoon IB
	No. 222 (F) Squadron	Blenheim IF, Spitfire
	No. 242 (F) Squadron	Hurricane I
	No. 247 (F) Squadron	Typhoon IB
	No. 258 (F) Squadron	Hurricane I
	No. 264 (F) Squadron	Defiant I
	No. 266 (F) Squadron	Spitfire VB, Typhoon IB
	No. 302 (F) Squadron	Hurricane I
	No. 310 (F) Squadron	Hurricane I
	No. 312 (F) Squadron	Hurricane I
	No. 601 (F) Squadron	Airacobra, Hurricane IIB
	No. 609 (F) Squadron	Spitfire VB, Typhoon IA
	No. 611 (F) Squadron	Spitfire I
	No. 1403 (MET) Flt.	Gladiator
	No. 1426 Enemy Aircraft Flt.	He.III, Ju.88, Bf.109, Bf.110
	Cambridge University Air Squadron	Tutor
	Imperial War Museum outstation	Variety of Aircraft
U.S.A.A.F.	78th Fighter Group, 8th A.F.	P.47C, P.47D, P.51D
	350th Fighter Group, 8th A.F.	P.39, Spitfire

EARLS COLNE, Essex

R.A.F.	No. 296 Squadron	Albemarle, Halifax III, ~~Horsa~~ *HAMILCAR GLID[?]*
	No. 297 Squadron	Albemarle, Halifax III, ~~Horsa~~ *HAMILCAR* "
U.S.A.A.F.	94th Bomb Group, 8th A.F.	B.17F
	323rd Bomb Group, 9th A.F.	B.26B

EAST WRETHAM, Norfolk

R.A.F.	No. 115 (B) Squadron	Lancaster B.I, B.II & B.III
	No. 311 (B) Squadron	Wellington IC
	No. 1429 Czech Training Unit	Wellington, Oxford
	No. 1657 H.C.U.	Lancaster B.II
	No. 1678 H.C.U.	Lancaster B.II
	Polish Resettlement Unit	
U.S.A.A.F.	359th Fighter Group, 8th A.F.	P.47D, P.51B, C, D, & K

ELLOUGH, Suffolk

R.A.F.	No. 15 Aircrew Holding Unit	
	No. 119 (RN) Squadron	Albacore
	No. 248 (B) Squadron	Mosquito

No. 254 (B) Squadron	Mosquito
No. 278 (ASR) Squadron	Walrus
No. 279 (ASR) Squadron	Warwick ASR, Sea Otter
No. 280 (ASR) Squadron	Warwick ASR, Sea Otter
No. 618 (B) Squadron	Mosquito IV
No. 810 (FAA) Squadron	Barracuda
No. 819 (RN) Squadron	Swordfish
No. 827 (FAA) Squadron	Barracuda
British Airways Helicopter Unit	

FELIXSTOWE, Suffolk

R.A.F.	No. 7 Recruit Training Centre	
	No. 22 (ASR) Squadron	Whirlwind ASR
	No. 209 (FB) Squadron	Singapore III
	No. 320 (CC) Squadron	Fokker T8W, Short S21 *Mercury*
	(R. Netherlands A.F.)	
	No. 928 (Balloon) Squadron	Balloons
	Marine Aircraft Experimental Establishment	All pre-war and some post-war flying boats, seaplanes and marine craft.
	No. 1103 Marine Craft Unit	Marine craft
	Flying Boat Modification Unit	Catalina, Sunderland

FELTWELL, Norfolk

R.A.F.	No. 3 F.T.S.	Prentice, Provost, Harvard, Tiger Moth
	No. 21 (B) Squadron	Ventura I
	No. 37 (B) Squadron	Harrow, Wellington I, Ia & Ic
	No. 57 (B) Squadron	Wellington Ic, Lancaster B.I.
	No. 75 (B) Squadron	Wellington I, Ia & III
	No. 77 (B) Squadron	Thor I.C.B.M.
	No. 92 (F) Squadron	Spitfire
	No. 192 (SD) Squadron	Wellington III, Halifax B.II & B.III, Mosquito B.IV, Mosquito PR.XVI
	No. 214 (B) Squadron	Harrow I & II, Wellington Ic
	No. 462 (B) Squadron	Halifax B.III, Halifax BVI
	No. 464 (B) Squadron	Ventura I & II
	No. 487 (B) Squadron	Ventura I & II
	No. 1473 (RCM) Flt.	
	No. 1519 (BAT) Flt.	Oxford
	No. 1688 Bomber Defence Training Flt.	Lancaster
	No. 3 Group Lancaster Finishing School	Lancaster B.III
	No. 3 Group G-H Training Flt.	Lancaster B.I, B.III
	Bomber Development Unit	Lancaster, Lincoln
	W.R.A.F. Training Unit	

FERSFIELD (Winfarthing), Norfolk

R.A.F.	No. 21 (B) Squadron	Mosquito
	No. 64 (F) Squadron	Mustang III
	No. 98 (B) Squadron	Mitchell III
	No. 126 (F) Squadron	Mustang III

AVIATION

	No. 140 (B) Squadron	Mosquito IV
	No. 180 (B) Squadron	Mosquito IV
	No. 226 (B) Squadron	Mitchell II & III
	No. 464 (B) Squadron	Mosquito
	No. 487 (B) Squadron	Mosquito
	No. 605 (B) Squadron	Mosquito IV
	No. 613 (B) Squadron	Mosquito IV
	No. 2 Group Support Unit	Boston IIIA, Mosquito, Anson, Mitchell, Hurricane, Martinet
U.S.A.A.F.	Aircraft Disbandment Centre	Several U.S.A.A.F. aircraft types
	3rd Division Detachment	B.17, B.24
	Robot Aircraft Project ANVIL, U.S.N.	PB4Y
	Robot Aircraft Project APHRODITE, U.S.A.A.F.	B.17, Ex-operational aircraft

FINMERE, Cambridgeshire

R.A.F.	No. 1473 Flt. (RCM)	Anson

FLIXTON (Bungay), Suffolk

R.A.F.	No. 53 Maintenance Unit	Bomb Storage
U.S.A.A.F.	446th Bomb Group, 8th A.F.	B.24D, B.24H

FOULSHAM, Norfolk

R.A.F.	No. 12 Glider Storage Unit	Horsa
	No. 98 (B) Squadron	Mitchell III
	No. 171 (B) Squadron	Halifax B.III, B.VI, & GT.III, Stirling BIII
	No. 180 (B) Squadron	Mitchell I & II, Mosquito B.XVI
	No. 192 (SD) Squadron	Halifax B.III & BV, Mosquito B.IV, B.III & B.XVI
	No. 199 (B) Squadron	Halifax B.III & B.VI
	No. 462 (SD) Squadron	Halifax B.III
	No. 514 (B) Squadron	Lancaster B.I, B.II & B.III
	No. 1473 (SD) Flt.	Halifax B.III, Mosquito IV, Wellington X
	No. 1679 H.C.U.	Lancaster B.I.
	Special Duties Radar Development Unit	
	Bomber Support Development Unit	Current Bomber aircraft types
U.S.A.A.F.	U.S.A.A.F. Special Unit	P.38
U.S.A.F.	U.S.A.F. Special Signals Unit	

FOWLMERE, Cambridgeshire

R.A.F.	No. 2 (AC) Squadron	Mustang I
	No. 19 (F) Squadron	Spitfire I & IB
	No. 111 (F) Squadron	Spitfire VB
	No. 133 (F) Squadron	Spitfire IIA
	No. 154 (F) Squadron	Spitfire IIA, IIB
	No. 174 (F) Squadron	Hurricane IIB

	No. 264 (F) Squadron	Defiant I
	No. 310 (F) Squadron	Hurricane
	No. 411 (F) Squadron	Spitfire VB
	No. 655 (AOP) Squadron	Auster AOP
U.S.A.A.F.	339th Fighter Group, 8th A.F.	P.51B, C. D. & K

FRAMLINGHAM, (Parham), Suffolk

U.S.A.A.F.	95th Bomb Group, 8th A.F.	B.17F
	390th Bomb Group, 8th A.F.	B.17F & G
	493rd Bomb Group, 8th A.F., Detachment	B.17G

GREAT ASHFIELD, Suffolk

U.S.A.A.F.	385th Bomb Group, 8th A.F.	B.17 F & G

GOSFIELD, Essex

R.A.F.	No. 271 (T) Squadron	Dakota
	No. 512 (T) Squadron	Dakota
	No. 575 (T) Squadron	Dakota
	No. 1677 (TT) Flt.	Martinet
U.S.A.A.F.	365th Fighter Group, 8th A.F.	P.47
	397th Bomb Group, 9th A.F.	B.26
	410th Bomb Group, 9th A.F.	A.20G

GREAT MASSINGHAM, Norfolk

R.A.F.	No. 18 (B) Squadron	Blenheim IV
	No. 90 (B) Squadron	Fortress I
	No. 169 (B) Squadron	Mosquito II, VI & XIX
	No. 180 (B) Squadron	Mitchell B.I & II, Mosquito B.XVI
	No. 342 (B) Squadron	Boston III, Mitchell III
	No. 1482 Bombing & Gunnery Flt.	Ventura, Blenheim IV, Mitchell, Martinet, Tomahawk
	No. 1692 Bomber Support Flt.	Defiant, Anson, Wellington XVIII, Beaufighter
	No. 1694 (TT) Flt.	Martinet
	Central Fighter Establishment	Current fighter aircraft types

GREAT SAMPFORD, Cambridgeshire

R.A.F.	No. 65 (F) Squadron	Spitfire VB
	No. 133 (F) Squadron, Eagle	Spitfire VB
	No. 616 (F) Squadron	Spitfire VB, Spitfire VI
	R.A.F. Regiment Battle School	
U.S.A.A.F.	335th Pursuit Squadron, U.S.A.A.F.	Spitfire VB
	336th Pursuit Squadron, U.S.A.A.F.	Spitfire VB

HALESWORTH, (Holton), Suffolk

R.A.F.	No. 758 (FAA) Squadron	Oxford, Beaufighter
	No. 762 (FAA) Squadron	Oxford, Beaufort, Sea Vampire
	No. 798 (FAA) Squadron	Oxford, Barracuda, Sea Vampire
U.S.A.A.F.	5th Emergency Rescue Squadron	P.47D, OA-10A, B.17G
	56th Fighter Group, 8th A.F.	P.47D

AVIATION

	489th Bomb Group, 8th A.F.	B.24 H & J
	496th Fighter Training Group	P.51

HARDWICK, Norfolk

U.S.A.A.F.	93rd Bomb Group, 8th A.F.	B.24 J, L & M
	310th Bomb Group, 12th A.F.	B.25
	329th Bomb Group, 8th A.F.	B.24

HARWICH, Essex

R.A.F.	No. 928 Balloon Squadron	24 Balloons

HETHEL, Norfolk

R.A.F.	No. 65 (F) Squadron	Spitfire LF.Ibe
	No. 126 (F) Squadron	Spitfire LF.Ibe
	No. 303 (F) Squadron	Mustang IV
	No. 316 (F) Squadron	Mustang III
U.S.A.A.F.	320th Bomb Group, 8th A.F.	B.26
	389th Bomb Group, 8th A.F.	B.24D, E, H, J, L, & M

HONINGTON, Suffolk

R.A.F.	No. 1 Transport Aircraft M.U.	Dakota, York
	No. 7 (B) Squadron	Valiant
	No. 9 (B) Squadron	Wellington I & III, Tornado
	No. 10 (B) Squadron	Canberra B.II & T.IV
	No. 12 Squadron	Buccaneer S.2B
	No. 15 (B) Squadron	Canberra B.II & T.IV
	No. 44 (B) Squadron	Canberra B.II
	No. 55 (B) Squadron	Victor B.IA
	No. 57 (B) Squadron	Canberra B.II & T.IV, Victor B.IA
	No. 75 (B) Squadron	Harrow
	No. 77 (B) Squadron	Wellesley I, Whitley B.III
	No. 90 (B) Squadron	Valiant B.I
	No. 94 M.U.	Armament
	No. 102 (B) Squadron	Heyford
	No. 103 (B) Squadron	Battle
	No. 105 (B) Squadron	Blenheim IV
	No. 199 (B) Squadron	Valiant B.I, Canberra B.II
	No. 204 (GR) Squadron	Shackleton
	No. 208 (B) Squadron	Buccaneer S.2A
	No. 215 (B) Squadron	Harrow, Wellington IA
	No. 237 O.C.U.	Buccaneer S.2A
	No. 311 (B) Squadron	Wellington IC
	No. 809 (RN) Squadron	Buccaneer
U.S.A.A.F.	364th Fighter Group	P.38J, P.51D
	B.17 Service Unit	B.17

HORHAM, Suffolk

R.A.F.	No. 25 M.U. Satellite	
	No. 262 M.U. Satellite	

U.S.A.A.F.	47th Bomb Group, 12th A.F.	A.20B
	95th Bomb Group, 12th A.F.	B.17D
	323rd Bomb Squadron, 12th A.F.	B.26B

HORSHAM ST FAITHS, Norfolk

R.A.F.	No. 9 (B) Squadron	Wellington IA
	No. 18 (B) Squadron	Blenheim IV
	No. 19 (F) Squadron	Spitfire I
	No. 21 (B) Squadron	Blenheim IV
	No. 23 (F) Squadron	Venom NF.III, Javelin FAW IV
	No. 34 (TT) Squadron	Beaufighter TT X
	No. 64 (F) Squadron	Mustang III, Mosquito T.III, Hornet
	No. 65 (F) Squadron	Spitfire LF IBe, Hornet
	No. 66 (F) Squadron	Spitfire I
	No. 74 (F) Squadron	Meteor F.III, Hunter F.IV & F.VI, Oxford
	No. 82 (B) Squadron	Blenheim IV
	No. 105 (B) Squadron	Blenheim IV, Mosquito I & IV
	No. 114 (B) Squadron	Blenheim IV
	No. 118 (F) Squadron	Spitfire
	No. 119 (F) Squadron	Mustang III
	No. 139 (B) Squadron	Blenheim IV & V, Mosquito B.IV
	No. 245 (F) Squadron	Meteor F.III & F.VIII
	No. 257 (F) Squadron	Meteor F.III
	No. 263 (F) Squadron	Meteor F.III
	No. 264 (F) Squadron, "A" Flt.	Defiant
	No. 275 (ASR) Squadron	Sycamore
	No. 307 (F) Squadron	Mosquito NF.XXX
	No. 500 (F) Squadron	Meteor F.IV
	No. 504 (F) Squadron	Meteor F.VIII
	No. 601 (F) Squadron	Meteor F.VIII
	No. 695 (TT) Squadron	Spitfire XVI, Oxford, Vengeance IV, Martinet, Hurricane, Lysander
	No. 1508 (BAT) Flt.	Blenheim IV, Oxford
	No. 1655 Mosquito Training Flt.	Blenheim VD, Mosquito IV
U.S.A.A.F.	56th Fighter Group, 8th A.F.	P.47C
	319th Bomb Group, 12th A.F.	B.26B
	458th Bomb Group, 8th A.F.	B.24H, J, L, & M
	Now Norwich Airport	
	Air Anglia Operations	

IPSWICH, Suffolk

R.A.F.	No. 3 (AATT) Flt.	Martinet
	No. 19 (F) Squadron	Spitfire VB
	No. 45 E. & R. T. S.	Tiger Moth
	No. 65 (F) Squadron	Spitfire VB
	No. 107 (B) Squadron	Blenheim IV
	No. 110 (B) Squadron	Blenheim IV
	No. 266 (F) Squadron	Spitfire VB
	No. 277 (ASR) Squadron	Lysander, Walrus

	No. 340 (F) Squadron	Spitfire VB
	No. 529 (AC) Squadron	Cierva C.30a
	No. 598 (AAC) Squadron	Martinet, Hurricane
	No. 652 (AOP) Squadron	Auster III
	No. 658 (AOP) Squadron	Auster III
	No. 679 (AAC) Squadron	Martinet, Hurricane, Barracuda, Vengeance
	No. 1499 Gunnery Flt.	Martinet
	No. 1508 (BAT) Flt.	Oxford
	No. 1517 (BAT) Flt.	Oxford
	No. 1616 (TT) Flt.	Henley
	Civil Air Guard	Tiger Moth
	Suffolk Flying Club	Auster, Cessna
	Horizon Flying Club	Tomahawk

KNETTISHALL, Norfolk

U.S.A.A.F.	388th Bomb Group, 8th A.F.	B.17 G, "Aphrodite" B.17, B.24

LAKENHEATH, Suffolk

R.A.F.	No. 20 O.C.U.	Wellington Ic
	No. 149 (B) Squadron	Stirling B.I, B.III
	No. 199 (B) Squadron	Stirling B.III, Wellington B.III
U.S.A.F.	2nd Bomb Group	B.29
	43rd Bomb Group	B.50A, KB.29M
	48th T.F.W.	F.100D, F.4D, F.III
	93rd Bomb Group	B.50D, KB.29P
	Support Units	C.97, C.74, B.36D, C.124, B.47, RB.36, RB.50, U-2, KC.97

LANGHAM, Norfolk

R.A.F.	No. 1 A.A.C.U.	Henley III TT, Defiant
	No. 2 Civil A.A. Co-op Unit	Beaufighter TT.X, Mosquito XXXV, Vampire TXI
	No. 112 Sub Storage Depot	
	No. 254 (CC) Squadron	Beaufighter
	No. 280 (ASR) Squadron	Warwick ASR:I, Anson, Hudson
	No. 407 (B) Squadron	Wellington XIV
	No. 455 (F) Squadron	Beaufighter
	No. 489 (F) Squadron	Beaufighter
	No. 519 (F) Squadron	Spitfire VI
	No. 521 (MET) Flt.	Fortress II, Gladiator
	No. 524 (B) Squadron	Wellington XIV
	No. 612 (GR) Squadron	Warwick
	No. 819 (FAA) Squadron	Swordfish
	No. 827 (FAA) Squadron	Barracuda
	No. 1402 (MET) Flt.	Hurricane
	Armament Practice Camp	
	Emergency Landing Ground	
	Royal Netherlands A.F. Training School	

LAVENHAM (Cockfield), Suffolk

U.S.A.A.F.	487th Bomb Group, 8th A.F.	B.24H & J, B.17G

LEISTON (Theberton), Suffolk

| U.S.A.A.F. | 357th Fighter Group, 8th & 9th A.F. | P.51D & K |
| | 358th Fighter Group, 8th A.F. | P.47D |

LITTLE SNORING, Norfolk

R.A.F.	No. 2 Civil A.A. Co-op Unit	Spitfire VB, Vampire T.XI
	No. 23 (B) Squadron	Mosquito VI
	No. 115 (B) Squadron	Lancaster B.I, II & V
	No. 141 (F) Squadron	Mosquito NF.XXX
	No. 169 (F) Squadron	Mosquito II & VI
	No. 274 M.U.	
	No. 515 (F) Squadron	Beaufighter II, Mosquito II & VI
	No. 1678 H.C.U.	Lancaster II
	No. 1692 Flt.	Defiant II, Beaufighter VI, Anson, Wellington XVIII, Mosquito IV
	Horsa Glider Storage Unit	Horsa

LITTLE WALDEN, Essex

U.S.A.A.F.	56th Fighter Group, 8th A.F.	P.47M
	361st Fighter Group, 8th A.F.	P.51B, C, D & K
	409th Bomb Group, 9th A.F.	A.20 Havoc
	493rd Bomb Group, 8th A.F.	B.17G

LORDS BRIDGE, Cambridgeshire

| R.A.F. | Relief Landing Ground | |
| | No. 22 E.F.T.S. | Tiger Moth |

LUDHAM, Norfolk

R.A.F.	No. 1 (F) Squadron	Spitfire F.XXI
	No. 19 (F) Squadron	Spitfire VB
	No. 91 (F) Squadron	Spitfire XII, Spitfire XXI
	No.152 (F) Squadron	Spitfire IIA
	No. 167 (F) Squadron	Spitfire VB
	No. 195 (F) Squadron	Typhoon IB
	No. 602 (F) Squadron	Spitfire XVI
	No. 603 (F) Squadron	Spitfire LF.IBe
	No. 610 (F) Squadron	Spitfire VB
	No. 611 (F) Squadron	Spitfire LF.VB

MARHAM, Norfolk

R.A.F.	No. 1 RNZAF (B) Squadron	Wellington IC
	No. 3 Group Fighter Affiliation Flt.	Battle
	No. 15 (B) Squadron	Washington
	No. 35 (B) Squadron	Lincoln BII, Washington B.I, Canberra B.II
	No. 38 (B) Squadron	Hendon, Wellington IC
	No. 44 (B) Squadron	Washington B.I
	No. 55 (B) Squadron	Victor K.IA
	No. 57 (B) Squadron	Washington B.I

AVIATION

	No. 90 (B) Squadron	Washington, Canberra
	No. 100 (B) Squadron	Canberra
	No. 102 (B) Squadron	Heyford
	No. 105 (B) Squadron	Blenheim IV, Mosquito IV
	No. 109 (B) Squadron	Mosquito
	No. 115 (B) Squadron	Harrow, Wellington I, Lincoln B.II, Washington B.I.
	No. 139 (B) Squadron	Mosquito B.III
	No. 147 (B) Squadron	Wellington I
	No. 148 (B) Squadron	Wellington IC, Valiant B.I,
	No. 149 (B) Squadron	Washington
	No. 207 (B) Squadron	Washington B.I, Valiant B.I., Canberra
	No. 214 (B) Squadron	Valiant B.I, Victor K.I
	No. 218 (B) Squadron	Battle, Wellington IC, Stirling I
	No. 231 O.C.U.	Canberra
	No. 232 O.C.U.	Victor IA & B.II
	No. 1418 (B) Flt.	Wellington B.III
	No. 1483 Bomber Defence Training Unit	Defiant II, Wellington B.III
	No. 1655 Mosquito Training Unit	Blenheim VD, Bisley, Oxford II, Mosquito III
	Central Bomber Establishment	Lancaster, Lincoln
	Washington Conversion Unit	Washington B.I.
U.S.A..F.	97th Bomb Group	B.29 Superfortress
	Bombing Exercise Units	B.29, B.50, B.47, B52D

MARTLESHAM HEATH, Suffolk

R.A.F.	No. 1 (F) Squadron	Typhoon I
	No. 3 (F) Squadron	Hurricane IIB & IIC
	No. 15 Squadron	Experimental, all types
	No. 17 (F) Squadron	Hurricane I & II
	No. 22 Squadron	Experimental, all types
	No. 22 (ASR) Squadron	Whirlwind HAR
	No. 25 (F) Squadron	Blenheim IF, Beaufighter NF.I
	No. 29 (F) Squadron	Blenheim INF
	No. 41 (F) Squadron	Spitfire VB
	No. 54 (F) Squadron	Spitfire VB
	No. 56 (F) Squadron	Hurricane I & IIB, Typhoon IB
	No. 64 (F) Squadron	Demon
	No. 65 (F) Squadron	Spitfire VB
	No. 71 (F) Squadron	Hurricane I & II, Spitfire VB
	No. 85 (F) Squadron	Hurricane I, Spitfire VB
	No. 92 (F) Squadron	Spitfire
	No. 110 (B) Squadron	Blenheim IV
	No. 111 (F) Squadron	Spitfire VB
	No. 121 (F) Squadron	Spitfire VB
	No. 122 (F) Squadron	Spitfire VB
	No. 124 (F) Squadron	Spitfire VB
	No. 132 (F) Squadron	Spitfire VB
	No. 151 (F) Squadron	Hurricane I

	No. 165 (F) Squadron	Spitfire VB
	No. 182 (F) Squadron	Hurricane I, Typhoon IA
	No. 198 (F) Squadron	Typhoon IB
	No. 222 (F) Squadron	Spitfire VB & IX
	No. 242 (F) Squadron	Hurricane I & IIB
	No. 257 (F) Squadron	Hurricane I
	No. 258 (F) Squadron	Hurricane II
	No. 263 (F) Squadron	Whirlwind I
	No. 264 (F) Squadron	Defiant I
	No. 266 (F) Squadron	Spitfire I & IIB
	No. 277 (ASR) Squadron	Lysander, Walrus, Defiant I
	No. 278 (ASR) Squadron	Walrus, Spitfire II, Anson
	No. 303 (F) Squadron	Spitfire VB
	No. 306 (F) Squadron	Spitfire IX
	No. 310 (F) Squadron	Hurricane IIB
	No. 312 (F) Squadron	Hurricane IIB
	No. 317 (F) Squadron	Spitfire VB
	No. 350 (F) Squadron	Spitfire VB
	No. 401 (F) Squadron	Spitfire IXB
	No. 402 (F) Squadron	Hurricane IIA
	No. 403 (F) Squadron	Spitfire VB
	No. 411 (F) Squadron	Spitfire VB
	No. 412 (F) Squadron	Spitfire VB
	No. 416 (F) Squadron	Spitfire VB
	No. 452 (F) Squadron	Spitfire VB
	No. 453 (F) Squadron	Spitfire VB
	No. 485 (F) Squadron	Spitfire VB
	No. 501 (F) Squadron	Spitfire VB
	No. 504 (F) Squadron	Hurricane I
	No. 604 (F) Squadron	Blenheim I & IV
	No. 605 (F) Squadron	Hurricane IIB
	No. 607 (F) Squadron	Hurricane IIB
	No. 610 (F) Squadron	Spitfire VB
	No. 613 (ASR) Squadron	Lysander
	No. 1488 Gunnery Flt.	Lysander, Defiant
	No. 2735 Squadron, R.A.F. Regiment	
	Blind Landing Experimental Unit	Dakota, Devon, Canberra, Lincoln Anson
	Bomb Ballistic Unit	Several experimental bomber types
	Rapid Landing Flt.	Meteor NF.XI & XIV
	Armament and Instrument Experimental Unit	Assorted fighter and bomber aircraft
	Battle of Britain Memorial Flt.	Hurricane II, Spitfire IX
	Air Training Corps Gliding School	Cadet gliders
U.S.A.F	356th Fighter Group, 8th A.F.	Spitfire IX, P.47D, P.51D & K

MATCHING, Essex

R.A.F.	Operational & Refresher Unit	Stirling IV, Halifax III, Horsa
U.S.A.A.F.	391st Bomb Group, 9th A.F.	B.26

AVIATION

MATLASKE, Norfolk

R.A.F.	No. 3 (F) Squadron	Tempest V
	No. 19 (F) Squadron	Spitfire IX, Mustang III
	No. 56 (F) Squadron	Typhoon IA, Tempest V
	No. 65 (F) Squadron	Mustang III
	No. 72 (F) Squadron	Spitfire VB
	No. 122 (F) Squadron	Mustang III
	No. 137 (F) Squadron	Whirlwind I
	No. 195 (F) Squadron	Typhoon IB
	No. 222 (F) Squadron	Spitfire IIB
	No. 229 (F) Squadron	Spitfire IX
	No. 245 (F) Squadron	Typhoon IB
	No. 266 (F) Squadron	Typhoon IA
	No. 278 (ASR) Squadron	Lysander, Walrus
	No. 453 (F) Squadron	Spitfire IX, XVI & LF.XVI
	No. 486 (F) Squadron	Tempest V
	No. 601 (F) Squadron	Hurricane IIB, Airacobra
	No. 602 (F) Squadron	Spitfire IXE
	No. 609 (F) Squadron	Typhoon IB
	No. 611 (F) Squadron	Spitfire LF.VB
U.S.A.A.F.	3rd Aviation Engineering Battalion	

MENDLESHAM, Suffolk

R.A.F.	No. 310 (F) Squadron	Spitfire LF.IX
	No. 312 (F) Squadron	Spitfire LF. IX
	No. 313 (F) Squadron	Spitfire IX
	No. 94 M.U. Storage Depot	Ammunition
U.S.A.A.F.	34th Bomb Group	B.24, B.17G

MEPAL, Cambridgeshire

R.A.F.	No. 7 (B) Squadron	Lancaster B.I & B.III
	No. 44 (B) Squadron	Lancaster B.I
	No. 49 (B) Squadron	Lancaster B.I, Lincoln B.I
	No. 75 (B) Squadron	Stirling I & III, Lancaster B.I & B.III
	No. 113 Squadron	Thor I.C.B.M.

METFIELD, Suffolk

U.S.A.A.F.	353rd Fighter Group, 8th A.F.	P.47D
	491st Bomb Group, 8th A.F.	B.24H, J, L & M
	European Air Division Transport Depot	C.47, C.54, B.24

METHWOLD, Norfolk

R.A.F.	No. 18 (B) Squadron	Blenheim IV
	No. 21 (B) Squadron	Blenheim IV, Ventura
	No. 37 (B) Squadron	Wellington IC
	No. 57 (B) Squadron	Wellington IC
	No. 75 (B) Squadron	Wellington IC
	No. 149 (B) Squadron	Lancaster B.I & B.III

	No. 207 (B) Squadron	Lancaster B.III
	No. 214 (B) Squadron	Wellington IC
	No. 218 (B) Squadron	Lancaster B.I
	No. 320 (B) Squadron	Mitchell II & III
	No. 464 (B) Squadron	Hudson GR.III, Ventura I & II
	No. 487 (B) Squadron	Ventura I & II
	Glider Storage Unit	Horsa

MILDENHALL, Suffolk

R.A.F.	No. 9 (B) Squadron	Wellington I
	No. 15 (B) Squadron	Stirling B.III, Lancaster B.I & B. III
	No. 21 (B) Squadron	Ventura
	No. 35 (B) Squadron	Lincoln B.I
	No. 38 (B) Squadron	Hendon, Heyford, Wellington I
	No. 44 (B) Squadron	Lincoln B.II
	No. 73 (F) Squadron	Gladiator
	No. 75 (B) Squadron	Wellington IC, Stirling B.I.
	No. 99 (B) Squadron	Heyford, Wellington IC
	No. 115 (B) Squadron	Wellington B.III, Lancaster B.I, Lincoln B.II
	No. 149 (B) Squadron	Heyford, Wellington IC, Stirling B.I & B.III Lincoln B.II
	No. 149 Conversion Flt.	Stirling
	No. 207 (B) Squadron	Lincoln B.II
	No. 211 (B) Squadron	Hind
	No. 218 (B) Squadron	Blenheim IV
	No. 401 (MET) Flt.	Gladiator
	No. 419 (B) Squadron	Wellington IC & B.III
	No. 622 (B) Squadron	Stirling B.III, Lancaster B.I & B.III
	No. 1403 (MET) Flt.	Gladiator
	No. 1503 (BAT) Flt.	Oxford
	No. 1505 (BAT) Flt.	Oxford
	H.Q. No. 3 Bomber Group	
U.S.A.F.	10th Airborne Command Control Squadron	EC.135H
	28th Weather Squadron	B.17
	53rd Weather Squadron	WB.50D, B.17
	93rd Bomb Wing	B.50D, B.47
	316th T.A.W.	C.130
	317th T.A.W.	C.130E
	513th T.A.W.	VT.29B, T.39A, C.130, EC.135
	2176th Communication Squadron	Transport types
	7511th Air Base Squadron	
	Military Airlift Command Terminal	C.97, C.118, C.124, C.130, C.133, C.141 & C.5
	U.S. Navy Logistic Support Unit	UC.45J, C.117D, C.131, CIA Trader
	322nd Air Division	C.124, C.118, C.97, C. 130, C.133, C. 141, C.5
	435th T.A.W.	C.130

AVIATION

	Civil Air Guard Units on Rotation	KC.135
	European Tanker Task Force	KC.135
	H.Q. U.S.A.F. 3rd Air Division	
	2nd Bomb Group	B.50D
	22nd Bomb Group	B.50D
	509th Bomb Group	B.50D

NEWMARKET HEATH, Suffolk

R.A.F.	No. 3 Lancaster Finishing School	Lancaster
	No. 7 (B) Squadron	Stirling B.I.
	No. 54 M.U. H.Q. Outstations in East Anglia	
	No. 75 (B) Squadron	Stirling B.I. & B.III
	No. 99 (B) Squadron	Wellington IC
	No. 107 (B) Squadron	Blenheim IV
	No. 138 (SD) Squadron	Hudson, Whitley, Lysander, Anson
	No. 149 (B) Squadron	Wellington I
	No. 161 (SD) Squadron	Lysander, Anson
	No. 215 (B) Squadron	Wellington IC
	No. 1419 (SD) Flt.	Whitley, Lysander, Anson
	No. 1483 Gunnery Flt.	Wellington X, Martinet, Spitfire V, Hurricane II
	No. 1688 Bomber Defence Training Unit	Wellington B.III & X, Hurricane, Spitfire, Lancaster B.I.
	Bomber Development Unit	Heavy bomber types
	Special Prototype Testing	Meteor prototype, Hamilcar prototype

NORTH CREAKE, Norfolk

R.A.F.	No. 171 (SD) Squadron	Stirling B.III, Halifax B.III, B.VI & GT.III
	No. 199 (SD) Squadron	Halifax B.III
	No. 274 M.U.	Storage
	Decoy Airfield Flt	

NORTH PICKENHAM, Norfolk

R.A.F.	No. 220 Squadron	Thor I.C.B.M.
	No. 258 M.U. (Sub-unit)	
	Kestrel Evaluation Unit	Kestrel
U.S.A.A.F.	491st Bomb Group, 8th A.F.	B.24L & M
	492nd Bomb Group, 8th A.F.	B.24H & J

OAKINGTON, Cambridgeshire

R.A.F.	No. 1 F.T.S.	Harvard
	No. 3 Photo Reconnaissance Unit	Spitfire Type F PR
	No. 5 F.T.S.	Vampire T.V, T.IX & T.XI, Varsity, Jetstream
	No. 5 F.T.S. Meteor Flt.	Meteor VII
	No. 7 (B) Squadron	Stirling B.I, Lancaster B.III
	No. 15 (B) Squadron	Stirling B.I

No. 24 (T) Squadron	Dakota, Valetta, York	
No. 27 (T) Squadron	Stirling V	
No. 30 (T) Squadron	Stirling V	
No. 46 (T) Squadron	Stirling V	
No. 86 (T) Squadron	Liberator	
No. 97 (B) Squadron	Lancaster B.I & B.III	
No. 101 (B) Squadron	Wellington IC	
No. 206 (T) Squadron	Liberator	
No. 218 (B) Squadron	Blenheim IV	
No. 238 (TC)	Stirling V	
No. 206 A.F.U. Squadron	Meteor III, IV & VII	
No. 242 (T) Squadron	York	
No. 571 (B) Squadron	Mosquito B.XVI	
No. 627 (B) Squadron	Lancaster B.I, B.II & B.III, Mosquito B.IV, B.IX, B.XVI & B.XXV, Boston III	
No. 657 Squadron	Gazelle, Lynx	
No. 1409 (MET) Flt.	Mosquito IV	

OLD BUCKENHAM, Norfolk

U.S.A.A.F.	453rd Bomb Group, 8th A.F.	B.24H, J, L & M

OULTON, Norfolk

R.A.F.	No. 18 (B) Squadron	Blenheim IV
	No. 21 (B) Squadron	Blenheim IV, Ventura B.I
	No. 88 (B) Squadron	Boston III
	No. 114 (B) Squadron	Hudson III
	No. 119 Sub-storage unit	Mosquito
	No. 139 (B) Squadron	Boston I, Blenheim IV
	No. 214 (SD) Squadron	Fortress B.II & B.III
	No. 223 (SD) Squadron	Fortress B.II & B.III, Liberator B.VI
	No. 236 (CC) Squadron	Beaufighter IC
	No. 1428 Hudson Conversion Unit	Hudson
	No. 1699 (SD) Flt.	Fortress B.II & B.III, Liberator B.VI
U.S.A.A.F.	803rd Radio Countermeasures Squadron	B.17F & G, B.24H & J, P.51

RACKHEATH, Norfolk

U.S.A.A.F.	467th Bomb Group, 8th A.F.	B.24H, J, L & M

RATTLESDEN, Suffolk

R.A.F.	Bloodhound Missile Unit	Bloodhound
U.S.A.A.F.	322nd Bomb Group, 8th A.F.	B.26B
	447th Bomb Group, 8th A.F.	B.17G

RAYDON, Suffolk

R.A.F.	Ministry Storage Depot	
U.S.A.A.F.	353rd Fighter Group, 8th A.F.	P.51D & K
	357th Fighter Group, 8th A.F.	P.51C & D

358th Fighter Group, 8th A.F.	P.47D
652nd Weather Squadron, 8th A.F.	P.51

RIDGEWELL, Essex

R.A.F.	No. 90 (B) Squadron	Stirling B.I
	No. 94 M.U.	
U.S.A.A.F.	4th Bomb Wing Substitution Unit	
	381st Bomb Group, 8th A.F.	B.17F

RIVENHALL, Essex

R.A.F.	No. 295 (T) Squadron	Stirling IV, Horsa	} 1944 - 45
	No. 570 (T) Squadron	Stirling IV, Horsa	
	No. 1677 (TT) Squadron	Martinet	
U.S.A.A.F.	363rd Fighter Group	P.51B	} 1942 - 43
	397th Fighter Group	P.51B	

BOMB GROOP   *B26 MARAUDER 1943 - 64*

ROCHFORD, Essex

R.A.F.	No. 19 (F) Squadron	Mustang III
	No. 41 (F) Squadron	Spitfire
	No. 54 (F) Squadron	Spitfire I & IIA
	No. 56 (F) Squadron	Hurricane I
	No. 64 (F) Squadron	Spitfire I, IIA & VB
	No. 74 (F) Squadron	Spitfire I
	No. 137 (F) Squadron	Hurricane IV
	No. 222 (F) Squadron	Spitfire VB, LFIXB
	No. 234 (F) Squadron	Spitfire VB
	No. 264 (F) Squadron	Mosquito NF.II
	No. 317 (F) Squadron	Spitfire IX
	No. 350 (F) Squadron	Spitfire VB
	No. 402 (F) Squadron	Hurricane IIA & IIB
	No. 403 (F) Squadron	Spitfire VB
	No. 411 (F) Squadron	Spitfire VB
	No. 453 (F) Squadron	Spitfire VB
	No. 603 (F) Squadron	Spitfire VA
	No. 611 (F) Squadron	Spitfire IIA
	No. 616 (F) Squadron	Spitfire I
	No. 17 Armament Practice Camp	

ROUGHAM, Suffolk

U.S.A.A.F.	47th Bomb Group, 12th A.F.	B.20B
	94th Bomb Group, 8th A.F.	B.17F
	322nd Bomb Group, 9th A.F.	B.26

SCULTHORPE, Norfolk

R.A.F.	No. 21 (B) Squadron	Mosquito B.IV & FB.VI
	No. 140 Squadron Aircraft Servicing Wing	
	No. 214 (B) Squadron	Fortress III

	No. 342 (B) Squadron	Mitchell III
	No. 464 (B) Squadron	Ventura B.I & B.II, Mosquito B.IV & FB.VI
	No. 487 (B) Squadron	Mosquito FB VI, Ventura B.I & B.II
	Glider Storage Unit	Horsa
U.S.A.A.F.	Radio Countermeasures Squadron, 8th A.F.	B.17F & G, B.24H & J, P51
U.S.A.F.	2nd Bomb Group	B.50D, KB.29M
	22nd Bomb Group	B.50D, KB29M
	19th T.R.S.	RB.45C, RB.66
	47th Bomb Group	RB45C, B.45
	43rd Bomb Group	B.50A, KB.29M
	49th Air Division	C.119, C.47, L.20, T.33
	92nd Bomb Group	B.29
	97th Bomb Group	B.50D, KB.29M
	301st Bomb Group	B.50D, KB.29M
	803rd Bomb Squadron	B.17F & G, B.24H & K, P.51
	8554th T.T. Flight	TB.26B, L.5
	Tanker Unit	KB.29P, KB.50D, KB.50J
	Radio Controlled Drone Unit	
	Storage Unit	F.100, Mystere, T.33
	7519th Combat Support Unit	

SEETHING, Norfolk

U.S.A.A.F.	448th Bomb Group, 8th A.F.	B.24H, J, L, & M

SHEPHERD'S GROVE, (Stanton), Suffolk

R.A.F.	No. 82 Squadron	Thor I.C.B.M.
	No. 89 (F) Squadron	Javelin FAW.VI
	No. 196 (T) Squadron	Stirling IV
	No.299 (B) Squadron	Stirling V
	No. 1657 H.C.U.	Stirling
	No. 1677 (TT) Squadron	Martinet
	Radio Warfare Establishment	Anson, Lancaster
U.S.A.F.	81st T.F.W.	F.84F, F.86A
	78th F.B.S.	F.84F

SHIPDHAM, Norfolk

R.A.F.	German P.O.W. Camp	
	Arrow Air Services	Light Civil Aircraft Services
U.S.A.A.F.	44th Bomb Group, 8th A.F.	B.24D & M
	319th Bomb Group, 12th A.F.	B.26B

SNAILWELL, Cambridgeshire

R.A.F.	No. 56 (F) Squadron	Typhoon IB
	No. 137 (F) Squadron	Whirlwind I
	No. 152 (F) Squadron	Spitfire IIA
	No. 168 (AC) Squadron	Tomahawk, Mustang I
	No. 170 (AC) Squadron	Mustang I

	No. 181 (F) Squadron	Typhoon IA
	No. 183 (F) Squadron	Typhoon IB
	No. 268 (AC) Squadron	Lysander, Tomahawk, Mustang I
	No. 309 (AC) Squadron	Mustang I
	No. 417 Repair and Salvage Unit	
	No. 609 (F) Squadron	Typhoon IB
	No. 613 (F) Squadron	Mustang III
	No. 614 (B) Squadron	Blenheim IV
	No. 527 Squadron	Blenheim IV, Hurricane, Hornet Moth
	No. 1426 Flt. Enemy Aircraft	He.III, Ju.88, Me.109, Bf.110
	Glider Maintenance Unit	
	Belgian A.F. Training Unit	Master II
U.S.A.A.F.	347th Fighter Squadron	P.39
	350th Fighter Group, 8th A.F.	Spitfire VB
	41st Base Complement Squadron	A.20G

SNETTERTON HEATH, Norfolk

R.A.F.	No. 262 M.U.	
U.S.A.A.F.	96th Bomb Group, 8th A.F.	B.17F
	386th Bomb Group, 8th A.F.	B.26B & C

STANSTED, Essex

R.A.F.	No. 263 M.U.	
	German P.O.W. Camp	
U.S.A.A.F.	344th Bomb Group, 9th A.F.	B.26
U.S.A.F.	30th Air Depot Group	
	803rd Engineering Aviation Battalion	
Civil	London Aero Motor Services	Halifax VIII
	Kemsley Airways	Dakota, Proctor
	Skyways	Tudor
	Aviation Traders	Carvair conversion
	B.E.A. & B.O.A.C. Training School	
	British United Airways (Trooping)	
	M.O.A. Fire Service Training School	

STRADISHALL, Suffolk

R.A.F.	No. 1 Air Navigators School	Varsity, Meteor XIV & XVII, Dominie T.I
	No. 1 (F) Squadron	Hunter F.VI & F.XVIII
	No. 7 (B) Squadron	Stirling I
	No. 9 (B) Squadron	Heyford, Wellington IA
	No. 35 (B) Squadron	Lancaster B.I
	No. 51 (T) Squadron	Stirling C.V.
	No. 54 (F) Squadron	Hunter F.VI
	No. 75 (B) Squadron	Wellington IA
	No. 85 (F) Squadron	Javelin FAW II & VI
	No. 89 (F) Squadron	Venom NF, Javelin FAW VI
	No. 101 (B) Squadron	Wellington B.III
	No. 109 (SD) Squadron	Halifax, Wellington III
	No. 111 (F) Squadron	Hunter IX

No. 115 (B) Squadron	Lancaster B.I
No. 125 (F) Squadron	Venom NF.V, Meteor NF.XI
No. 138 (SD) Squadron	Whitley, Hudson, Anson, Wellington
No. 148 (B) Squadron	Heyford, Wellesley I, Wellington I
No. 149 (B) Squadron	Lancaster B.I & B.III
No. 150 (B) Squadron	Battle
No. 152 (F) Squadron	Meteor NF.XIV
No. 158 (T) Squadron	Stirling C.V., York
No. 186 (B) Squadron	Lancaster B.I, B.III
No. 203 A.F.U.	Meteor IV, VII, Spitfire XIV, XVI, XIX, Vampire V, Harvard II
No. 207 (B) Squadron	Lancaster B.I, Lincoln B.II
No. 208 (F) Squadron	Hunter FGA, IX
No. 214 (B) Squadron	Stirling B.I
No. 215 (B) Squadron	Wellington I
No. 226 O.C.U.	Meteor IV & VII, Spitfire XIV, XVI, XIX, Vampire V, Harvard II, Meteor PR.IX, Tempest V, Beaufighter TT.X, Mosquito III, Hurricane, Martinet, Mosquito TT.35
No. 236 (B) Squadron	Blenheim IV
No. 245 (F) Squadron	Hunter F.IV
No. 253 (F) Squadron	Venom NF.II
No. 254 (F) Squadron	Blenheim IF
No. 258 (F) Squadron	Blenheim IV
No. 263 (F) Squadron	Hunter F.VI
No. 1419 (SD) Flt.	Whitley, Lysander, Maryland
No. 1521 (BAT) Flt.	Oxford
No. 1657 H.C.U.	Stirling B.I., Oxford
Today: H.M. Prison, Highpoint	

SWANTON MORLEY, Norfolk

R.A.F.	No. 1 Gliding Centre, A.T.C.	Cadet gliders
	No. 1 Air Signallers' School	Prentice
	No. 2 Group Support Unit	Mosquito, Boston III, Martinet, Hurricane, Anson
	No. 2 Group Command Flt.	Anson
	No. 3 (F) Squadron	Typhoon IB
	No. 4 Radio School	Anson, Proctor, Prentice
	No. 88 (B) Squadron	Blenheim IV, Boston III
	No. 98 (B) Squadron	Mitchell III
	No. 100 Group Mosquito Servicing Squadron	Mosquito
	No. 100 Group Command Flt.	Anson, Oxford
	No. 105 (B) Squadron	Blenheim IV, Mosquito B.IV
	No. 139 (B) Squadron	Mosquito B.IV
	No. 152 (F) Squadron	Spitfire IIA
	No. 226 (B) Squadron	Blenheim IV, Boston III
	No. 305 (B) Squadron	Mitchell III
	No. 320 (B) Squadron	Mitchell II

	No. 464 (B) Squadron	Mosquito IV
	No. 487 (B) Squadron	Mosquito IV
	No. 611 (ATC) Squadron	Gliding School
	No. 613 (B) Squadron	Mosquito IV
	No. 1482 B & G Flt.	Ventura III, Mosquito T.III
	No. 1508 (BAT) Flt.	Oxford
	No. 1515 (BAT) Flt.	Oxford
	Central Aircraft Servicing Establishment	
	"Window" Research Unit	
U.S.A.A.F.	15th Bomb Group	Boston III

SUDBURY, (Acton), Suffolk

U.S.A.A.F.	486th Bomb Group, 8th A.F.	B.24H & J, B.17G

SWANNINGTON, Norfolk

R.A.F.	No. 85 (B) Squadron	Mosquito XII, XVII & XXX
	No. 157 (B) Squadron	Mosquito XIX & XXX
	No. 274 M.U.	Mosquito

THORPE ABBOTS, Norfolk

U.S.A.A.F.	100th Bomb Group, 8th A.F.	B.17F
	106th Bomb Group, 8th A.F.	B.17F

TIBENHAM, Norfolk

R.A.F.	No. 214 (B) Squadron	Fortress II
	No. 342 (B) Squadron	Boston III, Havoc I & II
U.S.A.A.F.	445th Bomb Group, 8th A.F.	B.24H, J, L & M
U.S.A.F.	19th T.R.S.	RB.45C
	47th Bomb Wing	B.45, B.66
Civil	Norfolk Gliding Club	Gliders and sailplanes

TUDDENHAM, Suffolk

R.A.F.	No. 90 (B) Squadron	Stirling B.I & B.III, Lancaster B.I & B.III
	No. 107 Squadron	Thor I.C.B.M.
	No. 138 (B) Squadron	Lancaster B.I & B.III
	No. 149 (B) Squadron	Lancaster B.I & B.III
	No. 186 (B) Squadron	Lancaster B.I & B.III
	No. 207 (B) Squadron	Lancaster B.III

WATERBEACH, Cambridgeshire

R.A.F.	No. 1 (F) Squadron	Hunter FGA.IX
	No. 5 F.T.S.	Varsity
	No. 18 (T) Squadron	Dakota
	No. 24 (T) Squadron	York
	No. 25 (F) Squadron	Meteor NF.XII & XIV, Javelin FAW.VII & IX
	No. 46 (F) Squadron	Javelin FAW II
	No. 51 (T) Squadron	York

	No. 53 (T) Squadron	Dakota
	No. 54 (F) Squadron	Hunter FGA IX
	No. 56 (F) Squadron	Meteor F.IV, Swift FI & FII, Hunter F.V. & VI
	No. 59 (T) Squadron	Liberator II, VI & VIII
	No. 60 (F) Squadron	Javelin FAW VII
	No. 62 (T) Squadron	Dakota
	No. 64 (F) Squadron	Javelin FAW VII & IX
	No. 77 (T) Squadron	Dakota
	No. 99 (B) Squadron	Wellington B.I
	No. 153 (F) Squadron	Meteor NF.XIV
	No. 222 (F) Squadron	Meteor F.IV
	No. 253 (F) Squadron	Venom NF.IIA
	No. 514 (B) Squadron	Lancaster B.I, II & III
	No. 1651 H.C.U.	Stirling B.III
	No. 1678 H.C.U. Con. Flt.	Lancaster B.II
	Today Royal Engineers	

WATTISHAM, Suffolk

R.A.F.	No. 13 (AC) Squadron	Blenheim IV
	No. 16 Light Anti-Aircraft Squadron	R.A.F. Regiment
	No. 18 (B) Squadron	Blenheim IV
	No. 23 (F) Squadron	Phantom. Detached Falkland Islands
	No. 29 (F) Squadron	Lightning F.III
	No. 41 (F) Squadron	Javelin FAW.VIII
	No. 56 (F) Squadron	Meteor F.III, Lightning F.III & F.VI, Phantom
	No. 107 (B) Squadron	Blenheim IV
	No. 110 (B) Squadron	Blenheim IV
	No. 111 (F) Squadron	Hunter F.VI, Lightning IA & F.III, Phantom
	No. 152 (F) Squadron	Meteor NF.XIV
	No. 226 (B) Squadron	Blenheim IV, Boston III
	No. 236 (F) Squadron	Beaufighter VIC
	No. 245 (F) Squadron	Meteor F.III
	No. 257 (F) Squadron	Meteor F.VIII, Hunter F.II & F.V.
	No. 263 (F) Squadron	Meteor F.VIII, Hunter F.II & F.III
	No. 266 (F) Squadron	Meteor F.III
	No. 504 (F) Squadron	Hurricane I
	No. 1508 (BAT) Flt.	Blenheim IV
	Target Facilities Unit	Lightning
U.S.A.A.F.	68th Observation Group	P.39
	479th Fighter Group, 8th A.F.	P.38J, P.51D
	10th Air Depot Group	

WATTON, Norfolk

R.A.F.	No. 17 P.A.F.U.	Master II
	No. 18 (B) Squadron	Blenheim IV
	No. 21 (B) Squadron	Blenheim IV
	No. 34 (B) Squadron	Blenheim IV

	No. 51 Squadron, previously No. 192	
	No. 61 (B) Squadron, "B" Flt.	Hampden
	No. 82 (B) Squadron	Blenheim IV
	No. 90 (B) Squadron	Fortress I
	No. 98 Squadron, previously No. 245	
	No. 105 (B) Squadron	Blenheim IV
	No. 110 (B) Squadron	Blenheim IV
	No. 115 Squadron, previously No. 116	
	No. 116 (T) Squadron	Varsity, Anson, Mosquito
	No. 151 Squadron, previously Development Squadron	
	No. 192 (B) Squadron	Canberra, Washington, Comet, Mosquito, Lincoln
	No. 199 (B) Squadron	Lincoln B.I
	No. 245 Squadron, previously No. 527	
	No. 360 (B) Squadron	Canberra B.II & T.XVII
	No. 715 (Naval) Squadron	Avenger
	No. 751 (Naval) Squadron	Avenger, Venom, Gannet
	No. 527 (B) Squadron	Canberra
	No. 1508 (BAT) Flt.	Blenheim I
	Military Air Traffic Radar Calibration Squadron, Central Signals School	
	Radio Warfare Establishment	
U.S.A.A.F.	25th Bomb Group, 8th A.F.	B.24D, B.17G, Mosquito PR.XVI
	803rd Recc. Group	B.24D, B.17G, Mosquito PR.XVI
	3rd Strategic Air Depot	B.24

WENDLING, Norfolk

U.S.A.A.F.	392nd Bomb Group, 8th A.F.	B.24H, J, L & M

WEST RAYNHAM, Norfolk

R.A.F.	No. 1 (F) Squadron	Hunter FGA.IX
	No. 2 Group TT Flt.	Battle II, Lysander II
	No. 18 (B) Squadron	Blenheim IV
	No. 54 (F) Squadron	Hunter FGA.IX
	No. 66 (F) Squadron	Meteor F.VIII
	No. 75 (B) Squadron	Anson
	No. 76 (B) Squadron	Anson, Hampden
	No. 85 (F) Squadron	Javelin FAW.VIII, Canberra B.II & T.XIX
	No. 90 (B) Squadron	Blenheim IV, Fortress II
	No. 98 (B) Squadron	Mitchell II
	No. 100 (B) Squadron	Canberra B.II, T.IV & T.XIX
	No. 101 (B) Squadron	Blenheim IV, Wellington IC
	No. 114 (B) Squadron	Blenheim IV, Mitchell II
	No. 139 (B) Squadron	Blenheim IV
	No. 141 (B) Squadron	Mosquito II
	No. 141 (SD) Squadron	Beaufighter VIF, Mosquito II, IV & XXX
	No. 180 (B) Squadron	Mitchell II
	No. 239 (B) Squadron	Mosquito II, VII & NF.XXX

No. 342 (B) Squadron	Boston III & IIIA, Havoc I, Mitchell II
No. 610 (F) Squadron	Spitfire I
No. 614 (AC) Squadron	Blenheim IV
No. 1482 Bomber Defence Training Flt.	Defiant II, Boston III, Blenheim IV, Martinet, Ventura, Mitchell II, Blenheim V, Mosquito II
Air Fighting Development Squadron	Hunter F.I
Central Fighter Establishment	All types
Naval Fighter Development Unit	All naval fighters
Tripartite Squadron	Kestrel development
Day Fighter Leader School	Meteor F.IV & F.VIII
Day Fighter Combat School	Meteor F.IV & F.VIII
Fighter Leader School	Meteor F.IV & F.VIII
Night Fighter Leader School	Mosquito XXXVI, Meteor XI & XIV
Fighter Command Instrument Training Squadron	Oxford, Mosquito III & VII
Target Facilities Flt.	Canberra T.XI

WETHERSFIELD, Essex

R.A.F.	No. 196 (T) Squadron	Stirling IV
	No. 299 (T) Squadron	Stirling IV
	No. 1677 (TT) Flt.	Martinet

Blickling Hall, Norfolk, which became the home of No. 88 Squadron during 1943. *Mrs M. Martin*

	Operational & Refresher Training Unit	Halifax, Stirling
	No. 1385 H.C.U. (Unit above renamed)	
U.S.A.A.F.	416th Bomb Group, 9th A.F.	A.20J
U.S.A.F.	10th Tactical Recc. Wing	
	20th F.B.W.	F.84E, F.100D, F.100F
	23rd Rescue Squadron	H.21B, HH.43B
	66th Combat Support Wing	
	349th S.R.S., 100th S.R. Wing	U.2C

WITCHFORD, Cambridgeshire

R.A.F.	No. 115 (B) Squadron	Lancaster B.II & B.III
	No. 195 (B) Squadron	Lancaster B.II & B.III
	No. 196 (B) Squadron	Wellington X, Stirling B.III
	No. 514 (B) Squadron	Stirling B.III

WOODBRIDGE, (Sutton Heath), Suffolk

R.A.F.	No. 54 M.U. detachment	
	Bomb Ballistic Unit	Heavy Bomber types
	Blind Landing Experimental Unit	Dakota, Devon, Varsity, Anson, Canberra
	F.I.D.O. Operating Unit	
U.S.A.F.	20th F.B.W.	F.84G, F.100D
	67th A.R.R.S.	HC.130, HH.53
	78th T.F.S.	F.84F, F.101
	81st T.F.W.	F.4, A.10

WORMINGFORD, Essex

U.S.A.A.F.	55th Fighter Group, 8th A.F.	P.38J, P.51D
	362nd Fighter Group, 8th A.F.	P.47D

WRATTING COMMON, Cambridgeshire

R.A.F.	No. 90 (B) Squadron	Stirling B.I & B.III
	No. 195 (B) Squadron	Lancaster B.I & B.III

Various sites existed, in the region belonging to *No. 92 Group* and these consisted of Stores Equipment and Munition Depots and were positioned at places like R.A.F. Banham, R.A.F. Warren Wood and many other remote sites throughout North Suffolk and South Norfolk.

V-Bomber turned flying tanker, the Handley-Page Victor with its massive underwing tanks waits at Marham for its next refuelling operation with aircraft of the N.A.T.O. air forces.   *Myron Burak*

Fighter Command—East Anglia 1940-1960

The following tables give the disposition of Fighter Command Squadrons over the twenty year period 1940-1960, and the types of aircraft employed.

8th AUGUST, 1940

No. 11 Group

Martlesham Heath	No. 25 Squadron	Blenheim IF
	No. 85 Squadron	Hurricane I
Rochford	No. 56 Squadron	Hurricane I

No. 12 Group

Coltishall	No. 66 Squadron	Spitfire I
	No. 242 Squadron	Hurricane I
Duxford	No. 19 Squadron	Spitfire I

2nd JUNE, 1943

No. 11 Group

Bradwell Bay	No. 29 Squadron	Beaufighter IF
	No. 247 Squadron	Typhoon IB
Castle Camps	No. 605 Squadron	Mosquito II
Martlesham Heath	No. 501 Squadron	Spitfire VB

No. 12 Group

Coltishall	No. 68 Squadron	Beaufighter VI F
	No. 118 Squadron	Spitfire VB
Ludham	No. 195 Squadron	Typhoon IB
Matlaske	No. 56 Squadron	Typhoon IB
Snailwell	No. 170 Squadron	Mustang I
	No. 309 Squadron	Mustang I

6th JUNE, 1944 (D-Day)

No. 11 Group

Bradwell Bay	No. 219 Squadron	Mosquito XVII

No. 12 Group

Coltishall	No. 25 Squadron	Mosquito XVII
	No. 316 Squadron	Mustang III

No. 85 Group. (2nd Tactical Air Force)

	No. 124 Squadron	Spitfire VII

APPENDIX II

1st JUNE, 1950

No. 11 Group

Waterbeach	No. 56 Squadron	Meteor F4
	No. 63 Squadron	Meteor F4

No. 12 Group

Horsham St Faiths	No. 74 Squadron	Meteor F4
	No. 245 Squadron	Meteor F4
	No. 257 Squadron	Meteor F4
	No. 263 Squadron	Meteor F4

1st JUNE, 1955

No. 11 Group

Waterbeach	No. 56 Squadron	Hunter F.S
	No. 63 Squadron	Meteor F.8
	No. 253 Squadron	Venom NF.2a
Wattisham	No. 257 Squadron	Hunter F.2
	No. 263 Squadron	Hunter F.2, F.5
Stradishall	No. 125 Squadron	Meteor NF.11
	No. 152 Squadron	Meteor NF.12, NF.14
	No. 245 Squadron	Meteor F.8

No. 12 Group

Coltishall	No. 23 Squadron	Venom NF.2A
	No. 141 Squadron	Venom NF.3
Horsham St Faiths	No. 74 Squadron	Meteor F.8
Duxford	No. 64 Squadron	Meteor F.8
	No. 65 Squadron	Meteor F.8

1st JUNE, 1960

No. 11 Group

Waterbeach	No. 25 Squadron	Javelin FAW.7
	No. 46 Squadron	Javelin FAW.2
Wattisham	No. 56 Squadron	Hunter F.6
	No. 111 Squadron	Hunter F.6
Duxford	No. 64 Squadron	Javelin FAW.7
	No. 65 Squadron	Hunter F.6

No. 12 Group

Coltishall	No. 23 Squadron	Javelin FAW.7
	No. 41 Squadron	Javelin FAW.8
	No. 74 Squadron	Lightning F.1

No. 38 Group

Stradishall	No. 1 Squadron	Hunter FGA.9
	No. 54 Squadron	Hunter FGA.9

No. 11 Group embraced an area of England south of a line running east to west through Bedford, whilst *no. 12 Group* covered the area of the Midlands and East Anglia north of the line and as far as York.

Battle of Britain Memorial Flight

When formed at the former Battle of Britain airfield at Biggin Hill, Kent, in 1957 the Battle of Britain Flight boasted two Spitfire Mk. XVIs, two Spitfire PR Mk. 19s and a single Hurricane. During 1958 the unit moved to North Weald, Essex, and then after a short spell to Martlesham Heath, Suffolk, once the home of the Aeroplane and Armament Experimental Establishment. Whilst there the two Mk. XVIs were lost as the result of flying accidents.

During 1960 another move was made to Horsham St Faiths, Norfolk, where the flight was reduced to three aircraft when one of the PR Mk.19s was grounded. When Horsham St Faiths closed as an R.A.F. station in 1964 the flight moved once again to nearby Coltishall, which remained its home base for more than a decade. The flight is now based at R.A.F. Coningsby, the Lincolnshire bomber airfield which played so large a part in the bombing offensive against Occupied Europe in the Second World War.

The aircraft strength has gradually increased and the flight now has the following aircraft:-

Supermarine Spitfire Mk. VB AB.910	Built 1941
Coded QJ-J	No. 92 Squadron
Supermarine Spitfire MK.IIa P.7350	Built 1940
Coded UO-T	No. 266 Squadron. Battle of Britain
Supermarine Spitfire PR Mk.19 PM.631	Built 1945
Marked CA-D	No. 11 Squadron
Supermarine Spitfire Mk.19 PS.853	Built 1945
No Squadron marking. Painted PR blue	
Hawker Hurricane MK.IIc. LF.363	Built 1944
Coded LE-D	No. 242 Squadron. G/Capt. Douglas Bader's aircraft
Hawker Hurricane PZ.865	Built 1944
Coded DT-A	No. 257 Squadron. G/Capt. Stanford Tuck's aircraft
Avro Lancaster BI PA.474	No. 44 Squadron

The Lancaster, now named *City of Lincoln*, is the sole preserved example of this famous aircraft still in flying condition. It was formerly at Waddington but for economic reasons was moved to Coltishall in 1975 and has since resided with the Battle of Britain Memorial Flight.

The Flight aircraft have had notable careers, Spitfire AB.910 flying with No. 222 (Natal), No. 130 (Punjab), No. 133 (Eagle), No. 242 (Canadian), No. 416 (Canadian), No. 402 (Canadian) and No. 527 Squadrons. On 4th April 1945, it had the experience of taking a W.A.A.F. Flight Mechanic aloft astride the rear fuselage, when flying with No. 53 O.T.U. The pilot, Flight Lieutenant Cox, thinking that the mechanic A.C.W.2. Horton, who had been holding the tail down for taxi-ing purposes, was off the aircraft, opened up and took-off. To his dismay he saw the wind-swept W.A.A.F. still on the aircraft and flying very carefully round the airfield, landed and both were none the worse for the incident.

Spitfire P. 7350 is a true Battle of Britain aircraft being at Hornchurch during 1940 with No. 266 (Rhodesia) Squadron.

Hurricane LF.363 was specially built by the Hurricane designer, the late Mr Sidney Camm for Air Vice Marshal S. F. Vincent who as the Air Officer Commanding No. 11 Group, Fighter Command used it to visit all the stations in his Group.

The two earlier marques of Spitfire, the IIa and V, have speeds of 370 m.p.h. and 375 m.p.h. respectively, whilst the Mk.XIX can do 439 m.p.h. The Hurricane is more sedate at 350 m.p.h. whilst the Lancaster can make up a steady 275 m.p.h. on its 6,440 horse power.

Aircraft of the Battle of Britain Memorial Flight at Coltishall. These were photographed just prior to their moving to their new home at Coningsby, Lincs.

Above: The last aircraft to be evaluated at Martlesham Heath, the Avro 748 G-ARAY carries out a trial landing on a soft airfield surface during 1963. This type of aircraft was used by Channel Airways and operated from Ipswich Airport. *East Anglian Daily Times*

Right: The control tower at Martlesham Heath during the Second World War at the time U.S.A.A.F. fighter squadrons were based on the airfield. The control tower is now being restored as an aeronautical museum by the Martlesham Heath Air Museum Society. *U.S.A.F.*

Below: The Short Solent flying boat on the tarmac at R.A.F. Felixstowe in the early 1950s. *Ernest Graystone*

Above: A Hawker Siddeley Buccaneer which operated from R.A.F. Honington in Suffolk after being turned over from the Royal Navy to the Royal Air Force.   *Hawker Siddeley Limited*

Below: A spectacular piece of showmanship as a B.A.C. Lightning XP696 bursts up over the Hawker Siddeley Gnats of the Red Arrows display team during an air show at R.A.F. Wattisham in Suffolk.   *R.A.F.*

Bibliography

Air Defence of Great Britain. John R. Bushby (1973). Ian Allan.
Avro Aircraft since 1908. A. J. Jackson (1965). Putnam.
Battle of Britain. Marcel Jullian (1974). Cedric Chivers.
Black Lysander. Wing Commander John Nesbitt-Dufont (1973). Jarrolds.
Bomber Squadrons of the R.A.F. Philip Moyes (1964). Macdonald.
British Racing & Record Breaking Aircraft. Peter Lewis (1970). Putnam.
British Civil Aircraft. Vols. 1, 2 and 3. A. J. Jackson (1974). Putnam.
Camouflage and Markings U.S.A.A.F. Roger Freeman (1974). Ducimus Books.
Duel of Eagles. Peter Townsend (1970). Weidenfeld and Nicolson.
East Anglian Magazine. Various issues.
Essex at War. Harvey Benham (1945). Benham & Co.
Eyes of the Few. Daphne Carne (1960). Macmillan.
Famous Bombers of the Second World War. William Green (1960). Macdonald.
Fighter Squadrons of the R.A.F. J.D.R. Rawlings (1969). Macdonald.
Fly for your Life. Larry Forrester (1973). Frederick Muller.
Forewarned is Forearmed. T. E. Winslow (1948). William Hodge.
Great Yarmouth. Front Line Town. 1939–1945. Charles G. Box, O.B.E. (1946).
Hawker Aircraft since 1920. Francis K. Mason (1961–71). Putnam.
Here we are Together. Robert S. Arbib Jnr (1946). Green.
Hurricane at War. Chaz Bowyer (1971). Ian Allan.
I Fear no Man. Douglas Tidy (1972). Macdonald.
No. 74 Squadron R.A.F. Douglas Tidy (1972). Macdonald.
Know Aviation. Francis K. Mason, M. & M. C. Windrow (1973). George Philip.
Lancaster at War. Mike Garbett & Brian Goulding (1971). Ian Allan.
Lancasters. The Story of a Famous Bomber. Bruce Robertson (1964). Harleyford.
Lowestoft—Port War. Ford Jenkins (1945). W. S. Cowell.
Martlesham Heath. Gordon Kinsey (1975). Terence Dalton.
Moon Squadron. Jerrard Tickell (1973). George Mason.
Mosquito at War. Chaz Bowyer. Ian Allan.
Partners in Blue. Katherine Bentley Beauman (1971). Hutchinson.
Science at War. J. G. Crowther & R. Whiddington, C.B.E., F.R.S. (1947). H.M.S.O.
Spitfire at War. Alfred Price (1972). Ian Allan.
Spitfire Special. Ted Hooten (1972). Ian Allan.
Squadron Histories. Peter Lewis (1959). Putnam.
Storm from the Skies. Robert Jackson (1974). Arthur Barker Ltd.
Tempest & Typhoon at War. Ian Allan.
The Defence of the United Kingdom. Basil Collier (1957). H.M.S.O.
The Forgotten Pilots. Lettice Curtis (1971). G. T. Foulis.
The Mighty Eighth. Roger Freeman. Macdonald and Jane's.
The Royal Air Force in the World War. Vols. 1, 2, 3 and 4. Capt. Norman Macmillen, M.C., A.F.C. (1950). Harrap.
To Know the Sky. Prudence Hill (1962). William Kimber.
Twenty One Squadrons. The History of the Royal Auxiliary Air Force. Leslie Hunt (1972). Garnstone Press.
Twice Vertical. No. 1 Squadron R.A.F. Michael Shaw (1971). Macdonald.
Under the White Rose. The story of 609 Squadron. Frank H. Ziegler (1971). Macdonald.
Wingless Victory. Anthony Richardson (1953). 657 A.O.P. Squadron. Private.

General Index

(For Aeroplanes, Missiles and Airships see separate Index)

Index of Aeroplanes, Missiles and Airships

(Excluding Appendices I, II and III)

R.A.F. Squadrons and Units

Note: Squadron designations changed from time to time; for the sake of brevity, designations are not given in this index in such cases.

FOOTNOTE: (AAC) Anti-Aircraft Cooperation. (AC) Army Cooperation. (AOP) Air Observation Post. (ASR) Air Sea Rescue. (ATC) Air Training Corps. (B) Bomber. (BAT) Blind Approach Training. B.D.T. Bomber Defence Training. (CC) Coastal Command. (F) Fighter. (FB) Flying Boat. (GR) General Reconnaissance. H.C.U. Heavy Conversion Unit. (MET) Meteorological. O.C.U. Operational Conversion Unit. R.C.M. Radio Counter Measures. (S.A.R.) Search and Rescue. (SD) Special Duties. (T) Transport.

U.S.A.A.F. and U.S.A.F. Units

2nd B.G., 246, 252, 255
3rd Strategic Air Depot, 260
3rd Div. Detachment, 242
3rd Aviation Engineering Battalion, 250
4th F.G., 239
4th B.W. Subs. Unit, 254
5th Aerial Port Squadron, 187
5th Emergency Rescue Sqdn, 172, 243
9th B.G., 108
10th Air Depot Group, 61, 259
10th Airborne Command Control Sqdn, 187, 251
15th B.G., 258
15th B.S., 101
19th T.R.S., 255, 258
20th T.F.W., 262
22nd B.G., 252, 255
23rd Rescue Sqdn, 262
25th B.G., 260
25th Recce Group, 124
28th Weather Sqdn, 186, 251
30th Air Depot Group, 256
34th B.G., 131, 250
41st Base Complement Sqdn, 256
43rd B.G., 246,, 255
44th B.G., 108, 118, 255
47th B.G., 245, 254, 255
47th B.W., 258
48th T.F.W., 184, 246
49th Air Div, 255
53rd Weather Sqdn, 251
55th F.G., 120, 262
56th F.S., 103
56th F.G., 111, 127, 234, 243, 245, 247
66th Comb. Supp. Wing, 262
67th A.R.R.S., 177, 189, 190, 262
68th Obs. Grp., 101, 259
78th F.B.S., 187, 189, 262
78th F.G., 240
78th F.S., 103, 255
79th F.S., 214
81st F.B.W., 187, 233
81st T.F.W., 187, 188, 189, 233, 255, 262
87th F.I.S., 233
91st F.B.S., 187, 233
92nd F.B.S., 187, 233
92nd B.G., 108, 255
93rd B.G., 235, 244, 246
93rd B.W., 251
94th B.G., 105, 109, 126, 240, 254
95th B.G., 110, 115, 124, 243, 245

96th B.G., 131, 232, 256
97th B.G., 248, 255
100th B.G., 110, 115, 258
106th B.G., 258
285th B.G., 115
301st B.G., 255
310th B.G., 235, 244
316th T.A.W., 251
317th T.A.W., 251
319th B.G., 232, 245, 255
320th B.G., 244
322nd B.G., 232, 253, 254
322nd Air Div., 251
323rd B.G., 240
323rd B.S., 245
329th B.G., 235, 244
329th B.S., 102
335th P.S., 243
336th P.S., 243
339th F.G., 127, 243
340th B.S., 181
341st B.S., 181
342nd B.S., 181
344th B.G., 256
347th F.S., 256
349th S.R.S., 262
350th F.G., 101, 240, 256
351st B.G., 112
352nd F.G., 234
353rd F.G., 111, 120, 134, 250, 253
354th F.G., 115, 235
355th F.G., 235
356th F., 111, 112, 127, 129, 249
356th Wing, 41
357th F.G., 114, 116, 117, 130, 133, 253
358th F.G., 134, 254
359th F.G., 113, 122, 240
361st F.G., 113, 234, 247
362nd F.G., 114, 262
363rd F.G., 254
363rd F.S., 114
364th F.G., 244
364th F.S., 114, 116
365th F.G., 243
381st B.G., 110, 254
385th B.G., 120, 126, 130, 243
386th B.G., 234, 239, 256
387th B.G., 236, 239
388th B.G., 109, 246
389th B.G., 108, 244
390th B.G., 106, 110, 112, 128, 131, 132, 171, 242
391st B.G., 249

392nd B.G., 118, 260
394th B.G., 234
397th B.G., 243, 254
409th B.G., 247
410th B.G., 243
416th B.G., 262
435th T.A.W., 251
445th B.G., 113, 120, 125, 258
446th B.G., 113, 128, 235, 242
447th B.G., 113, 120, 253
448th B.G., 113, 118, 255
452nd B.G., 239
453rd B.G., 253
458th B.G., 115, 126, 245
466th B.G., 232
467th B.G., 118, 153
479th F.G., 259
486th B.G., 120, 121, 131, 258
487th B.G., 120, 121, 126, 246
489th B.G., 244
490th B.G., 126, 235
491st B.G., 250, 252
492nd B.G., 120, 252
493rd B.G., 128, 238, 243, 247
496th B.G., 244
509th B.G., 252
513th T.A.W., 186, 187, 251
549th B.S., 126
563rd B.S., 109
568th B.S., 132
569th B.S., 132
570th B.S., 132
571st B.S., 132
652nd Weather Sqdn, 254
803rd B.S., 151, 255
803rd Aviation Eng. Batt., 256
803rd Recc. Group, 260
803rd Radio CM Sqdn, 253
2176th Comm. Sqdn, 251
7511th Air Base Sqdn, 251
7519th Combat Support Unit, 255
8554th T.T. Flt, 255
Aircraft Disbandment Centre, 242
B.17 Service Unit, 244
Military Airlift Command Terminal, 251
Radio Counter Measures Sqdn, 255
Robot Aircraft Project "Anvil", 242
Robot Aircraft Project "Aphrodite", 242
U.S.A.F. Transportation Centre, 190
U.S. Navy Logistic Support Unit, 251

A.R.R.S. Aerospace Rescue and Recovery Squadron. B.G. Bomb Group. B.S. Bomb Squadron. B.W. Bomb Wing. F.B.S. Fighter Bomber Squadron. F.B.W. Fighter Bomber Wing. F.G. Fighter Group. F.I.S. Fighter Interceptor Squadron. F.S. Fighter Squadron. Ob Group. Observation Group. P.S. Pursuit Squadron. Recc. Group. Reconnaissance Group. S.R.S. Strategic Reconnaissance Squadron. T.A.W. Tactical Airlift Wing. T.F.S. Tactical Fighter Squadron. T.F.W. Tactical Fighter Wing.

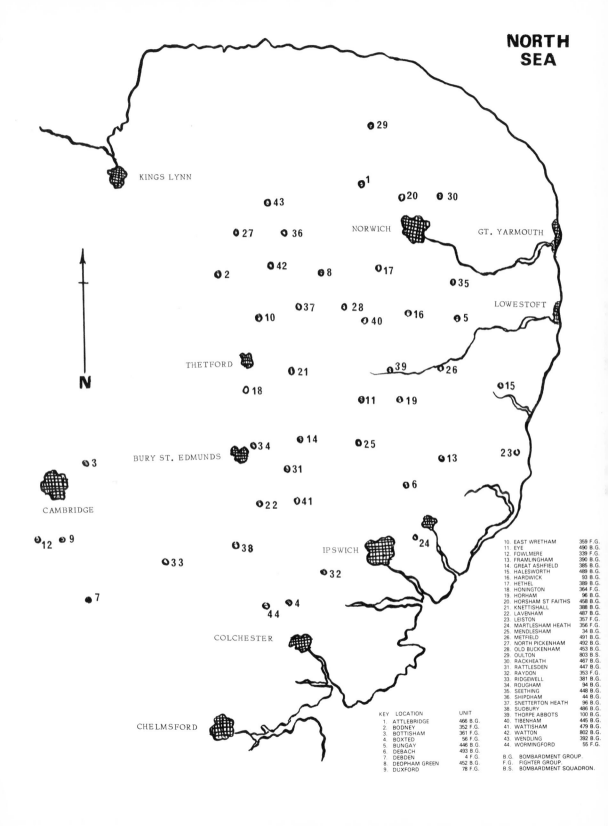

1.	ANDREWSFIELD	51.	LITTLE WALDEN
2.	ATTLEBRIDGE	52.	LUDHAM
3.	BECCLES	53.	MARHAM
4.	BENTWATERS	54.	MARTLESHAM HEATH
5.	BIRCH	55.	MATLASKE
6.	BIRCHAM NEWTON	56.	MATCHING
7.	BODNEY	57.	MENDLESHAM
8.	BOREHAM	58.	MEPAL
9.	BOTTISHAM	59.	MILDENHALL
10.	BOXTED	60.	METFIELD
11.	BRADWELL BAY	61.	NEWMARKET HEATH
12.	BUNGAY	62.	NORTH CREAKE
13.	CAMBRIDGE	63.	NORTH PICKENHAM
14.	CASTLE CAMPS	64.	OAKINGTON
15.	CHEDBURGH	65.	OLD BUCKENHAM
16.	CHIPPING ONGAR	66.	ORFORDNESS
17.	COLTISHALL	67.	OULTON
18.	DEBACH	68.	RACKHEATH
19.	DEBDEN	69.	RATTLESDEN
20.	DEOPHAM GREEN	70.	RAYDON
21.	DOCKING	71.	RIDGEWELL
22.	DOWNHAM MARKET	72.	RIVENHALL
23.	DUXFORD	73.	ROCHFORD
24.	EARLS COLNE	74.	ROUGHAM
25.	EAST WRETHAM	75.	SCULTHORPE
26.	EYE	76.	SEETHING
27.	FELIXSTOWE	77.	SHEPHERDS GROVE
28.	FERSFIELD	78.	SHIPDHAM
29.	FOULSHAM	79.	SNAILWELL
30.	FOWLMERE	80.	SNETTERTON HEATH
31.	FRAMLINGHAM	81.	STANSTED
32.	GOSFIELD	82.	STRADISHALL
33.	GREAT ASHFIELD	83.	SUDBURY
34.	GREAT DUNMOW	84.	SWANNINGTON
35.	GREAT MASSINGHAM	85.	SWANTON MORLEY
36.	GREAT SAMPFORD	86.	TIBENHAM
37.	GREAT YARMOUTH	87.	THORPE ABBOTS
38.	HALESWORTH	88.	TUDDENHAM
39.	HARDWICK	89.	WATERBEACH
40.	HETHEL	90.	WATTON
41.	HONINGTON	91.	WATTISHAM
42.	HORHAM	92.	WENDLING
43.	HORSHAM ST FAITHS	93.	WESTLEY
44.	IPSWICH	94.	WEST RAYNHAM
45.	KNETTISHALL	95.	WETHERSFIELD
46.	LAKENHEATH	96.	WITCHFORD
47.	LANGHAM	97.	WOODBRIDGE
48.	LAVENHAM	98.	WRATTING COMMON
49.	LEISTON	99.	WORMINGFORD
50.	LITTLE SNORING		